Independence Movements and Their Aftermath

Self-Determination and the Struggle for Success

Editors
Jon B. Alterman
Will Todman

CSIS | CENTER FOR STRATEGIC & INTERNATIONAL STUDIES

ROWMAN & LITTLEFIELD
Lanham • Boulder • New York • London

Center for Strategic & International Studies
1616 Rhode Island Avenue, NW
Washington, DC 20036
202-887-0200 | www.csis.org

Published by Rowman & Littlefield
A wholly owned subsidiary of The Rowman & Littlefield Publishing Group, Inc.
4501 Forbes Boulevard, Lanham, MD 20706
www.rowman.com

Unit A, Whitacre Mews, 26-34 Stannary Street, London SE114AB

© 2019 by the Center for Strategic and International Studies.

All rights reserved. No part of this book may be reproduced in any form or by any electronic or mechanical means, including information storage and retrieval systems, without written permission from the publisher, except by a reviewer who may quote passage in a review.

ISBN 978-1-4422-8079-3 (cloth alk. paper)
ISBN 978-1-4422-8080-9 (paperback)
ISBN 978-1-4422-8081-6 (electronic)

Contents

Acknowledgments	vii
1. Introduction *Jon B. Alterman*	1
2. Bangladesh: Two Independence Movements *Howard and Teresita Schaffer*	10
3. Eritrea: The Independence Struggle and the Struggles of Independence *Terrence Lyons*	36
4. Timor-Leste: A Nation of Resistance *Miks Muižarājs*	53
5. Kosovo: An Unlikely Success Still in the Making *Daniel Serwer*	81
6. South Sudan: The Painful Rise and Rapid Descent of the World's Newest Nation *Richard Downie*	100
7. The Importance of Being Balanced: Lessons from Negotiated Settlements to Self-Determination Movements in Bosnia, Macedonia, and Kosovo *Erin Jenne and Beáta Huszka*	117
8. Generalizing the Findings *Will Todman*	138
9. Self-Determination and U.S. Choices *Will Todman*	160

10. Conclusion 193
   Jon B. Alterman

Index 203

About the Authors 211

Advisory Board Members 215

About CSIS 217

ACKNOWLEDGMENTS

This book would not have been possible without invaluable contributions from a distinguished group of international policy practitioners and experts. The project's advisory board offered continued guidance and substantive feedback to the research team throughout the project. Members included Professor Henri Barkey, the Bernard L. and Bertha F. Cohen Professor of International Relations at Lehigh University; General Wesley Clark (USA, Ret.), CEO of Wesley K. Clark & Associates and NATO's former supreme allied commander; Ambassador Marc Grossman, vice chairman of the Cohen Group and former undersecretary of state for political affairs; Dr. Claudia Hofmann, a professorial lecturer at the School of International Service at American University; Ambassador Beth Jones, an adviser with ExxonMobil and former assistant secretary of state for European and Eurasian affairs; Clare Lockhart, director and cofounder of the Institute for State Effectiveness; Ambassador Princeton Lyman, senior adviser to the president of the United States Institute of Peace and former U.S. special envoy for Sudan and South Sudan; Dr. Jodi Nelson, senior vice president for policy and practice at the International Rescue Committee; Ambassador Thomas Pickering, vice chair of Hills & Company and former undersecretary of state for political affairs; Ambassador David Pressman, partner at Boies, Schiller, & Flexner and former deputy U.S. ambassador to the United Nations; Professor Nicholas Sambanis, Presidential Distinguished Professor of Political Science at the University of Pennsylvania; Ambassador Alan Solomont, the Pierre and Pamela Omidyar Dean of the Tisch College of Civic Life at Tufts University and former U.S. ambassador to Spain; and Anne Witkowsky, former deputy assistant secretary of defense for stability and humanitarian affairs in the Office of the Undersecretary of Defense for Policy.

Special appreciation is extended to Dr. Molly Inman for her invaluable assistance with the quantitative section, to Professor Stephen Saideman, Rick Scott, and Ambassador Molly Phee for their helpful comments on the case studies, to Haim Malka for his thoughtful feedback, and to Susan Bennett for editing the case studies. We are also grateful to Brian Adeba for his contributions.

Additionally, particular credit and a great deal of thanks goes to the following contributors: Emily Grunewald, Caroline Amenabar, Abby Kukura, Amber Atteridge, Aaron Ach, Sumaya Almajdoub, Razieh Armin, Caroline Bechtel, Mark Berlin, Aaron Christensen, Kerry Dugandzic, Claire Harrison, Jonathan Thrall, and Ben Westfall.

We are grateful to the CSIS Brzezinski Institute on Geostrategy for its generous support of this study and to CSIS Trustee Fred Khosravi for his intellectual guidance and financial support.

Although this book benefited greatly from the guidance of numerous individuals, the content is the sole responsibility of the authors and should not be construed to represent the opinions of anyone associated with the project. Any remaining mistakes are the sole responsibility of the authors.

1. INTRODUCTION
Jon B. Alterman

After weeks of intense, determined expressions, protesters have broken out in smiles and tears of joy. Hardened young men fire weapons as instruments of celebration, their gunshots joining car horns, songs, ululations, and chants of "God is great," in a cacophony of joy.[1] Some break into dance. The streets around them glow as the colors of the flag are waved above heads, painted on cheeks, and worn over shoulders.[2] Cars inch slowly through the crowd, covered with celebrants like floats in a parade.[3] To the outside observer, the scene might be reminiscent of patriotic rallies past. But celebrants like Wanis Agouri will tell you that civic engagement was no more than a forced ritual in the past, "but today people want to be here, it's from the heart."[4] As the sun sets, the light begins to dazzle. Drivers flip their headlights on to ignite the streets as a dancefloor; fireworks illuminate it from above.[5] Taking a moment from the revelry, Karim Ennarah pauses to consider how this moment could possibly be. He bursts into tears. The road was long and painful, he remarks. "But we held our ground. We did it."[6]

The moment of unalloyed joy that comes from a hard-fought political victory seems spontaneous, even as it is predictable. In fact, the passage above is not a single celebration, but a montage of four different ones, in Egypt, South Sudan, Iraqi Kurdistan, and Libya. In the first and the last, a dictator fell. In the middle two, independence seemed imminent, although in the former case it preceded warfare and, in the latter, it never arrived at all. The jubilation expressed at the moment of apparent triumph is one of the rewards of political activity.

Yet politics is merely a bridge to governance. One price of governance is appreciating that things often get better, but also can worsen significantly. That reality can hit hard, either because things do not improve, or because they improve only for a few while many fall into misery. What follows here is an effort to improve the chances that political joy is sustained, and that it leads to effective governance.

The challenge is an increasingly common one. The world has seen many celebrations like the ones described above, in part because over the last 200 years politics have become more universal. The spread of literacy and communications, combined with expanding suffrage, increasingly has connected citizens to their governments and given citizens a sense of their country's place in the world. Communications also help inform citizens and subjects of the failures of their rulers. In this context, the number of independent states is rising.

When the Paris Peace Conference set the terms for the end of World War I, just 27 nations were in attendance.[7] The Russian Federation was absent from Versailles because it had already concluded a peace treaty with the four Central Powers nine months before, and the vanquished Central Powers were excluded. Those 32 countries controlled almost the entire globe and virtually all the world's population. It is hard to imagine more than a small fraction of that population had any idea that the conference was occurring. Just over 25 years later, 51 countries were founding members of the United Nations, almost a doubling of the number at Versailles. Today, the United Nations has 193 member states, almost a quadrupling of the number in 1945.[8]

It is tempting to see growing self-determination as an inexorable trend. The uneducated and remote populations of a century ago are now increasingly sophisticated, networked, and cosmopolitan. Social entrepreneurs are resurrecting identities and repurposing them for the modern period. Heterogeneous populations remain the norm for most countries, and in many societies, activists agitate to break the nation into smaller more homogenous units. Should trends continue, the math would be daunting. If 50 countries in 1945 gave rise to 193 today, we might expect to see 750 countries by the dawn of the twenty-second century.[9]

The mere prospect of such a scenario would prompt us to rethink what it is to have self-determination, and what statehood would even mean in that context. We would be hard-pressed to predict how a world with 750 states would operate, how effectively individual states might operate, or how those states would interact with each other. In a world in which so much that is now domestic would necessarily be international, how could cooperation be fostered? What would happen when cooperation broke down? What kind of blocs would emerge, how stable would they be, and how would they relate to states outside of those blocs?

Before putting too much energy into such a thought experiment, we would do well to recall that self-determination movements do not proceed along some inevitable exponential curve. Many forces that led to waves of self-determination projects largely exhausted themselves. Colonialism died decades ago, and most large multiethnic empires have broken apart. Some self-determination movements, such as in Québec, seem to have reconciled with enjoying significant autonomy. While many groups seek self-determination, achieving independence is a relatively rare occurrence that often has been tied to large external events.

The most common cause of independence has been the passing of empires, which occurred in four waves: when Spain abandoned its empire in the Americas in the early nineteenth century; when the Versailles Treaty and its aftermath carved up the Central Powers' empires after World War I; when the European powers abandoned their empires after World War II; and when the Soviet Union fell.[10] The last case is an extreme one: The Soviet Union's collapse created 15 sovereign states where there had only been one, and untied the Balkans from a single united Yugoslavia into seven (although some say six) independent nations.[11]

The rubble of crumbled empires is not the only soil from which independence has emerged. More sporadically, independence has come from secession movements such as the one that split the North American colonies from Great Britain. Often, these movements have at their root an ethnic or sectarian difference, driven by a sense of economic grievance—or opportunity.[12] A sense of marginalization in East Pakistan, and a similar sense of marginalization combined with the prospect of oil wealth in South Sudan, helped drive successful secession movements in both places. For the time being, secession movements in Scotland, Catalonia, and the Basque country are on hold. The overall history of secession movements tends to be one of unfulfilled aspirations, however. From Sri Lankan Tamils to Nigerian Igbo, and from Tibetans to Chechens, central governments have frequently resisted efforts to fracture their territory.

A record of successful and unsuccessful efforts at political change has produced a trove of political science literature on civil war, ethnic conflict, and self-determination and secession movements. Utilizing large datasets, myriad studies seek to untangle what factors contribute to movements' success in gaining independence. They conclude that independence remains a relatively unlikely outcome of self-determination movements.[13]

When states emerge from independence struggles, they are often fragile—although fragility may also arise from poverty, warfare, drought, or myriad other causes. A profusion of political science literature also exists on these states and what factors contribute to their resilience or struggles.[14]

Surprising, though, is the scarcity of writing on what might seem to be the most important question for those seeking independence, which links the two literatures above: what factors contribute to "successful" states—however one might define them—emerging from self-determination movements? That is to say, if one thinks of self-determination as a necessary but insufficient aspect of success, what aspects of the self-determination movement contribute to success *after* self-determination has been won? Understanding what the precursors are of peaceful and resilient states would be a major contribution both to those who aspire to independence and to those on the outside who are considering their approaches to independence struggles.

There is no clear definition of success. One might define it merely by measuring internal violence[15] or economic growth or interstate warfare. One also can define it by poll numbers that suggest subjects find the new government legitimate. One can use indicators of governmental capacity, as well, giving an indication of future trajectory. There is some variance within societies, as specific individuals and groups certainly will have much better outcomes than others. Tolstoy opens *Anna Karenina* by judging, "All happy families are alike; each unhappy family is unhappy in its own way." That seems not to apply much to states. All happy states are different, and all states, by their nature, are constantly striving for improvement. Overall, we concluded that success after self-determination is never complete, but it remains fairly easy to separate from failure.

At the core of this project is a contention that leaders of independence movements have agency.[16] They make choices all the time about where to invest resources, what skills to hone, and what alliances to forge. They often cannot determine the circumstances of their independence, but they certainly can influence what their group looks like at the time of independence. Does the group have a functioning bureaucracy? Is it relatively unified within the areas that it seeks to make independent? Do the group's members have strong trade relations and neighbors that want them to succeed? Has the group made effective contact with world powers, and has it won sympathy, if not outright support? All these things are within the purview of self-determination movements to develop, and movements have gone forward with varying degrees of having developed them. With an understanding of these factors in hand, leaders may wish to accelerate or delay independence until circumstances are more promising for their ultimate success. Many may feel that opportunities are so rare that they must be seized whenever they appear, but in so doing they may make eventual independence less likely.

Leaders also may consider the factors at hand and determine that the odds of success after independence are long. It may be impossible to gain the support of surrounding states, the economic context may be forbidding, or the geography or demography may pose unusual obstacles. In such cases, leaders may consider whether complete independence is the most desirable outcome. The attractiveness of something short of independence can increase with creative approaches to sovereignty and autonomy, especially in circumstances in which supranational structures such as the European Union exist alongside traditional national ones.

There is no simple way to approach these kinds of questions systematically. One of the most promising approaches is to take a large sample of independence movements (or fragile states) and understand what factors are associated with failure and success. Failure in these cases is much easier to categorize than success. War and famine are clear signs of failure, but what are the appropriate metrics for success, what thresholds separate success and failure, and what time frame should be used?

In addition, such database-heavy research invariably minimizes the importance of context. If there were four major waves of independence in the past, how might one code for being in the midst of such a global wave or not? And what does the particular context in which earlier movements gained independence tell us about the conditions of independence movements in the future? What global trends will sweep the next movements along, and what trends will pull them backward? How will the recent track record of independence movements—positive or negative—affect expectations for their own failure or success, and how will those expectations shape levels of internal and external support?

This study takes a more qualitative approach to the problem, taking five self-determination movements that achieved independence and analyzing them in a standardized framework. Because our intended audience is principally policymakers seeking to enrich their understanding of problems they are facing, we chose case studies that provided a range of initial conditions and a range of outcomes. As a consequence, some have natural resources while others do not, some enjoyed extensive international support while others did not, and some occurred rather quickly while others were slow. The analytical framework applied to these cases included an assessment of the underlying identities that gave rise to these movements, the existing political and economic contexts, the roles that violence and external actors played, and the extent to which a charismatic leader was central to the movement's appeal. Our goal was to help shape and structure policy discussions rather than advance the political science literature, and we emphasized comprehendibility over comprehensiveness. While no case study was an unqualified success, we were able to identify factors that contributed to success after independence, and factors that tended to undermine success.

Writing about Bangladesh, Ambassadors Howard and Teresita Schaffer find that the marriage between East and West Pakistan was always fragile, but the decisive factors that led to partition were from outside Pakistan itself: Secretary of State Henry Kissinger's China diplomacy and India's intervention. The country faced tremendous political polarization, economic challenges, and military tensions. A combination of charismatic leadership, unexpectedly strong economic growth, and an extant and vibrant NGO sector helped guide the country forward.

Terrence Lyons finds that Eritrea emerged surprisingly resilient after a brutal 30-year war, in part because it established many of the institutions of a state throughout the war.[17] When the government of Ethiopia stumbled at the end of the Cold War, Eritrea not only won independence, but did so with the support of the government from which it was seceding. The new state enjoyed broad international support for many years, but a border war with Ethiopia seven years after independence plunged Eritrea into an authoritarian grip from which the country has been unable to escape.

Timor-Leste is one of the more unlikely self-determination efforts described here. In Miks Muižarājs' analysis, Western governments were uniformly opposed to Timorese self-determination efforts because of the Marxist ideology that the independence movement embraced. Sophisticated diplomacy that included a papal visit, the end of the Cold War, the Asian financial crisis, and a political shift in Indonesia all combined to create an opening for Timorese independence. Very large-scale international support from the United Nations and elsewhere, combined with a Timorese ability to avoid the pitfalls of such assistance, helped lay the groundwork for a largely successful state-building effort.

Daniel Serwer finds that Kosovo's independence was the improbable consequence of a confluence of factors, including rebellion, repression, state dissolution and collapse, NATO intervention, Western support, Russian weakness, and UN administration. Among the case studies collected in this volume, Kosovo seems to have had the strongest assist from exogenous factors that led to independence.

The final independence case study considered here is Richard Downie's examination of South Sudan. There, the Sudanese government's ostracization was a key factor that promoted the secession of the South. As the Khartoum government became more rigidly Islamist in orientation and harbored terrorists, governments such as the United States viewed the largely Christian and animist South as a victim deserving of liberation. The South was not well prepared for independence, with a weak economy, rampant corruption around the oil industry, and poor infrastructure. In addition, politicians failed to protect revenues from the predations of political parties. Soon, disputes within the leadership, combined with hostility between Khartoum and Juba, helped plunge the country into civil war.

In addition to the case studies of independence movements, Erin Jenne and Beáta Huszka compare the different outcomes of three different approaches to self-determination in the Balkans. Examining Bosnia, Macedonia, and Kosovo, they conclude that minority communities can prosper as autonomous units provided the state retains adequate powers of sovereignty, majorities' interests are preserved, and the regional and international environment is supportive.

Two additional chapters round out the analysis. In one, Will Todman analyzes 70 states that won their independence after 1960 to determine what kinds of factors would predict success in the immediate aftermath. Seeking to understand if geostrategic location, the conditions of independence, international aid, international peacekeeping missions, or natural resources played a significant role in states' trajectories in the years after independence, he finds that no overall patterns emerge, but he helpfully identifies ways in which the same factor might cut in different ways in different conditions.

Finally, Todman also sketches out a playbook for U.S. government decisionmakers, highlighting factors they might want to weigh when deciding whether to support or suppress self-determination movements, and the tools at their disposal to do so.

We conclude not with a formula, but with a set of concerns that should guide those involved in self-determination movements. These include international environment, regional environment, economic and political context, security context, and a bucket of social issues. None is by itself dispositive, but we present a policy tool that allows one to visualize the prospects for success.

The policy tool is a spider chart with eight different axes. The further along all the axes an aspiring state is, the better its anticipated result after statehood is accomplished. That is to say, the more of the chart that is covered, the better the odds are. Contrarily, an aspiring state that covers little of the chart, or where some axes are only scantily developed, should expect a more difficult time after independence. The chart identifies visually where some of the important shortcomings are and where energy should be devoted.

Political celebrations are especially exultant when they mark an end to repression, or the results are unexpected. Self-determination movements fit both criteria by definition. A sense of grievance drives every such movement, and history shows that the odds against winning self-determination are long. Globalization, increasing mobility, and the rise of supranational structures such as the European Union have not visibly diminished groups' desire for self-determination. If anything, these trends seem to have fed them. As has been the case for centuries, self-determination seems likely to remain the ambition of many and the accomplishment of few. The authors hope this volume contributes to greater levels of peace and security in the instances in which it is achieved.

NOTES

1. Edmund Blair and Samia Nakhoul, "Egypt Protests Topple Mubarak after 18 Days," Reuters, February 10, 2011; Chris McGreal and Jack Shenker, "Hosni Mubarak Resigns—and Egypt Celebrates a New Dawn," *The Guardian*, February 11, 2011.
2. Alan Taylor, "South Sudan: The Newest Nation in the World," *The Atlantic*, July 11, 2011.
3. Alex MacDonald, "'Bye Bye Iraq': Erbil Celebrates as Polls Close in Kurdish Independence Vote," *Middle East Eye*, September 25, 2017.
4. Ian Black, "Benghazi's Moment of Joy as Libya's Tyranny Ends," *The Guardian*, October 23, 2011.

5. Alexander Dziadosz and Jeremy Clarke, "South Sudanese Dance to Celebrate Independence," Reuters, July 8, 2011.

6. McGreal and Shenker, "Hosni Mubarak Resigns."

7. "The Treaty of Peace with Germany (Treaty of Versailles, 1919)," in Charles Bevans, ed., *United States Treaties and International Agreements: 1776–1949*, Volume 2 (Washington, DC: U.S. Department of State, 1969), 43–240.

8. United Nations, "Growth in United Nations Membership, 1945–Present," http://www.un.org/en/sections/member-states/growth-united-nations-membership-1945-present/index.html.

9. This may seriously overstate the case. Nicholas Sambanis et al. count only 464 self-determination movements between 1945 and 2012, the overwhelming majority of which were unsuccessful. To arrive at a number like 750, a large number of new movements would need to emerge, especially given the relatively low success rate of such movements historically. See Nicholas Sambanis, Micha Germann, and Andreas Schädel, "SDM: A New Data Set on Self-Determination Movements with an Application to Reputational Theory of Conflict," *Journal of Conflict Resolution* 62, no. 3 (2018): 656–686.

10. Bridget Coggins suggests four waves but omits Latin America and splits the post–World War II cohort into states that immediately won independence after the war and those that won it more gradually through the 1970s. Bridget Coggins, "Friends in High Places: International Politics and the Emergence of States from Secession," *International Organization* 65 (Summer 2011): 436–447.

11. Ian Traynor, "Montenegro Vote Finally Seals Death of Yugoslavia," *The Guardian*, May 21, 2006. The states are Croatia, Slovenia, Macedonia, Bosnia and Hercegovina, Macedonia, and Montenegro. Kosovo's status as an independent state is disputed.

12. Paul Collier and Anke Hoeffler, *The Political Economy of Secession* (Washington, DC: World Bank, 2002); Nicholas Sambanis and Branko Milanovic, *Explaining the Demand for Sovereignty*, Policy Research Working Paper 5888 (Washington, DC: World Bank, 2011).

13. For example, see Bridget Coggins, "Friends in High Places: International Politics and the Emergence of States from Secessionism," *International Organization* 65 (Summer 2011): 433–467; Ryan Griffiths, *Age of Secession: The International and Domestic Determinants of State Birth* (Cambridge: Cambridge University Press, 2016); and Jason Sorens, *Secessionism: Identity, Interest, and Strategy* (Kingston, ON: McGill-Queen's University Press, 2012).

14. For example, see David Chandler and Timothy Sisk, eds., *The Routledge Handbook of International Statebuilding* (New York: Routledge, 2013); Louise Anderson, Bjørn Møller, and Finn Stepputat, eds., *Fragile States and Insecure People: Violence, Security, and Statehood in the Twenty-First Century* (New York: Palgrave MacMillan, 2007); Michael Doyle and Nicholas Sambanis, *Making War and Building Peace: United Nations Peace Operations* (Princeton, NJ: Princeton University Press, 2006); and Julia Raue and Patrick Sutter, eds., *Facets and Practices of State-Building* (Leiden, Netherlands: Nijhoff Publishers, 2009).

15. Jaroslav Tir, "Dividing Countries to Promote Peace: Prospects for Long-Term Success of Partitions," *Journal of Peace Research* 42, no. 5 (2005): 545–562.

16. This point is made more narrowly in Stephen M. Saideman, Beth K. Dougherty, and Erin K. Jenne, "Dilemmas of Divorce: How Secessionist Identities Cut Both Ways," *Security Studies* 14, no. 4 (2005): 607–636.

17. For examples of proto-state institutions in South Sudan, Sri Lanka, and the Congo, see, for example, Zacharia Cherian Mampilly, *Rebel Rulers: Insurgent Governance and Civilian Life during War* (Ithaca, NY: Cornell University Press, 2011); for Colombia, see Ana Arjona, *Rebelocracy: Social Order in the Colombian Civil War* (Cambridge: Cambridge University Press, 2016).

2. BANGLADESH: TWO INDEPENDENCE MOVEMENTS
Howard and Teresita Schaffer

TIMELINE

August 14, 1947	Pakistan is established, with East Bengal as part
September 1948	Muhammad Ali Jinnah, Pakistan's founder, dies
February 21, 1952	Students in Dhaka riot, demanding equal status for Bangla language
March 1954	Awami League leads the victorious United Front in the East Pakistan Legislative Assembly election
September 1954	Constituent Assembly declares Urdu and Bangla to be the official languages of Pakistan
October 1958	General Mohammad Ayub Khan (later Field Marshal) declares martial law in Pakistan
1963	Sheikh Mujibur Rahman becomes leader of Awami League
February 1966	Mujib sets out Six Point Program, calling for two separate autonomous states in Pakistan
February/March 1969	Ayub invites Mujib and other opposition leaders to Round Table Conference, which collapses March 13
March 25, 1969	General Agha Mohammad Yahya Khan becomes president of Pakistan on resignation of Ayub

November 1970	Massive cyclone strikes East Pakistan
December 7, 1970	Pakistan national parliamentary elections; Awami League wins all but two seats in East Pakistan, and a majority of the national parliament
March 1, 1971	Yahya cancels initial sitting of the new parliament
March 25, 1971	Awami League is banned, brutal crackdown is implemented; kicks off nine-month civil war
March 26, 1971	Sheikh Mujib pens Bangladeshi Declaration of Independence, which is read the next day; he is arrested
November 1971	India provides sanctuary to Awami League militants
December 3, 1971	Pakistan attacks three airfields in Indian Punjab; India intervenes
December 10, 1971	Pakistani governor of East Pakistan makes last-ditch attempt to obtain a cease-fire without surrendering
December 15, 1971	Indian army enters Dhaka
December 16, 1971	Pakistan's commanding general, General Niazi, signs the Instrument of Surrender
December 28, 1971	Sheikh Mujib and other Awami League leaders are released from jail
January 10, 1972	Mujib returns to Bangladesh
March 26, 1972	Bangladesh nationalizes property of Pakistanis who fled to West Pakistan, as well as Bengali-owned industrial assets over a certain size
July 2, 1972	Simla Agreement signed by India and Pakistan opens the way to repatriation of Bangladeshis interned in Pakistan
August 1972	Bangladesh joins the World Bank and International Monetary Fund (IMF)
December 16, 1972	Constitution is adopted
February 1974	Prime Minister Bhutto announces recognition of Bangladesh

October 1974	Bangladesh joins the United Nations
December 1974	Sheikh Mujib declares state of emergency
January 1975	The Fourth Amendment is passed, making Sheikh Mujib president in a one-party state
August 15, 1975	Sheikh Mujib and most of his family are assassinated
November 1975	A coup kills four of Sheikh Mujib's closest associates; Chief Justice A. S. M. Sayem is appointed president and chief martial law administrator
January 1976	Bangladesh and Pakistan establish diplomatic and economic relations
1976–1977	Multiple coup attempts thwarted
1977	A. S. M. Sayem resigns due to ill health
1978	General Ziaur Rahman is elected president
1979	Zia's party wins two-thirds majority in elections
1981	Zia is assassinated
1982	General H. M. Ershad assumes control of Bangladesh in a coup
1990	Ershad is forced from office by a popular movement headed by Sheikh Hasina, daughter of Sheikh Mujib, and by Begum Khaleda Zia, widow of General Zia; Begum Zia becomes prime minister; the two women, bitter political opponents, alternate in power until 2015, when Sheikh Hasina wins a second term in a controversial election

Bangladesh's independence in 1971 shocked the world with its violence and the callousness of U.S. policy, inspired a unique Beatles concert, and became a feature in a major shift in relations among the United States, China, the Soviet Union, and India. But the Bangladesh movement did not arise in a vacuum. Instead, it grew out of the fragmented geographic, ethnic, and power structure left behind from its first independence movement, when the subcontinent was partitioned into India and Pakistan in 1947.

Figure 2.1. Map of Bangladesh

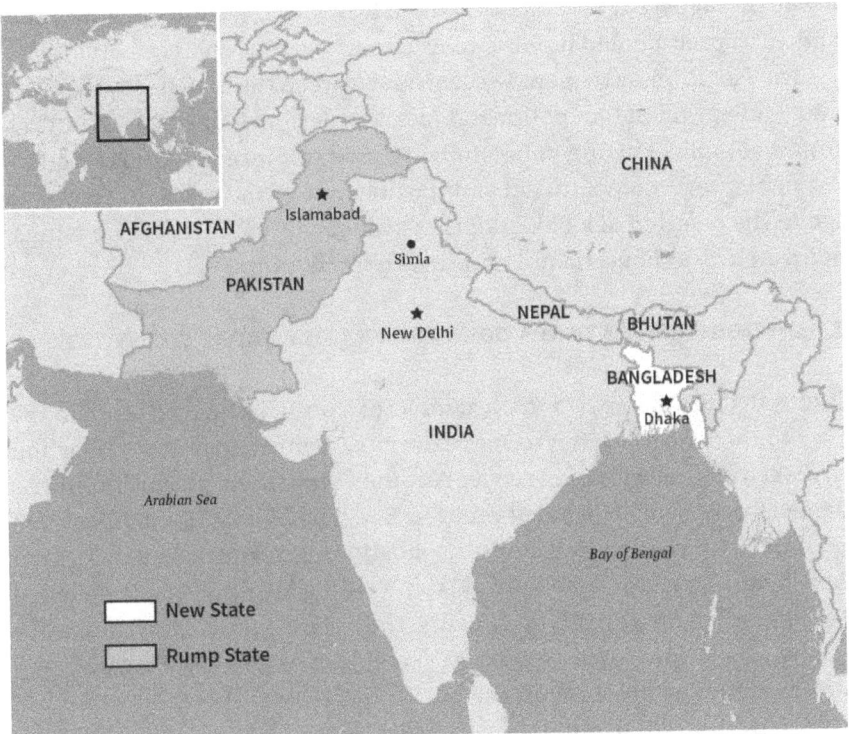

After independence, Bangladesh was expected to be a "basket case." Relatively successful economically, its political trajectory has been more volatile, albeit more promising than other countries studied for this project. However, many issues that shaped the Bangladesh movement—the second of the country's two independence movements—still stalk Bangladeshi politics four decades after its bloody creation.

THE FIRST INDEPENDENCE MOVEMENT: CREATING PAKISTAN

In the wake of the Second World War, the British concluded that they would have to "Quit India." They aspired to leave behind a united subcontinent, long a jewel in their imperial crown. But by the spring of 1947, political realities on the ground forced the British to accept the demands of the subcontinent's sizable Muslim minority for a separate, independent homeland to be called Pakistan. The hastily carried out Partition that followed in August 1947 was accompanied by widespread violence, murder, and an unprecedented number of refugees.[1]

The Partition settlement worked out between the British government and contending Indian political forces was designed to place the bulk of imperial India's Muslim population in Pakistan. Since the major Muslim-majority areas were situated at opposite ends of the subcontinent, this led to the creation of a Pakistan that awkwardly comprised two wings, separated by a thousand miles of Indian territory.[2]

TWO-WINGED PAKISTAN: A COUNTRY FRAGILE FROM THE START

Issues that ultimately led to the demise of a united Pakistan arose in the new country's earliest days. One of the most immediate was the question of Pakistan's national language. Another was the composition of the armed forces, which included very few Bengalis. What little industry and commerce existed in Pakistan was mostly in the West and was held in non-Bengali hands. Although Pakistan's ruling Muslim League included some prominent Bengali politicians, they were overshadowed by Muhammad Ali Jinnah, the venerated "Great Leader" (Quaid-e-Azam), who dominated the government, the party, and all aspects of Pakistani national life until his untimely death in September 1948.

The Language Issue

Controversies over the designation of a national language have bedeviled many emerging countries, notably those of the multilingual former British possessions in South Asia. In East Pakistan, Bengali pride in the Bangla language had an unusually important political dimension. Culture, rather than competition for jobs, was the most contentious aspect of this divisive issue.

Jinnah was adamant about having one national language for Pakistan and rejected Bengali demands for equal status for Urdu and Bangla. After his death, the language issue sparked lengthy, acrimonious debates in the Constituent Assembly, the parliamentary body charged with framing a constitution for the new country. In early 1952, students demanding equal status for Bangla rioted in the streets of Dhaka. Several were killed by police. The date of what Bangladeshis consider the students' martyrdom,

"Ekushay" (for the 21st of February), is an annual remembrance still observed with great solemnity in Bangladesh.

In September 1954, the Constituent Assembly finally designated two official languages for Pakistan—Urdu and Bangla. But the bitter debate leading up to this compromise had damaged Pakistan's fragile unity and birthed a strong cultural movement in East Pakistan that significantly contributed to the growth of Bengali nationalism.

The Military

The ethnic composition of the Pakistani armed forces reflected the long-standing British practice of recruiting Indians exclusively from the so-called martial races. Since their disloyalty to the Raj during the 1857 Mutiny, Bengalis—both Muslim and Hindu—were largely excluded. As a result, the Pakistani military mostly consisted of officers and other ranks drawn from the Punjabi and Pashtun ethnic groups and from Urdu-speaking families of northern India. Bengalis were virtually excluded from senior positions.

The military and their West Pakistani civilian allies dominated Pakistan's governing institutions, determining security, foreign, and economic policies. That resulted in Pakistan's 1954 alignment with the U.S.-led Western bloc in the global confrontation between the "Free World" and the forces of international Communism. This support was more popular in West Pakistan than in the East. Bengalis were increasingly convinced that their Western compatriots were profiting more from the alliance than they were.

East Pakistanis were also troubled by the military leaders' strategy in the event of another war with India. The military argued the only effective way to defend East Pakistan would be to attack India from the West, stationing only a small force in the East. Understandably, this strategy did not allay East Pakistanis' concerns that their wing could easily be overrun by vastly superior Indian forces.

Economic Grievances

Another major concern for East Pakistanis was the widespread conviction that most of the economic assistance from the United States and its allies ended up in the western wing. Per capita gross domestic product

(GDP) in East Pakistan was about 20 percent higher than in the West in 1960, when Pakistan's treaty relations with the United States were fully in place. But by 1970, the East lagged 20 percent behind the West in GDP. More than half of its GDP came from agriculture throughout the 1960s. By contrast, agricultural production in the West had fallen as industrial production surged.[3]

FIRST STIRRINGS OF THE INDEPENDENCE MOVEMENT

East Pakistanis increasingly believed they were victims of deliberate and unfair discrimination by their more privileged West Wing compatriots. They relied on political organization and legal change as their methods for demanding a more equitable role in national affairs. They found an early opportunity in the March 1954 election for the East Pakistan Legislative Assembly.

This provincial election pitted the incumbent Muslim League against a newly organized United Front of disparate opposition leaders and parties. The strongest of these parties was the Awami (People's) Muslim League, soon to be renamed the Awami League and opened to Hindu and other non-Muslim members. Its leader, veteran politician Huseyn Shaheed Suhrawardy,[4] chose the charismatic, up-and-coming young Sheikh Mujibur Rahman as one of his principal lieutenants. When Suhrawardy died in 1963, Sheikh Mujib, as he was widely called, became party leader. Eight years later he led Bangladesh to independence.

Conducted under universal suffrage but with separate balloting for Muslim and non-Muslim voters, the provincial election resulted in an upset, landslide victory for the United Front. It won 223 of the 237 Muslim seats to the Muslim League's seven, and also enjoyed substantial support among the provincial assembly's considerable Hindu membership. Awami Leaguers won the bulk of the United Front seats. Successful candidates of its ally the Krishak Sramik Party (KSP), led by veteran politician Fazlul Haq, made up the second largest group. Despite the Awami League's stronger performance at the polls, Haq became chief minister.[5]

The United Front platform demanded provincial autonomy except in defense, foreign affairs, and currency. It called for recognition of Bangla as a national language and its use in instruction at all levels, the creation of a directly elected constituent assembly, agricultural reforms, the ending of restrictions on trade with and travel to India, freedom of trade in jute, and the withdrawal of provisions permitting political arrests and detentions.[6] Most of these demands were, of course, largely or totally unacceptable to the West Pakistani generals, senior civil servants, and politicians who dominated the central government in Karachi.

This establishment was unwilling to tolerate a United Front government in Dhaka or dissidence from Bengalis and others at the national level. The United Front enjoyed only a brief, troubled life. Severe rioting at East Pakistani jute mills between Bengali and non-Bengali workers and accusations that Haq was collaborating with the Indians led the central government to dismiss him and his provincial government before any of the United Front's major demands could be satisfied or addressed. The assembly was suspended, then dissolved a few months later. The East Pakistani government came to be led by a succession of political groupings that reflected both the instability of alignments in the assembly and frequent intervention by the central government.[7]

GENERAL AYUB KHAN TAKES CHARGE

Mohammad Ayub Khan, a former commander of the Pakistan Army and defense minister in civilian-led governments in the 1950s, declared martial law in October 1958.[8] Ayub would rule Pakistan as president for the next 11 years. The pro–West Pakistan biases of earlier governments continued to dominate his approach. He relied on an inner circle drawn from the West Pakistani military and civil service elite. West Pakistanis approved of Ayub's anti-corruption measures, the rapid economic growth he generated, and his establishment of Pakistan as a poster child for economic development and political stability among Third World countries.

By contrast, sentiment in East Pakistan was much less positive. Bengalis had only limited roles in running the country, sensed they were falling behind the West in economic development, and felt largely neglected by the aid-giving world. With the deaths in the 1960s of Suhrawardy and Fazlul Haq, they also lost two of their most respected leaders.

Ayub did, however, make several decisions that pleased Bengalis. Most importantly, in his final years as president, he significantly increased recruitment of East Pakistanis into commissioned ranks of the armed forces and senior civil service. He also boosted East Pakistan's industrial and agricultural development, though it continued to lag behind the West.

AYUB'S DECLINE AND FALL

Ayub's seemingly invulnerable position declined in the mid-1960s. His reputation as a statesman and military leader was badly damaged after the short war with India to win control over Kashmir ended in stalemate. He also suffered from the changing perception in West Pakistan of his government's economic performance. Resentment grew toward the beneficiaries of the new wealth, seen in today's terms as "crony capitalists."[9]

As support for Ayub weakened, frustrated Bengalis took action. At a conference of opposition party leaders from East and West Pakistan in Lahore in February 1966, Sheikh Mujib, then president of the Awami League, radically changed the focus of Bengali demands. He and others representing East Pakistan concluded that the West Pakistani establishment's domination of the national government meant that sharing power was no longer a feasible way for the Bengalis to attain their political and economic objectives.

The Six Point Program that Sheikh Mujib set out exceeded the limited autonomy the United Front had proposed in its 1964 provincial election campaign. It called for two sovereign autonomous states, limiting the power of the federal government, new currency provisions, autonomous taxation and revenue collection, a new foreign exchange arrangement, and the establishment of an East Pakistani armed force.

Not surprisingly, President Ayub called the Six Point Program a scheme for East Pakistan's secession and threatened force to block its adoption. Sheikh Mujib and other Awami Leaguers were jailed, leading to province-wide demonstrations and clashes in which students played a leading role.[10] Facing mounting turbulence, Ayub invited opposition leaders from both wings, including the recently released Sheikh Mujib, to a round table conference. Held in February and March 1969, the bitterly divided conference ultimately failed when President Ayub declared that fundamental constitutional questions could be decided only by elected representatives.[11]

Soon afterward, Ayub announced his resignation as president. The 1962 constitution he had promulgated was abrogated, the National Assembly was dissolved, and martial law was proclaimed. Ayub handed over the presidency to General Agha Mohammad Yahya Khan, the army's commander-in-chief.

THE END OF UNITED PAKISTAN

Yahya Khan was the last president of Pakistan as delineated in the 1947 Partition of India. His three years in power ended with his resignation after Pakistan's military defeat by India in 1971 and the emergence of an independent Bangladesh. He was a man of limited ability and unsteady character who proved unable to deal with the enormous problems Pakistan faced. Nonetheless, he received strong support from the administration of President Richard Nixon.

Yahya got off to a promising start. He pledged early elections for a National Assembly that would be required to draft a new constitution within 120 days of the balloting. The new president also issued an important decree stipulating that provincial representation in the newly chosen body would be allocated on the basis of population. For the first time, East Pakistan would choose a majority of the members of a national Pakistani assembly.

In East Pakistan, the Awami League's battle cry in the campaign was the Six Point Program. Sheikh Mujib's party's strong appeal there was boosted by widespread resentment at the central government's failure to deal adequately and promptly with the devastating impact of the worst cyclone and tidal wave in eastern Bengal in living memory.[12] When polling took place starting in early December 1970, the Awami League swept the East, winning 160 of the province's 162 National Assembly seats. Results were less decisive in the West, where Zulfikar Ali Bhutto's Pakistan People's Party won 81 of 138 seats. Importantly, the Awami League won no seats in the West, nor did the PPP win any in the East.

The outcome surprised Yahya and his military commanders. They were troubled by the Awami League's sweep in East Pakistan and all that implied for the division of power between the East and West and for the military's parochial interests. A series of talks involving Yahya, Sheikh Mujib, and Bhutto followed the elections, but made no progress in resolving the deadlock on the establishment of a civilian-led, constitutional government. Under pressure from Bhutto and his military colleagues, Yahya postponed indefinitely the inaugural session of the National Assembly scheduled for March 1, 1971, in Dhaka. At the same time, he sent military reinforcements to East Pakistan and prepared diplomatic groundwork for an eventual crackdown there.[13]

The postponement sine die of the National Assembly triggered an Awami League–directed shutdown of all normal activity in East Pakistan. Violence flared and hundreds were killed. Sheikh Mujib continued to urge restraint, but also began to speak of a "struggle for independence" in speeches to supporters in Dhaka.

The deadlock was broken on March 25 when the Awami League was banned, all political activity proscribed, and a brutal crackdown implemented. The reinforced Pakistan Army killed thousands of Bengali civilians. Sheikh Mujib and his principal associates were arrested a few days later. Bhutto, fully supporting Yahya's action, told the press, "By the Grace of God, Pakistan has at last been saved."[14] He was wrong. Instead, the military action led to a nine-month civil war and, in December 1971, to the liberation of East Pakistan and its emergence as independent Bangladesh.

THE INTERNATIONAL TAPESTRY

The development of the Bangladesh movement grew out of the structure of the Pakistan state as first created and how united Pakistan was governed. Unhappiness in East Pakistan fueled calls for separation. Pakistan and Bangladesh found themselves at the confluence of two international forces: Cold War politics, specifically Henry Kissinger's China diplomacy, and India's response to Pakistan's fragility. The Cold War connection added drama and international significance to the events surrounding Bangladesh's independence, and India's intervention proved to be decisive.

The Cold War Dimension

Secretary of State Kissinger's determination to pursue a dramatic reversal of major power relationships was the driving force behind the United States' pro-Pakistan policy. For some time, the United States had been exploring an opening to China, hoping to secure Chinese cooperation against the Soviet Union. Pakistan was one of two countries being considered as possible intermediaries. Kissinger would not countenance any policy moves distasteful to Pakistan lest they interfere with his larger strategic aims. In October 1970, before the crackdown in East Bengal, President Nixon asked for Pakistan's assistance.[15] In July 1971, Kissinger, with the help of Yahya's government, made a secret visit to China. Soon after Kissinger returned to Washington, his visit to Beijing was announced, along with the news that Nixon planned to visit China. Pakistan's role in brokering the U.S. opening to China became publicly known.

Evidence of increasingly close U.S.-Pakistan ties set off alarms in New Delhi. On August 9, 1971, India signed a Treaty of Friendship and Cooperation with the Soviet Union.[16] Such a pact had apparently been under discussion for six years.[17] But Washington's pro-Pakistan policy provided an important argument for this clear deviation from India's traditional posture of nonalignment, shaping an environment where India decided to intervene in the Bangladesh war.

Indian and Pakistani Diplomacy

Indian and Pakistani diplomacy intensified in August 1971. The Awami League, with its principal leaders in jail in Pakistan, had formed a provisional government. Close ties were established with the Indian government, which provided offices in Calcutta and assigned a liaison officer from the Ministry of External Affairs. Indian diplomats hoped to heal splits and ease tensions within the pro-Bangladesh movement. India also had begun training pro-independence guerrillas.

India's policy toward Pakistan hardened, largely confined to diplomacy. Pakistan also made overtures to Bangladesh movement leaders, working through George Griffin, an official at the U.S. Consulate General in Calcutta. Pakistan sought a face-saving arrangement but refused to release Sheikh Mujib from jail or to grant Bangladesh independence—both nonstarters in light of the violence of Pakistan's crackdown a few months earlier.[18]

Refugees, most of them Hindu, began pouring into India, an estimated 7 million of them by July 1971. By October, India felt that time was running out. India had always sought to maintain regional primacy. Washington was still in Pakistan's corner. Concerned about a preemptive U.S. gambit, Prime Minister Indira Gandhi preferred to make the first move. Once convinced that her military could achieve a decisive and quick victory, she had them prepare in earnest. Government and public opinion solidly backed her. By November, India was providing sanctuary to Awami League paramilitaries conducting operations against the Pakistan Army. With intervention looming, India and pro-Bangladesh forces created a joint command. In the end, Pakistan's decision to attack three airfields in Indian Punjab on December 3 triggered India's full-scale intervention.[19]

Last-Minute Diplomacy

The most dramatic U.S. moves came after India's intervention. On December 3, the United States cut off economic aid to India and dispatched the aircraft carrier *Enterprise* to provide a show of force in the Indian Ocean. The UN Security Council got involved. A U.S.-sponsored resolution calling for a cessation of hostilities was vetoed by the Soviet Union, supporting India. The General Assembly eventually approved a cease-fire resolution by a huge majority.

Kissinger made two moves. On Nixon's direct instructions, he attempted an unsuccessful bid to induce Soviet pressure on India to pull back. The other came on December 10, when Kissinger told the Chinese ambassador to the United Nations that "if the People's Republic were to consider the situation on the Indian subcontinent a threat to its security ... [the United States] would oppose efforts of others to interfere with the People's Republic." The United States, in other words, was prepared to act as China's quasi-ally. The Chinese, however, showed no interest.[20] Next the Pakistani governor of East Pakistan made a last-ditch effort to obtain a cease-fire and to install a Bangladeshi government without a formal surrender from the Pakistan Army. In the end, an independent Bangladesh was inevitable.

Maneuvering among the United States, India, China, and the Soviet Union influenced the foreign policy of these nations and impacted their ties with Bangladesh. In particular, U.S. policies toward events that reshaped the politics of the Indian subcontinent were driven almost entirely by extra-regional issues.[21]

The End of the War

On December 15, 1971, the Indian Army entered Dhaka. The next day, General Niazi, commander of the Pakistani forces, approached the U.S. Consulate General in Dhaka to ask its help in communicating a cease-fire proposal to his Indian counterparts. Once again, Pakistanis tried to accomplish this without use of the word "surrender"—in vain.[22] From India's intervention to the surrender took only 13 days.

ESTABLISHING THE NEW STATE

Sheikh Mujib and other senior Awami League leaders were released from prison in Pakistan starting December 28, 1971. Sheikh Mujib returned to a victorious Bangladesh on January 10.[23] He had been an iconic rebel leader, exemplified by his oft-used title, "Bangabandhu," or Friend of Bengal. Now he needed to create a state, establish authority, and reinvigorate the economy.

Laying the Groundwork

The first steps in establishing national institutions occurred immediately after the brutal Pakistan Army crackdown. Just before his arrest, Sheikh Mujib had begun a state-in-waiting.[24] In mid-April 1971, the leaders still at liberty announced the formation of a provisional government and swore in a roster of officeholders—Sheikh Mujib as president in absentia, Syed Nazrul Islam as acting president, and Tajuddin Ahmed as prime minister. They also published a Declaration of Independence that Mujib issued the day after the massacre. Provisional government leaders put Colonel Osmany, a Bengali officer retired from the Pakistan Army, in charge of military affairs. He set up an organizational structure and regional commands for the military personnel who had left the Pakistan Army.[25]

In the nine months between the crackdown and the end of the war, many Bengali foreign service officers assigned to Pakistani missions abroad left their posts. Most were permitted to stay in their host countries.[26] The provisional government—and after the surrender, the new government—used these people to make contact with other governments. Some wound up playing major roles in independent Bangladesh. The most senior Bengali in the embassy in Washington, the economist A. M. A. Muhith, went on to senior positions, and at this writing is finance minister in Sheikh Hasina's government.[27]

Many civil servants who had run the East Pakistan government came from the West. The few Bengali civil servants physically in Bangladesh, who were disproportionately junior in rank, remained in place. Bengali civil servants stationed in West Pakistan, like their military counterparts, were not repatriated to Bangladesh until after 1973. Besides these structural problems, East Bengal had only had a provincial government in the pre-independence period. Civil servants were suddenly faced with larger responsibilities that came with running a sovereign state—but with far fewer resources than most states enjoy.

Writing a Constitution

Much of the energy of the Bangladesh movement focused on dissatisfaction with Pakistan's constitutional arrangements, so a constitution for the new country loomed large for post-independence leaders. Writing the constitution was entrusted to lawyers trained, like so many in the subcontinental elite, in Britain. Soon after Sheikh Mujib's return, the provisional authorities—those who had been elected to the ill-fated National Assembly in 1970—were incorporated as a Constituent Assembly. To provide interim governing rules, they also proclaimed a provisional constitutional instrument and established a Supreme Court.

The constitution, adopted on the first anniversary of Pakistan's surrender—December 16, 1972—created a parliamentary system, with the prime minister as the chief executive and a unicameral legislature. Drafters struggled to avoid mistakes they felt Pakistan's constitution had made, detailing principles often left implicit. The constitution made significant use of symbolism: besides the date, the drafters made a major effort to find a lawyer capable of writing the document in Bangla.[28]

Separating from Pakistan, Joining the World

Transitioning from surrender to peace was the subject of negotiations between India and Pakistan, culminating in a conference at Simla in the summer of 1972.[29] The Simla Agreement is best remembered for providing "rules of the road" for India-Pakistan relations. It mandated India's release of 93,000 Pakistan troops who were in the East when the war ended and taken to India as prisoners of war. Simla also created a framework for Pakistan's return to Bangladesh of interned Bengalis who had been in the Pakistani civil service or military.[30]

These exchanges of personnel were delayed by the larger drama of settling Bangladesh's place in international institutions and dividing assets and liabilities between Pakistan and Bangladesh. The first breakthrough came in February 1974. With a meeting of the Organization of the Islamic Conference (OIC) fast approaching, a delegation of Islamic ministers traveled to Dhaka, seeking to broker an agreement between the two Muslim states. When the delegation went on to Lahore the next day, Pakistan's Prime Minister Bhutto announced his recognition of Bangladesh, thus removing the major obstacle to personnel exchanges, which took place over the next year.[31]

Pakistani recognition also accelerated the process of separating Bangladeshi and Pakistani international debt. Bangladesh had joined the International Monetary Fund and the World Bank after the Simla conference, in August 1972. This brought access to desperately needed aid resources, while the World Bank provided a formula for dividing the debt. Bangladesh's application to join the United Nations, previously vetoed by China, finally gained approval in October 1974.[32] Pakistan and Bangladesh established diplomatic relations and trade in January 1976.

GOVERNING INDEPENDENT BANGLADESH: SHEIKH MUJIB'S TURBULENT RULE AND BLOODY END

Sheikh Mujib was an extraordinary leader of the Bangladesh movement. He gave millions of his countrymen hope, leadership, and unity. Yet he was burdened by the high expectations his political leadership created in the Bangladeshi public. He spoke of "four pillars" of Bangladesh: nationalism, socialism, secularism, and democracy. He was not the first iconic leader, however, to discover that governing a country beset by desperate problems is a different and more arduous challenge. Sheikh Mujib's tenure as head of a new government was extraordinarily volatile because of an agricultural sector far from capable of feeding the country, few foreign exchange–earning assets, a desperate shortage of human and financial resources, fractious politics, divisions in the army, and the continuing presence of armed activists.

On March 26, 1972—exactly one year after the bloody crackdown on Dhaka that marked the official birth of Bangladesh—the government decided to nationalize the property of Pakistanis who had returned to West Pakistan, as well as Bengali-owned industrial assets over a certain size, the first step in a hoped-for socialist transformation.[33]

In the elections of 1973, the Awami League once again won nearly all of the 300 seats in parliament and 73 percent of the votes. The economy, however, remained a disaster. The middle class, once the backbone of the Awami League, and donors, which the government depended on for funding, pushed back. Spreading law and order problems led Sheikh Mujib to declare a state of emergency in December 1974. He changed the constitution to increase his authority. The Fourth Amendment, passed overwhelmingly in January 1975, declared him president, and instituted a one-party state. He also created the personal security group, Jatiyo Rakkhi Bahini.[34]

On August 15, 1975, a group led by four army officers assassinated Sheikh Mujib and almost his entire family. Only his two daughters, both in Europe at the time, survived. One, Sheikh Hasina, has served three times as prime minister. Accounts of the assassination focused more on personal factors than on the institutional problems of the army. Two of the officers involved had recently been separated from the army and had personal scores to settle.[35]

THE ZIA YEARS: ECONOMIC SUCCESS, MILITARY CRACKDOWN, A BLOODY END

The few months that followed Sheikh Mujib's assassination were chaotic. Another coup in early November, again led by an army officer, killed four of Sheikh Mujib's closest associates in Dhaka Central Jail. A few days later, the officer who had led the first coup was killed in a counter-coup. Soon afterward, Chief Justice A. S. M. Sayem was appointed president and chief martial law administrator. The army chief of staff, General Ziaur Rahman, soon emerged as the next power figure and became president after Sayem's resignation due to ill health in 1977.

Over an extended period, generals ruled Bangladesh. Zia's rule began with martial law, and he put down coup attempts in 1976 and 1977. Elected president in 1978, he then founded his own party, now one of the two major contending parties in Bangladeshi democratic politics. Zia's party won a two-thirds majority in the 1979 elections.

Three issues marked Zia's time in power and represented significant departures from Sheikh Mujib's era. First, he softened the emphasis on secularism that had represented one of Mujib's "pillars." He incorporated into his party former members of the Muslim League—the founding party of Pakistan, regarded as traitorous by freedom parties.

Second, Zia devoted enormous energy, indeed ruthlessness, to restoring discipline in the armed forces. Developing a unified army was one of the central tasks that consumed the early Bangladeshi governments.

Finally, Zia made major changes in Bangladeshi economic policy, including relaxing restrictions on private investment and reversing much of the Mujib-era nationalization. This led to a resurgence of the economy that would have astonished anyone familiar with pre-independence years.

In 1981, Zia too was assassinated, again by army officers. As with Sheikh Mujib, the ringleader had a history of tensions with Zia. The immediate succession to Zia followed the constitutional order. But within about a year, General H. M. Ershad had taken over, again in a coup. Ershad left office in 1990, forced out by a popular movement spearheaded by Sheikh Hasina, daughter of Sheikh Mujib, and by Begum Khaleda Zia, widow of General Zia. For a decade and a half, these two women, representing two political dynasties of Bangladesh, alternated in power, with elections widely praised for fairness. Between elections, the political situation remained highly polarized.

Sheikh Hasina, elected prime minister in 2008, was able to secure reelection in 2014 in a controversial election, the first time since 1990 that a civilian political leader had served two successive terms. The opposition declined to take part in the 2014 election; this means that she wields power with no significant counterweight. Bangladesh under her leadership has continued to do well economically—far better than anyone expected at its birth.

THREE CENTRAL CHALLENGES: ARMY, ECONOMY, AND GOVERNANCE

Those who have governed Bangladesh have faced many difficulties in launching a new nation. Three stand out: creating a disciplined and unified army; enabling a desperately poor economy to support one of the densest populations on earth; and governance, including in particular forging a governing consensus. Broadly speaking, the country met the first two quite successfully. The governing consensus, however, remains elusive.

The Army

Bangladesh had three types of armed organizations at independence. The first two consisted of Bengalis who had been in the Pakistan Army. Within days after the March 25, 1971 army crackdown, five Bengali battalions based in East Pakistan left the Pakistan Army and joined the rebellion. The East Pakistan Rifles, a paramilitary formation with members dispersed around the country, followed quickly. All joined independence forces as units, including Bengali officers and enlisted troops. They formed the nucleus of the forces organized by Colonel, later General, Osmany. They are referred to as Freedom Fighters or, in Bangla, Mukti Bahini.

A second ex-Pakistan Army group consisted of Bengali military officers and troops who were stationed in West Pakistan when the crackdown took place. They were interned and brought back to Bangladesh between 1973 and 1975. They were known in Bangladesh as Repatriates.

Integrating these two groups after independence took more than three decades. In consideration of their role in achieving independence, Freedom Fighters were granted two years of backdated seniority, with the result that some repatriated officers were suddenly junior to those they had previously outranked. Freedom Fighters were suspicious of the more numerous Repatriates, and the latter did not always share the strong personal loyalty to Mujib that most of the Freedom Fighters espoused. Repatriates, on the other hand, resented the prominence given the Freedom Fighters.[36]

The third set of armed groups were guerrilla organizations that had taken part in the liberation war. Some were civilian volunteers with minimal training who were not integrated into the regular army, though a few volunteered. These included young people with radical political views sharply at variance with those who had served in the military. The latter had little patience with talk of "a revolutionary army."

Other guerrillas had been more professionally trained by India in the run-up to the war. Mujib recognized these forces could be a threat to his authority. A week after his return to Bangladesh, he called on the Freedom Fighters outside the regular defense forces to surrender their arms. He presided over a ceremony in which perhaps the most powerful Mukti Bahini leader, Kader "Tiger" Siddiqui, surrendered arms to the new government.

The army was where classic "insider/outsider" problems simmered and flared. Freedom Fighters led the army for a decade after independence. General Zia carried out a discipline campaign that led to the execution of hundreds of military officers. He also integrated the Jatiyo Rakkhi Bahini into the army. In his stewardship of the army, he leaned more heavily on Repatriates.[37] General Ershad, who took power in a 1982 military coup and was the first Repatriate to head the army, came down hard on the Freedom Fighters.[38] Mutinies and other problems traceable to the different groups in the army continued for four decades.

The army has played an important role in politics at various times, especially through its involvement in the interim government of 2007–2008 and its role in the unsuccessful effort to banish the two principal political leaders, Sheikh Hasina and Begum Zia, from political life.

The Economic Surprise

The immediate impact of independence was an economic disaster. In 1972, its first year of independence, newly independent Bangladesh saw a 13 percent drop in its GDP, a 10 percent fall in agricultural production, and a 46 percent reduction in industrial production. Agricultural land had been pillaged and burned. The transportation network suffered vast destruction.[39] The new government's decision to take over most of the country's industrial assets deepened the economic trough.

The big surprise was how successfully the economy turned around. A few years after independence, aid resources began to flow in much greater quantity. The World Bank began lending to Bangladesh in 1973, although about two-thirds of the new money was allocated to reconstruction of wartime and cyclone damage.[40] What really fueled the resurgence were the growth of a vibrant and effective NGO sector and the rise of the textile industry.

The NGO story predates Bangladeshi independence. East Pakistan had a lively NGO scene. Its best-known institution was the Academy of Rural Development in Comilla, in eastern Bangladesh, launched in 1959 and headed by the charismatic Akhtar Hameed Khan, who hailed from the far northwest of West Pakistan. He developed a model for using cooperatives as an economic development tool and was widely believed to be one inspiration for the microcredit model, used with considerable success by several pathbreaking NGOs.[41] The oldest of these, BRAC, founded by Sir Fazle Hassan Abed in 1972, now claims the title of the world's largest NGO; Grameen Bank, founded by Muhammad Yunus, is also internationally renowned. The success of these NGOs owed a great deal to successive Bangladeshi governments' decisions to adopt policies that provided space to bear fruit, not just in microcredit, but also in tremendously successful programs for literacy and family planning. Many benefited from foreign funding.

Table 2.1. Growth of Bangladesh Ready-Made Garments Industry, 1982–1993[a]

Year	Gross Exports (millions of USD)	Percentage of Total Exports
1981/82	7.0	1.1
1982/83	10.8	1.6
1983/84	32.0	3.8
1984/85	116.0	12.8
1985/86	131.0	16.0
1986/87	299.0	27.8
1987/88	433.0	35.2
1988/89	471.0	36.6
1989/90	609.0	40.0
1990/91	736.0	42.8
1991/92	1,064.0	53.4
1992/93	1,240.5	52.0

[a] Bangladesh Garment Manufacturers and Exporters Association and Bangladesh Bureau of Statistics, cited in World Bank, *Bangladesh: From Stabilization to Growth* (Washington, DC: World Bank, 1995), 77.

The decision of the post-Mujib governments to reverse much of the earlier nationalization policy set the stage for the extraordinary success of the ready-made garment industry in Bangladesh. Zia, before becoming president, was under considerable pressure from aid donors to ease conditions for private investment—both domestic and foreign. As early as December 1975, the government eliminated the ceiling on individual private investments and removed a number of industries from the category reserved for the public sector. Further legislative changes were enacted over the next few years.[42]

The private sector responded. The first ready-made garment factory to register was a South Korean-Bangladeshi joint venture, Daewoo-Desh. By 1983, 21 factories had been registered. By this time, the industry was overwhelmingly homegrown. Joint ventures were greatly outnumbered by Bangladeshi investments. Labor in these plants was entirely Bangladeshi, consisting largely of women who were the first female wage-earners in their families.

Export figures illustrate the impact of this surging industry on the Bangladeshi economy. By 1993, ready-made garments accounted for 52 percent of Bangladeshi exports.

Bangladeshi GDP has continued to grow. The country also has achieved another goal no one expected: it is able to feed itself and even to export rice most years. National leaders have begun speaking about Bangladesh as a "middle-income country," and young people think of themselves as part of the next cyber generation.

Struggling with Governance

History still shapes politics in Bangladesh. Many issues that led to the breakup of the two-wing Pakistan are still part of the fabric of the country. Some, such as the language issue, are rallying points for Bangladeshis. Ideological divisions that roiled the Bangladesh movement at independence, such as the argument over whether Bangladesh should seek a socialist revolution or a revolutionary army, have eased.

The first decade of independence left a legacy of deep political polarization. The two principal political parties, Sheikh Mujib's Awami League, which brought the country to birth, and the Bangladesh Nationalist Party (BNP), created by Zia seven years later, have carried on a bitter contest for power over three decades. Both continue to be led and dominated by members of the founders' families. Both are prepared to use every means available to retain their power.

Politics is a winner-take-all affair in Bangladesh. Both parties have ensured that positions of power remain firmly in the hands of their sympathizers. In the early years, Bangladesh was often at the bottom of the Transparency International Corruption Perceptions Index—perceived as corrupt more often and in more ways than any other country covered.[43]

The tradition of polarized politics goes back to Bangladesh's first independence struggle—the partition of British India. One of Bangladesh's most respected political scientists told the authors that Bangladesh's politicians got their start in British times as opponents of the established order, opponents who had no chance of taking power. This same brand of hopeless opposition was typical of many Bengali political activists during the days of united Pakistan. The result was an environment in which purity is prized and compromise is a dirty word.[44] That persists to this day.

The country was founded with an ethos of secularism. Though Zia was the first leader to call Bangladesh an Islamic republic, he departed little from the overall ethos of tolerance and secularism. The BNP's tactical alliance with some Islamist parties brought the issue of Islamic extremism into the already overheated political arena and also played into the politics of history. The July 2016 attack on a popular café in a Dhaka neighborhood, carried out by young Bangladeshis professing adherence to the Islamic State, was a shock to the government and to many Bangladeshis, demonstrating that Islamic extremism now has some Bangladeshi roots.

Polarization is likely to remain strong. Over the past two decades, areas of agreement among Bangladeshis have dwindled. Yet there remains wide acceptance of the push for literacy and empowerment that built the NGO movement; family planning, one of the country's early successes, maintains support across the board; and entrepreneurship that benefits country and its economy is vibrant. Still to be determined is whether the personalities involved in these efforts can work together on common goals while avoiding controversy. Americans today should have some sympathy for the difficulty of operating in this environment, but in this respect, the early dreams of Bangladesh have become harder to achieve.

NOTES

1. Although these tragic developments attracted international attention, the degree of coverage in that pre-television, pre-social media world was much more limited than it would have been later (and was, we shall see, a quarter century afterward during the war for Bangladesh's independence). There was no outcry for outside humanitarian relief, let alone for the intervention of foreign powers. Partition and its immediate aftermath were considered a "British show" for London and the emerging South Asian successor states to deal with on their own. Nor did the events figure in the Cold War confrontation between the communist and noncommunist powers that was then in its earliest stages. This would change over time, especially when the confrontation between India and Pakistan over the disputed princely state of Kashmir attracted the diplomatic attention of Washington and Moscow.

2. Coined in the early 1930s, the term "Pakistan" was based on an acronym derived from Punjab, Afghania (the North-West Frontier Province), Kashmir, Sindh, and the "stan" of Baluchistan. Significantly, the acronym did not include any reference to Bengal or other parts of eastern India. In its original form, which was accepted by the Muslim League at its session in Lahore in 1940, the so-called "Pakistan Resolution" stated that if the condition of Muslims in the provinces of India ruled by the Indian National Congress did not improve, India should be divided into Muslim and non-Muslim areas with two independent sovereign Muslim-majority states carved out of the rest of India in the northwest and the east. It did not call for a single, united Pakistan, nor indeed did it include the term "Pakistan." In 1946, the resolution was rescinded and reissued as a call for a single Pakistan state. For a detailed study of this important historic background to the formation of Pakistan, see Craig Baxter, *Bangladesh: A New Nation in an Old Setting* (Boulder, CO: Westview, 1984), 25–27.

3. Economic statistics in this paragraph are taken from the World Bank database on the Website of the World Bank, http://data.worldbank.org/indicator/NY.GDP.PCAP.CD?locations=BD-PK.

4. Suhrawardy had been Muslim League premier (chief minister) of the Bengal Province of British India in the pre-Partition years before Jinnah ousted him for supporting a failed last-ditch effort by Bengali Hindu and Muslim political leaders to set up a sovereign, independent, single United Bengal outside both India and Pakistan. He had subsequently remained behind in Calcutta for several years after Partition before moving to East Pakistan.

5. Haq's party's name means Farmer and Worker Party. Suhrawardy briefly served as a member of Haq's provincial government before becoming prime minister of Pakistan.

6. Baxter, *Bangladesh*, 41–42.

7. Baxter, *Bangladesh*, 43.

8. Initially, Iskandar Mirza, Pakistan's president, and Ayub were coleaders of the martial law administration. But within three weeks Ayub, doubting Mirza's loyalty, packed him off to London, ending what would probably have been an unworkable duumvirate.

9. The list was compiled in 1968 by Dr. Mahbub ul Haq, then chief economist at the Planning Commission of Pakistan. According to Haq, these 22 families controlled 66 percent of Pakistan's industrial assets and 87 percent of its banking assets. Almost all of the 22 families were based in West Pakistan or had West Pakistani origins.

10. Agartala, where the conspiracy was allegedly hatched, is a town in northeastern India close to the international border. In February 1969, the Pakistani government withdrew all charges against Mujib and others. He was rapturously welcomed by huge crowds in Dhaka. For a detailed personal account of how the trial played out, see Kamal Hossain, *Bangladesh: Quest for Freedom and Justice* (Dhaka: University Press, 2013), Chapter 4.

11. Aside from the issue of provincial autonomy, the conference also grappled (unsuccessfully) with the long contentious issue of the administration of West Pakistan. This matter pitted the Punjabis, who favored a "One Unit" arrangement that they would dominate, against representatives of the smaller ethnic groups—Sindhis, Pashtuns, and Baluchis—whose provinces had been amalgamated into a unified, Punjabi-dominated West Pakistan province in the 1950s, over their strong objection.

12. An estimated quarter million died in the storm. Sheikh Mujib declared that the destruction and its aftermath had brought into sharp focus "the basic truth that every Bengali has felt in his bones, that we have been treated so long as a colony and a market." Asked by a foreign correspondent if his statement could be read as a call for independence, Mujib replied "No, not yet." Quoted in Srinath Raghavan, *1971: A Global History of the Creation of Bangladesh* (Cambridge, MA: Harvard University Press, 2013), 32.

13. As India had closed its airspace to traffic between the two wings of Pakistan, the planes had to refuel in Sri Lanka en route.

14. Articles in *Dawn* and the *Pakistan Times*, both March 27, 1971, quoted in Raghavan, *1971*, 51.

15. Gary J. Bass, *The Blood Telegram: Nixon, Kissinger, and a Forgotten Genocide* (New York: Alfred A. Knopf, 2013), 103.

16. Ministry of External Affairs, Government of India, http://mea.gov.in/bilateral-documents.htm?dtl/5139/Treaty+of.

17. J. N. Dixit, *India-Pakistan in War and Peace* (New Delhi: Books Today, 2002), 176.

18. George G. B. Griffin, interview, ADST Oral History Project (April 30, 2002), 34–58; Dixit, *India-Pakistan in War and Peace*, 188.

19. Bass, *The Blood Telegram*, 205–235; Dixit, *India-Pakistan in War and Peace*, 199–204.

20. Bass, *The Blood Telegram*, 302–303; Raghavan, *1971*, 205, 240–256.

21. Raghavan, *1971*, 252–255.

22. Raghavan, *1971*, 257–262.

23. For a moving account of their imprisonment, release, and intermediate stops in London and Delhi, see Hossain, *Bangladesh*, 105–122. Kamal Hossain, a close associate of Mujib, was imprisoned and in solitary confinement for eight months. He later became Mujib's foreign minister and remained active in Awami League politics until the mid-1990s.

24. Hossain, *Bangladesh*, 134. Zia was the first to declare an independent state with himself as head, on March 27, a statement that he corrected the next day, stating that the new state was operating under the guidance of Sheikh Mujibur Rahman. See text on the Website of the party he founded, the BNP, at http://en.bnpbangladesh.com/2016/05/28/life-of-shahid-president-ziaur-rahman/.

25. Hossain, *Bangladesh*, 134–135; Bangladesh Defence, "History of Bangladesh Army," http://www.defencebd.com/2010/11/history-of-bangladesh-army.html. The provisional government was often referred to as a "government in exile" because it also enjoyed facilities in India.

26. Despite the strong U.S. pro-Pakistan policy, the United States did accommodate the Bengali diplomats in Washington who left the Pakistan embassy. The State Department assigned an officer to maintain liaison with them, Craig Baxter, selected in part because he was a South Asia expert but was not then working in the Bureau of Near Eastern and South Asian Affairs. This kept the effort at a safe distance from the White House.

27. Muhith, in an interview with one of the authors, made clear that he considered this period one of the most important of his life.

28. Hossain, *Bangladesh*, 135–156. He was one of the authors of the constitution.

29. Ministry of External Affairs, India, "Simla Agreement, July 2, 1972."

30. Raghavan, *1971*, 270.

31. T.S. Cheema, *Pakistan-Bangladesh Relations* (Nagar, India: Unistar Books, 2013), 72–73.

32. The People's Republic of China was only admitted to the United Nations on October 25, 1971.

33. Stanley A. Kochanek, *Patron-Client Politics and Business in Bangladesh* (New Delhi: Sage, 1993), 75–88.

34. Baxter, *Bangladesh*, 57–59.

35. Baxter, *Bangladesh*, 59; Marcus Franda, *Bangladesh: The First Decade* (New Delhi: South Asian Publishers, 1982), 53–63.

36. Kamal Hossain gives the number of these ex-Pakistan Army Freedom Fighters as 25,000 (Hossain, *Bangladesh*, 126). Much larger figures, ranging from 51,000 to 120,000, are cited in Bangladesh Genocide Archive, "Freedom Fighters," http://www.genocidebangladesh.org/freedom-fighters/, though this source appears to combine ex-army personnel and guerrillas. Bangladesh Defence, "History of Bangladesh Army," cites a figure of 28,000 for the Repatriates. Shamsher Chowdhury believes the relative size of the Freedom Fighter group was smaller. See also Ziaur Rahman's party biography, Bangladesh Nationalist Party, "Life of Shahid President Ziaur Rahman," http://en.bnpbangladesh.com/2016/05/28/life-of-shahid-president-ziaur-rahman/.

37. Franda, *Bangladesh: The First Decade*, 276. Franda claims that Zia himself admitted to 406 executions (306). See also Global Security, "Bangladesh Army History," http://www.globalsecurity.org/military/world/bangladesh/army-history-3.htm, which claims over 1,000.

38. Global Security, "Bangladesh Army History," http://www.globalsecurity.org/military/world/bangladesh/army-history-3.htm; Bangladesh Defence, "History of Bangladesh Army," http://www.defencebd.com/2010/11/history-of-bangladesh-army.html.

39. World Bank database.

40. World Bank, *Annual Report 1973* (Washington, DC: World Bank, 1973), 126, 131.

41. Bangladesh Academy for Rural Development (BARD), Comilla, "About the Founder," http://www.bard.gov.bd/About_the_Founder.php. Ironically, Akhtar Hameed went back to Pakistan after Bangladeshi independence, and tried out his cooperative model in a poor neighborhood in Karachi—only to fall afoul of the governmental and religious authorities. He was revered in Bangladesh, especially in Comilla, until and beyond his death in 1999, in contrast to the low profile he had in Pakistan.

42. Kochanek, *Patron-Client Politics*, 91.

43. Transparency International, "Corruption Perceptions Index," https://www.transparency.org/research/cpi/overview.

44. Najma Chowdhury, professor of political science (retired), Dhaka University, conversations with authors.

3. ERITREA: THE INDEPENDENCE STRUGGLE AND THE STRUGGLES OF INDEPENDENCE

Terrence Lyons

TIMELINE

1952	UN federates Eritrea with Ethiopia after British and Italian administration
1962	Eritrean Assembly votes to join Ethiopia fully
Early 1960s	War for independence begins; the Eritrean Liberation Front (ELF) is founded
1970	Eritrean People's Liberation Front (EPLF) founded as an alternative rebel group
1974	The Derg military committee takes power in Ethiopia and abolishes the monarchy
1975	Tigrayan People's Liberation Front (TPLF) forms to fight the Derg
Mid-1970s	Ethiopian forces drive Eritrean rebels from the cities
1981	EPLF defeats the ELF and becomes the dominant Eritrean rebel faction
1989	TPLF occupies much of northern Ethiopia and creates the Ethiopian People's Revolutionary Democratic Front (EPRDF)
1991	EPRDF takes Addis Ababa and EPLF takes Asmara, effectively ending the war; Isaias and Meles agree to a referendum on Eritrea's future status

1993	UN referendum finds overwhelming support for independence; Eritrea formally declares independence and receives international recognition
1994	EPLF transforms itself into a political party, the People's Front for Democracy and Justice, making Eritrea a one-party state
1997	Draft constitution ratified by the constituent assembly
1998	Tensions over port access, borders, and currency trigger the Eritrean-Ethiopian war; estimated 70,000–100,000 people are killed
June 2000	Cease-fire agreement between Ethiopia and Eritrea
December 2000	Algiers Agreement ends the war and creates the Eritrea-Ethiopia Border Commission (EEBC)
September 2001	Eritrean government officials and their supporters are arrested for a letter criticizing Isaias and calling for his resignation
2002	EEBC determines that Badme belongs to Eritrea
2009	United Nations, with African Union and U.S. support, imposes sanctions on Eritrea; the economy collapses

Eritrea's saga of achieving independence in 1993 entails a brutal 30-year war and the mobilization of a remarkable national liberation movement. In the late nineteenth century, this small state in the Horn of Africa suffered under the colonial domination of the Italians, followed by Ethiopia's imperialism and military rule. Self-determination, not secession, was sought by Eritrean nationalists because they never accepted colonial rule or Ethiopia's sovereignty. After a war that included near victory in the mid-1970s, internecine splits, and a strategic retreat to a mountain redoubt in the far northwest, the Eritrean People's Liberation Front (EPLF) defeated the Soviet-backed Ethiopian army and seized control of all of Eritrea in May 1991.

The postwar independence era started with great hopes, a referendum in which 99 percent of the population voted in favor of independence, the

Figure 3.1. Map of Eritrea

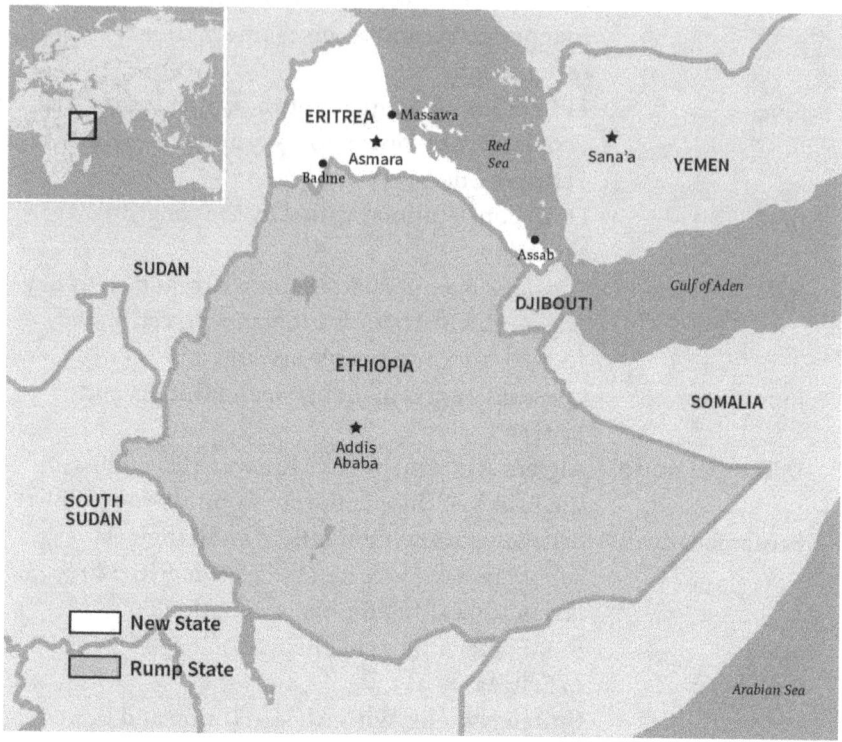

conversion of the rebel movement into a ruling party, and the creation of a consultative process to write a new constitution. In 1998, however, a border war broke out with Ethiopia, resulting in the almost complete militarization of Eritrean society. In 2001, a group of leaders who played key roles in the liberation war demanded political reforms and were arrested by President Isaias Afwerki. Since then Eritrea has experienced the complete closure of political space, economic decline, international sanctions, and isolation. It ranks near the bottom of global assessments regarding democracy, human rights, religious freedom, and free media.

THE ORIGINS OF ERITREA

Eritrea's population of 4 to 6 million is divided into nine officially recognized ethnic groups. The Tigrinya population makes up approximately

50 percent of the total and the Tigre approximately 30 percent. The remaining 20 percent is distributed across the Saho, Afar, Bilen, Nara, Rashaida, Hedareb, and Kunama. Four religions are recognized—Orthodox Christianity, Islam, Catholicism, and Lutheranism. Geographically, Eritrea includes a central highland plateau largely populated by Tigrinya agriculturalists, the western lowland inhabited by Tigre, and the southeastern territory along the Red Sea by Afar and Saho. Historically, these divisions often made Eritrean unity difficult and provided the basis for divide-and-rule tactics by both the Italians and Ethiopians. But the protracted struggle for independence created a strong sense of a unified Eritrean identity.

Eritrea's existence as a political entity began with the creation of the Italian colony along the Red Sea. Prior to that time, today's Eritrea had links to Ottoman authorities along the coast and with Ethiopian royal authorities in the central highlands. Italy did not enter the race for colonies until the 1880s when it established its foothold in the Red Sea port of Massawa. Following the Battle of Adwa in 1896, Italy consolidated its colony with the agreement of Ethiopian emperor Menelik.

During the imperial period, Italy regarded Eritrea as a settler colony, investing in infrastructure (notably the Asmara–Massawa railroad) and manufacturing in urban areas. After the British army defeated Italian forces in East Africa in 1943, these investments ended and the British Military Administration (BMA) removed and sold industrial plants and equipment. The BMA, however, did allow Eritreans to form political parties (often along religious lines), labor unions, and other independent social organizations.

The BMA governed Eritrea until 1952, when a controversial UN decision federated the former colony with Imperial Ethiopia. The norm that former colonies should be given independence was not in place in the early 1950s, and the United States, along with other major powers, thought its security interests would be best served by linking Eritrea with Ethiopia. Some lowland Eritreans, mobilized in the Muslim League, opposed the federation while some highlanders and those linked to the Orthodox Church supported closer ties with Ethiopia's Christian elites. The Italian and British administrations had left Eritreans with an assembly, political parties, commercialized agriculture, and a manufacturing sector unlike any in Ethiopia. The Eritrean-Ethiopian Federation existed as an awkward hybrid, merging an autonomous region that had an elected assembly with an imperial, absolutist system. In 1962, the Eritrean Assembly voted—in a cloud of controversy, bribery, coercion, and boycotts—to end the federation and join Ethiopia as its fourteenth province.[1]

The Eritrean independence movement was born out of the absolutism of the Ethiopian imperial state and a growing sense of Eritrean nationalism and grievance. Emperor Haile Selassie ruled through a feudal system of local nobility, close relations with the Orthodox Church, and a series of clients. A repressive security apparatus arrested dissidents and limited independent political and civic space. External powers, most notably the United States, which had an important military communications facility in Eritrea, supported Haile Selassie.

By the late 1960s, dissent within Ethiopia and Eritrea grew among the increasingly educated youth and university students. The Ethiopian Student Movement raised fundamental questions about the nature of imperial rule.[2] Ethiopian and Eritrean students in the United States and Europe brought home commitments to Marxism-Leninism and a frustration at what they viewed as their backward homelands. Highly politicized students demanded land reform, as captured in the popular demand for "Land to the Tiller." They engaged in heated debates around the "nationalities question," which asked whether or not Eritreans had the right to self-determination. By the mid-1970s, opposition had spread in the form of military mutinies, mass demonstrations, and demands for the arrest of top government officials. The military formed a committee (known as the Derg) that eventually seized power in what was labeled the "Creeping Coup." The emperor was then deposed.

THE ARMED STRUGGLE: 1961 TO 1991

The Eritrean rebellion against Ethiopian rule began in the early 1960s. The Eritrean Liberation Front (ELF) led the struggle in its early years. This insurgent movement was organized initially by students in Cairo and had strong support from Muslim, lowland Eritreans, and from some leaders in the Arab world.[3] The exiled leadership controlled the flow of weapons and financial support from Ba'athist states such as Syria and Iraq, but the soldiers were recruited locally on the basis of clan and religious networks. The ELF organized its struggle by establishing autonomous military units, following the model of the Algerian National Liberation Front

(FLN). In practice, these divisions tended to replicate ethnic, religious, and regional identities.

In the late 1960s and early 1970s, the ELF attracted more and more recruits from the Christian highlands, creating a tension that contributed to an internal crisis in the early 1970s. These divisions eventually led to the creation of a breakaway faction in 1970, known as the Eritrean People's Liberation Front (EPLF). The leadership of the EPLF tended to draw from highland Tigrinyas and to be more leftist in its orientation, reflecting the general direction of the Ethiopian Student Movement. The EPLF first defined itself as a revolutionary vanguard but later as a broad front that included a range of ideological positions unified around the independence issue.[4]

During the 1970s, the ELF and EPLF coexisted, although often with high levels of hostility. The insurgents seemed close to victory in the mid-1970s as Ethiopia went through a revolution that provoked armed conflict on several fronts simultaneously. A bloody internecine conflict for dominance within the liberation movement raged from 1972 to 1974. This intra-Eritrean fighting "reproduced communal divisions as leaders and fighters sought to defend their positions through a reliance on relatives, clans, and tribes."[5] With significant assistance from the Soviet Union and Cuba, Ethiopia successfully pushed the rebels out of Asmara into their mountain redoubts in the northwest. In 1981, the EPLF eventually defeated the ELF and served as the dominant rebel organization engaging in the armed struggle for Eritrean independence until victory in 1991.

The EPLF operated as a highly disciplined, hierarchically organized insurgent force. The armed movement helped overcome the societal divisions of Eritrea to create a united liberation movement. The rebel force exercised strict democratic centralism. The organization was marked by its "clandestinity and an endemic culture of public silence" during the war.[6] The insurgents developed complex systems of administration in territory that they liberated, particularly in the northwestern Sahel. Political education and socialization were given priority. Trained cadres maintained links between the political and military struggles. The EPLF was proud of the medical services it provided to soldiers and civilians. Small-scale workshops, hidden in caves, produced uniforms, sandals, and parts for captured weapons.[7] The EPLF committed itself to equality, and an estimated 30 percent of its fighters were women.[8]

In many ways, the EPLF operated as a proto-state during the armed struggle, running its own economic and social policies and providing "government" services. In liberated areas, the EPLF introduced land reform, rural cooperatives, and locally elected councils.[9] Organization served both to provide autonomous administration and to control the population in order to serve the armed struggle. The EPLF's reach extended to refugees in camps in Sudan, and the front had a strong presence within the diaspora in North America and Europe, where it engaged in lobbying and extensive fund-raising.

While the Muslim–Christian dichotomy reflected the underlying diversity of the Eritrean population and different ethnic identities were recognized, the EPLF positioned itself as a national liberation movement that framed its struggle as fighting for the united Eritrean nation. The movement insisted, "There are no differences among Eritreans on the goal of national independence."[10] Some groups, notably the Kunama and the Afar, included segments that were more ambivalent about Eritrean nationalism and that retained ties to kin in Ethiopia. However, people from all ethnic and religious backgrounds participated in the armed struggle and contributed to the construction of a new Eritrean identity that grew out of the enormous sacrifices experienced during the war.

The Eritrean independence struggle lacked major international supporters. Many in Africa regarded with suspicion any effort seeking to redraw lines of sovereignty. The Organization of African Unity (OAU) explicitly rejected any change to colonial boundaries. After the Ethiopian revolution (1974 to 1977), the United States and the Soviet Union switched clients in the Horn of Africa, with Moscow shifting its support from Somalia to Ethiopia. Washington did not provide military assistance to the EPLF or to the rebels in Ethiopia, perceiving these groups to be Marxist and therefore not good candidates for the anti-Soviet Reagan Doctrine.

The Eritrean liberation struggle did receive some critical international support. Perhaps most importantly, Sudan allowed the EPLF to use its territory to ship supplies, and the Sudanese town of Kassala became a major hub for the movement. Large numbers of Eritreans fled to refugee camps in Sudan as well. During the famine of the mid-1980s, Eritrea received cross-border humanitarian support from northern European donors through the Emergency Relief Desk.[11] The Eritrean diaspora served as a key wing of the movement, lobbying and raising funds in Europe and North America. Finally, the EPLF had a complicated set of relationships with the Tigrayan People's Liberation Front (TPLF) in northern Ethiopia and, to a lesser extent, the Oromo Liberation Front. While contentious, the relationships benefited the EPLF by making it harder for the Ethiopian army to resupply its troops in Eritrea.[12]

In the mid-1970s, internal divisions within the Eritrean liberation movement and massive support from the Soviet Union allowed the Derg to rebalance itself and push the EPLF out of the cities and towns and toward the sparsely populated northwest around the town of Nakfa. The Ethiopian military unleashed massive military campaigns but could not remove the EPLF from dug-in positions in the mountains. Following classic Maoist guerrilla doctrine, the EPLF organized a "strategic retreat," giving up land rather than engaging Ethiopian forces in combat.

By the late 1980s, Ethiopia's military was in shambles. President Mengistu Haile Mariam had executed its most competent generals after a failed coup attempt and morale had plummeted.[13] The Soviet Union, undergoing its own transformation under President Mikhail Gorbachev, informed Mengistu that Moscow would not renew its defense and cooperation agreement with Ethiopia. In 1988, the EPLF won a major battle at Afabet, which shifted the military balance. The TPLF transformed from a relatively small force capable of hit-and-run attacks to an insurgent army that occupied most of Tigray (the region that borders Eritrea to the south) by 1989. Afterward, the TPLF created the Ethiopian People's Revolutionary Democratic Front (EPRDF) and began to move toward Addis Ababa. By 1990, the EPLF controlled most of Eritrea and the TPLF-led EPRDF moved toward the Ethiopian capital.

PEACE AND THE LEGACIES OF THE ARMED STRUGGLE, 1991 TO 1998

Mengistu fled Addis Ababa in May 1991. It was then clear the EPLF would be victorious in its war to liberate Eritrea and that the EPLF's allies in the TPLF-led EPRDF would lead the next government in Ethiopia. U.S. assistant secretary of state for African affairs Herman Cohen convened a meeting in London of major rebel groups and what was left of the Derg regime. By the time the talks commenced, military reality on the ground had already determined the outcome.[14]

The EPLF took control of Eritrea's capital, Asmara, on May 24, 1991, effectively ending the 30-year struggle. The EPRDF seized power in Addis

Ababa four days later. Isaias Afwerki announced that his movement would cooperate with, but not join, the transitional government organized by the EPRDF. The EPLF established a separate provisional government, which it framed as merely "formalizing an administration that has existed in Eritrea for 15 years."[15] The government of the de facto independent state of Eritrea waited until the United Nations organized a referendum in April 1993 to officially declare de jure independence. The outcome was never in doubt: the United Nations certified that 99.83 percent of the ballots had been cast for independence. The process of holding a referendum mattered to the Eritrean movement because it regarded the UN decision to federate the former Italian colony with Ethiopia as the beginning of the struggle for decolonization and independence. In this framing, Eritrea had been denied its legitimate independence first by the Ethiopian empire and then by the Derg regime of Mengistu Haile Mariam. However, the legitimacy of its claims for self-determination rested on its status as a former colony.

International recognition followed immediately and with little drama for two reasons. First, the EPLF had won the war and occupied all of Eritrea. Military domination, rather than international diplomacy or law, determined Eritrea's independence and recognition. Second, the new Ethiopian regime led by Meles Zenawi and the EPRDF welcomed the referendum and supported independence for Eritrea. Ethiopia was the first state to recognize the new state after the 1993 referendum. Without any objection from the state that was notionally "losing" a province, it was untenable for other international actors to object.[16]

The new regime initially enjoyed widespread international support. Having defeated the brutal regime of Mengistu Haile Mariam, the change in leadership offered an opportunity for pragmatic governing along with a renewed commitment to its people. Washington saw Eritrea (along with Ethiopia and Uganda) as a group of "impressive new leaders" in Africa and worked with these three states in pursuit of regional objectives, notably the containment of the National Islamic Front regime in Sudan.[17]

Eritrea's international support came despite Asmara's deep criticism of international organizations. The EPLF did not forget that it had had few supporters among the major powers or international organizations and prided itself on self-reliance and autonomy during the war. EPLF leader Isaias Afwerki said in his inaugural speech to the OAU that joining it "was not spiritually gratifying" because it was a "nominal organization that has failed to deliver on its pronounced goals and objectives."[18] Many in the West saw this stance as a refreshing commitment to pursuing development on its own terms rather than acquiescing to international policy agendas.

From 1991 until 1998, Ethiopia and Eritrea had what appeared to be cooperative relations. The two states and their leaders appeared ready to put aside past conflicts and to work together on a broad range of economic and diplomatic issues. Initially, both used the same currency (the Ethiopian birr) and Ethiopia retained access to the Eritrean port of Assab. Large numbers of Eritreans living in Ethiopia participated in the 1993 Eritrean referendum, with polling stations set up in Addis Ababa and around the country, and these citizens retained their Ethiopian passports.

In 1994, the EPLF formally transformed itself from an insurgent organization to a ruling party and launched the People's Front for Democracy and Justice (PFDJ). In the immediate postwar period, the ruling party was enormously popular, having delivered the independence so many Eritreans desired. Former rebel movement leaders became the leadership of the provisional government. The PFDJ was established as the sole legal political party in Eritrea. It ruled first through a party-selected central committee and then (after the PFDJ's third congress in 1994) by a party-selected transitional parliament.[19] The PFDJ initiated a consultative process to write the first constitution for independent Eritrea. A 50-member commission and 10-member executive committee oversaw the process. It was charged with the duty to organize and manage "a wide-ranging and all-embracing national debate and education through public seminars and lecture series on constitutional principles and practices."[20] After two years of public consultation, the commission sent the draft to the constituent assembly, which quickly ratified the constitution on May 23, 1997. While ratified, the constitution has yet to be implemented.

Economically the new state started from a very low base, having suffered through 30 years of war. It had, however, a significant and strategically important Red Sea coastline, the prospect of obtaining considerable revenue in port fees, and optimistic expectations regarding the development of gold and other natural resources. The Eritrean diaspora remained a crucial source of revenue. Ruling authorities envisioned Eritrea, with its industrious and hardworking population, as developing into a Red Sea

Singapore or a state like the Asian Tigers. The Eritrean state retained ownership of all land—rural and urban—making its role in the economy overwhelmingly dominant.[21]

Eritrea's history of achieving independence without significant external assistance led it to value autonomy and to view international financial institutions and nongovernmental organizations with suspicion. The PFDJ's National Charter of 1994 emphasized "self-reliance in all fields" and, in terms of the economy, "to rely on internal capabilities and develop internal capacities." Fear of dependency made the regime wary of traditional international assistance. Autonomy, the movement long argued, enhances independent thinking, innovation, perseverance, and pride in work and struggle.[22] International nongovernmental organizations were kicked out of Eritrea and relations with international financial institutions were difficult.

While independence served as a core source of cohesion and support for the PFDJ's rule, there was growing disquiet among some top party leaders over the authoritarian tendencies of President Isaias Afwerki and those in his immediate circle. Human rights concerns and delays in implementing the constitution, scheduling elections, and convening a party congress raised questions about whether the powerful and disciplined insurgent army could transform itself into a democratic regime capable of tolerating dissent and engaging in meaningful consultation.[23]

THE BORDER WAR

Questions about postwar governance, however, were shelved as war with Ethiopia erupted again. The warm relations between Eritrea and Ethiopia immediately after 1991 had degenerated by 1998. Disputes between Addis Ababa and Asmara arose over landlocked Ethiopia's access to Eritrean ports, questions of how the new Eritrean currency related to the existing Ethiopian currency, and disagreements over the precise location of their poorly demarcated border. Some tensions recalled the acrimonious relationship during the civil war. The classic imperatives of state- and nation-building drove both regimes to set forth unconditional goals and refuse compromise on the vital issues of territoriality, legitimacy, and identity. Reliance on solidarity between the two heads of state rather than a more institutionalized set of coordinating mechanisms left the interstate relationship personalized and fragile.[24]

In May 1998, Eritrean armed forces attacked the disputed border town of Badme. This use of military force quickly escalated into full-scale war.[25] Historical links and rivalries between the two populations, ruling parties, and leaders made the violence particularly bitter. An estimated 70,000 to 100,000 people were killed, 1 million were displaced, and a generation of development opportunities was squandered. After a period of military stalemate and unproductive negotiations, Ethiopia launched a major offensive in May 2000, broke through defenses, and forced Eritrea to pull its troops back to prewar positions. Following a June 2000 cease-fire agreement, the warring parties signed an internationally brokered agreement in Algiers in December 2000.[26]

The Algiers Agreement put in place a cease-fire, established a border zone to be patrolled by a UN peacekeeping mission, and created the Eritrea-Ethiopia Border Commission (EEBC). Under the agreement, the EEBC was tasked with demarcating a border based on colonial maps. Its judgment was final and binding. In April 2002, the EEBC issued its determination that the town of Badme was on Eritrea's side of the border. While not a strategically or economically important location, both regimes used Badme as the marker of whether it had "won" or "lost" the war, and hence whether the terrible sacrifices each had made in the conflict were justified or in vain.[27] The Ethiopian government initially objected to the decision, then accepted the agreement in principle while calling for more talks about implementation. Since then, the border conflict has been in an expensive stalemate, with regular eruptions of tension that create concerns about a return to war.

AFTER THE BORDER WAR

In March 2001, shortly after the Algiers Agreement was signed, a group of 15 senior Eritrean officials, several of whom had played major roles in the liberation struggle, signed a letter that criticized President Isaias and called for greater democracy. Among their demands was a congress of the ruling party, something that had last taken place in 1993. The letter was leaked. Eleven signatories and a number of their supporters were arrested in September 2001. They have been held incommunicado and without charge since then. The G-15 letter appealed to public opinion to remove Isaias, and it is unclear what the dissidents thought Isaias's reaction would be. Rather than stepping down or opening negotiations, the leader responded as he had to threats during the armed struggle, seeking to eliminate the challenge.

The Eritrean government became highly repressive and isolationist. International human rights groups, monitors of religious persecution, and media watchdogs list Eritrea among the most repressive regimes in the world.[28] Today, a very small leadership circle around President Isaias dominates all aspects of political, economic, and social life. Power is concentrated in individuals, not institutions, making the regime unaccountable and capricious. Tronvoll and Mekonnen conclude that the regime's "nationalist ideology and populist appeal have been replaced by brute force, repression, and structural surveillance."[29]

Scholars have characterized Eritrea as a "garrison state," emphasizing the degree of militarization of all aspects of society and the overarching preoccupation with security.[30] Since the 1998–2000 border war, the regime has justified postponing planned moves toward constitutional rule and elections and the imposition of de facto martial law as necessary to protect Eritrea's independence. All citizens are required to perform national service, which often takes the form of lifelong military conscription. These harsh conditions and the absence of economic prospects have contributed to an extraordinary exodus of Eritreans seeking asylum and generating a refugee crisis in Europe.

Besides its border war with Ethiopia, Eritrea has had disputes with Yemen and Djibouti. International economic relations suffered after 2009 when the United Nations, with the support of the African Union and the United States, imposed sanctions against Eritrea. These sanctions arose from Eritrea's support for the Shabaab militant group in Somalia. Eritrea denied any involvement, but the United Nations imposed sanctions and began a contentious series of annual reviews. Asmara refused to cooperate with the United Nations in this process.

The 1998–2000 border war, the 2001 crackdown, and international sanctions led to the virtual collapse of the Eritrean economy. In 2008, for example, its economy contracted by nearly 10 percent, resulting in a shortage of basic commodities and necessitating rationing. These economic restrictions resulted in the development of a massive illicit economy that relied upon corruption at high levels of the security forces. Key income from mining, notably the Bisha gold mine, which began operation in 2011 with the support of investment from the Canadian firm Nevsun, holds promise. In an effort to curb black market activity, the government removed all old currency from circulation and issued new notes in 2015.

The Eritrean diaspora has been a critical source of support for the EPLF regime. Eritreans in the diaspora effectively pay a 2 percent tax that subsidizes the Eritrean state. Many in the diaspora send money voluntarily, given their strong support for Eritrea's independence and the role the regime has played in defending Eritrea's sovereignty. Others, however, pay the tax in order to obtain visas and other consular services that allow them to visit relatives in Eritrea. More than just about any other state, the politics and economics of Eritrea are shaped in significant measure by Eritreans living abroad.[31]

CONCLUSION

Eritrea's story reflects an extraordinary liberation struggle. The outcome of the war was determined by the 30 years of armed resistance by the Eritrean Liberation Front and later the Eritrean People's Liberation Front. These insurgent groups fought Emperor Haile Selassie and then the Derg regime until the Ethiopian army was exhausted and unable to fight. The liberation of Eritrea by military force was followed by an internationally monitored referendum in which 99 percent of Eritreans voted for independence. International recognition and support quickly followed.

The first eight years after victory represented a time of considerable hope and promise. The EPLF transformed itself into a political party, the PFDJ, and set up a consultative process to write Eritrea's first constitution. Asmara developed a friendly relationship with Addis Ababa and most Western powers. The commitment to autonomy and independence was powerful and resulted in some successes, as exemplified by the rebuilding of the railroad from Asmara to Massawa without international assistance. The war-torn country started the process of demobilizing its armed forces and rebuilding its shattered economy, with considerable support from the international community and the Eritrean diaspora.

In hindsight, the growing tensions between Ethiopia and Eritrea are clear. However, at the time there was a sense that Isaias and Meles—two comrades in arms—would resolve their differences. In the end, a border skirmish in 1998 near Badme quickly escalated into full-scale war, leaving

Eritrea again highly militarized and now increasingly isolated. The nonimplementation of the Eritrea-Ethiopia Border Commission demarcation created a very costly stalemate with Ethiopia. Repression increased, as seen in the 2001 arrests of senior leaders of the armed struggle who advocated for a political opening. In the 2010s, international sanctions, an economic crisis that required rationing of basic commodities, and a massive outflow of migrants left Eritrea as one of the poorest and most authoritarian states in the world.

National liberation movements such as the EPLF, with their legacies of intense socialization, solidarity, and vertical command structures, have produced some of the world's strongest authoritarian parties. During the civil war, rivals are defeated rather than tolerated, creating precedents and expectations that shape postwar politics. In Eritrea, the legacies of the victorious rebel movement created a ruling system without mechanisms to foster open debate within the leadership or consultations with the population. Dissidents became traitors and questioning leaders were seen as acting on behalf of the enemies of Eritrea's independence. In this way, the very strengths that fostered the EPLF's ability to win the war were hindrances to postwar accountability and democracy.

NOTES

1. Tekeste Negash, *Eritrea and Ethiopia: The Federal Experience* (New Brunswick, NJ: Transaction, 1997). See also Michela Wrong, *I Didn't Do It for You: How the World Betrayed a Small African Nation* (New York: HarperCollins, 2005).

2. Bahru Zewde, *The Quest for Socialist Ethiopia: The Ethiopian Student Movement c. 1960–1974* (Addis Ababa: James Currey, 2014).

3. Ruth Iyob, *The Eritrean Struggle for Independence: Domination, Resistance, Nationalism 1941–1993* (Cambridge: Cambridge University Press, 1995).

4. Michael Woldemariam, *Insurgent Fragmentation in the Horn of Africa: Rebellion and Its Discontents* (Cambridge: Cambridge University Press, 2018).

5. David Pool, *From Guerrillas to Government: The Eritrean People's Liberation Front* (London: James Currey, 2001), 55.

6. Ruth Iyob, "The Eritrean Experiment: A Cautious Pragmatism?" *Journal of Modern African Studies* 35, no. 4 (December 1997): 647–673; see also Fouad Makki, "Nationalism, State Formation, and the Public Sphere: Eritrea 1991–1996," *Review of African Political Economy* 23, no. 70 (1996): 475–497.

7. James Firebrace and Stuart Holland, *Never Kneel Down: Drought, Development, and Liberation in Eritrea* (Trenton, NJ: Red Sea Press, 1985).

8. Victoria Bernal, "Equality to Die For? Women Guerrilla Fighters and Eritrea's Cultural Revolution," *Political and Legal Anthropology Review* 23, no. 2 (November 2000): 61–76; Tanja Müller, *The Making of Elite Women: Revolution and Nation Building in Eritrea* (Boston: Brill, 2005).

9. Dan Connell, *Against All Odds: A Chronicle of the Eritrean Revolution with a New Afterword on the Postwar Transition* (Trenton, NJ: Red Sea Press, 1997).

10. Government of Eritrea, *Eritrea: Birth of a Nation* (Asmara: Government of Eritrea, 1993).

11. Mark R. Duffield and John Prendergast, *Without Troops and Tanks: The Emergency Relief Desk and the Cross-Border Operations into Eritrea and Tigray* (Trenton, NJ: Red Sea Press, 1994).

12. Kjetil Tronvoll, *War and the Politics of Identity in Ethiopia: The Making of Enemies and Allies in the Horn of Africa* (London: James Currey, 2009); John Young, *Peasant Revolution in Ethiopia: The Tigray People's Liberation Front* (Cambridge: Cambridge University Press, 1997).

13. Fantahun Ayele, *The Ethiopian Army: From Victory to Collapse* (Evanston, IL: Northwestern University Press, 2014).

14. Terrence Lyons, "The Transition in Ethiopia," *CSIS Africa Notes* 127 (1991).

15. Isaias Afewerki quoted in Blaine Harden, "Eritrean Rebels to Form Own Rule, Separate from Ethiopian Government," *Washington Post*, May 30, 1991.

16. It is notable that the EPRDF's position on Eritrean independence was highly controversial among Ethiopian nationalists and remained as a rallying cry of opposition to the ruling party in Addis Ababa. But this domestic opposition within Ethiopia did not determine the international community's stance toward recognizing Eritrea's independence.

17. Marina Ottaway, *Africa's New Leaders: Democracy of State Reconstruction?* (Washington DC: Carnegie Endowment for International Peace, 2000); Peter Woodward, *US Foreign Policy and the Horn of Africa* (Burlington, VT: Ashgate, 2006).

18. "OAU Summit Opens to Criticism from Newest Member Eritrea," Agence France-Presse, June 28, 1993.

19. Richard Reid, "Caught in the Headlights of History: Eritrea, the EPLF, and the Post-War Nation-State," *Journal of Modern African Studies* 43, no. 3 (September 2005): 467–488.

20. Bereket Habte Selassie, "Constitution-Making in Eritrea: A Process-Driven Approach," in *Framing the State in Times of Transition: Case Studies in Constitution Making*, ed. Laurel E. Miller (Washington, DC: U.S. Institute of Peace Press, 2010).

21. Kidane Mengisteab and Okbazghi Yohannes, *Anatomy of an African Tragedy: Political, Economic and Foreign Policy Crisis in Post-Independence Eritrea* (Trenton, NJ: Red Sea Press, 2005).

22. Firebrace and Holland, *Never Kneel Down*.

23. The challenge of transforming victorious insurgents into democratic ruling parties is not limited to Eritrea. For more see Terrence Lyons, "The Importance of Winning: Victorious Insurgent Groups and Authoritarian Politics," *Comparative Politics* 48, no. 2 (January 2016): 167–185.

24. Gilbert M. Khadiagala, "Reflection on the Ethiopia-Eritrea Border Conflict," *Fletcher Forum* 23, no. 2 (Fall 1999): 39–56.

25. This was the judgment of the Eritrea-Ethiopia Claims Commission established by the Algiers Peace Agreement.

26. Terrence Lyons, *Avoiding Conflict in the Horn of Africa: U.S. Policy toward Ethiopia and Eritrea* (New York: Council on Foreign Relations, 2006).

27. Some mockingly likened the war to "two bald men fighting over a comb," but as a symbol of sacrifice Badme was very valuable.

28. The Committee to Protect Journalists labeled Eritrea "one of the world's worst jailers of journalists." Reporters without Borders ranked Eritrea 166 out of 168 counties in its 2006 Worldwide Press Freedom Index. Freedom House ranked the state as "not free" in its 2007 report. The U.S. Department of State's "International Religious Freedom Report 2007" says that the Eritrean Government "continued to harass, arrest, and detain members of independent evangelical groups, Pentecostals, Jehovah's Witnesses, and a reform movement within the Eritrean Orthodox Church."

29. Kjetil Tronvoll and Daniel R. Mekonnen, *The African Garrison State: Human Rights and Political Development in Eritrea* (London: James Currey, 2014).

30. Tronvoll and Mekonnen, *The African Garrison State*.

31. Victoria Bernal, "Eritrea On-Line: Diaspora, Cyberspace, and the Public Sphere," *American Ethnologist* 32, no. 4 (2005): 660–675; Amanda Poole, "Ransoms, Remittances, and Refugees: The Gatekeeper State in Eritrea," *Africa Today* 60, no. 2 (Winter 2013): 66–82.

4. TIMOR-LESTE: A NATION OF RESISTANCE

Miks Muižarājs

TIMELINE

1515	Portuguese settlers arrive on the island of Timor
1851	After a series of colonial wars, Portugal and the Netherlands begin border negotiations; Portugal gains dominion over the eastern half of Timor
1945	After a three-year-long invasion during World War II, Japan is expelled from East Timor and Portuguese colonial rule resumes
1974	A military coup overthrows Portuguese regime and commits to decolonization
August 1975	After a brief civil war in East Timor, Portuguese complete withdrawal
November 28, 1975	FRETILIN unilaterally declares independence
December 7, 1975	Indonesia invades East Timor, commencing a 24-year civil war
1975–1976	UN Security Council passes two resolutions condemning the invasion and calling for self-determination
1979	Last FRETILIN base falls to Indonesian forces
October 1989	Pope John Paul II visits Dili, sparking a wave of protests

December 1989	Australia and Indonesia sign the Timor Gap Treaty, and begin joint oil exploration and production
1991	Santa Cruz massacre leaves 270 protestors dead and is televised around the world
1996	José Ramos-Horta and Bishop Belo are awarded Nobel Peace Prize
1997	Asian financial crisis
April 1998	The Timorese National Resistance Council (CNRT) is formed with Gusmão as president
May 20, 1998	President Suharto of Indonesia resigns; replaced by B. J. Habibie
May 5, 1999	Indonesia and Portugal agree to hold popular consultation on East Timor
August 30, 1999	Timorese reject special autonomy in referendum that opens door to independence; kicks off retribution violence by pro-Jakarta militia
September 15, 1999	UNSC 1264 authorizes deployment of INTERFET to East Timor
September 20, 1999	INTERFET deploys 12,600 troops in East Timor
October 1999	UNTAET assumes sovereign authority in East Timor
May 20, 2002	Democratic Republic of Timor-Leste declares independence
April 2006	Riots in Dili kick off a wave of unrest
May 2006	Fighting breaks out between F-FDTL and PNTL
May 25, 2006	International peacekeeping forces arrive in Timor-Leste
February 11, 2008	Failed coup attempt; President Ramos-Horta severely wounded

At the turn of the twenty-first century, a small half-island nation emerged from the chaos of conflict against monumental odds. Within just 15 years of independence, Timor-Leste managed to become the most democratic nation in Southeast Asia.[1] Its success was possible due to the skill of its

Figure 4.1. Map of Timor-Leste

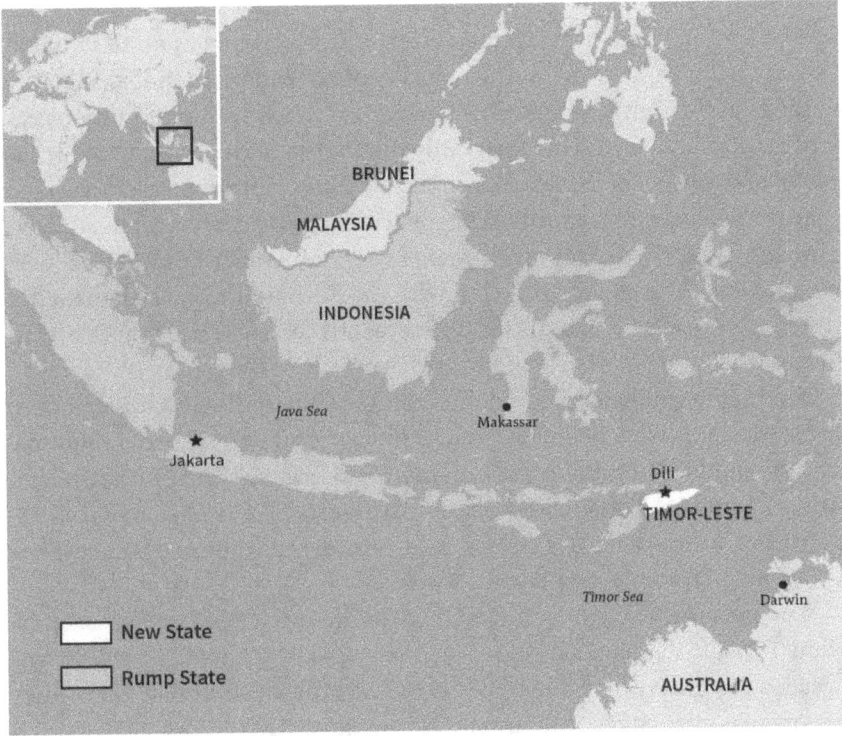

leaders, shifts in geopolitics, and unprecedented levels of international support. Leaders were able to unite East Timor's ethnically and politically divided society and transform it into a powerful resistance network that coalesced military, clandestine, diplomatic, and activist efforts at a critical juncture in history. A successful campaign to win the hearts and minds of the global audience and the realignment of powerful interests after the Cold War culminated in considerable pressure on Indonesia to release its grip. Brief UN administration and considerable commitments from Australia, Portugal, the United States, and other nations to construct institutions and deploy troops helped prevent a return to violence. Timor-Leste's savvy and dynamic leadership capitalized on this international support and managed to use its considerable oil reserves to overcome fragility. Despite centrifugal forces, the leadership continues to share aspirations of building a sovereign and prosperous nation.

THE GENESIS OF A NEW STATE

The island of Timor was inhabited by various groups of settlers, most notably from Papua New Guinea, the Pacific Islands, and Indochina. Due to the island's highly mountainous terrain, these waves of migration created a number of ethno-linguistically distinct societies. When the Portuguese arrived in the sixteenth century, colonial administrators decided against overhauling traditional governance structures, instead governing indirectly through the preexisting patchwork of competing local kings (*liurai*). After a series of wars with the Netherlands, a settlement between the two empires in the mid-nineteenth century sliced the island in half, with Portugal preserving control over the eastern part.

Portugal's imposition of a poll tax in 1901 led to the first anticolonial, proto-nationalist movement, which incorporated multiple chiefdoms. The Portuguese put down the rebellion with force, killing an estimated 25,000 people. Although unsuccessful, this struggle created a shared experience of resistance to external rule, reinforced when the Japanese invaded East Timor during World War II.[2]

The postwar external political environment created favorable conditions for self-determination. After the 1945 UN Charter called for increased autonomy of colonial territories, Portugal rebranded East Timor an "overseas province" to maintain legitimate control. Lisbon also boosted access to education,[3] contributing to heightened levels of political consciousness, with organized cells of educated elite secretly discussing the poor economic conditions and the lack of opportunities for political participation.

In 1974, a military coup overthrew the Portuguese regime and the new government adopted a policy of decolonization. In the political environment that ensued, Timorese elites created political parties. These emerged with contrasting ideological and geopolitical allegiances.[4] Jakarta exacerbated animosities between them by launching targeted information campaigns against the pro-independence Timorese Social Democratic Association (ASDT) party, in part due to its Marxist ideology, which was considered a potential threat to the national security of Indonesia.[5] Tensions resulted in a brief civil war between ASDT (renamed the Revolutionary Front for an Independent East Timor, FRETILIN) and the Timorese Democratic Union (UDT) in August 1975, which led to the complete withdrawal of the Portuguese administration. In the void of administrative authority and having decisively defeated UDT, FRETILIN unilaterally declared independence on November 29, 1975.

The independent Democratic Republic of Timor-Leste lasted only nine days. On December 7, 1975, the Indonesian National Armed Forces (ABRI) invaded East Timor, commencing a 24-year civil war. FRETILIN and ABRI clashed throughout the country, with especially heavy civilian casualties in the two largest Timorese urban centers of Dili and Baucau, as well as in eastern districts of the island. ABRI's superior firepower and numbers forced FRETILIN to withdraw inland. After four years of relentless ABRI air assaults and ground offensives, FRETILIN's last mountain base fell in 1979. Of the original force of about 15,000 FRETILIN fighters, only 700 survived, dispersed in small pockets across the territory.[6] The total number of casualties, including deaths by hunger and disease, was estimated between 104,000 and 204,000 out of a pre-invasion population of 664,223 (1974).[7]

One of the few surviving FRETILIN leaders, Xanana Gusmão, oversaw internal restructuring. The armed resistance fully adopted guerrilla tactics. Relying on the civilian population for intelligence, a clandestine network of operatives emerged, which allowed FRETILIN to carry out surgical hit-and-run strikes, a tactic FRETILIN would maintain well into the 1990s. These were followed by brutal crackdowns that further alienated the population.[8]

After incorporating East Timor into its administrative structures, Indonesia's economic policies contributed to growing dissatisfaction. Investment was targeted at rehabilitation of physical infrastructure and human capital in an attempt to legitimize the occupation and to integrate the largely cashless rural households into the macroeconomy. These plans led to increased school enrollment and the development of infrastructure, but the economy was dominated by the military and geared toward its own needs. Corruption was rife, with ABRI holding a monopoly on lucrative coffee exports and controlling transfers from Indonesia. Corruption further deterred foreign direct investment and contributed to high unemployment, especially among Timorese youth. These economic grievances provided additional kindling to the pro-independence protests that erupted during the 1990s.

The lure of East Timor's natural resources provided economic incentives for foreign intervention. British and Australian companies conducted onshore oil exploration in East Timor throughout the twentieth century, but the few existing wells produced low yields, preventing large-scale investment. After the Indonesian invasion in 1975, Australia and Indonesia began negotiating the Timor Gap Treaty, which would permit joint offshore oil production and revenue sharing that had previously failed due to Lisbon's reluctance to participate in talks.

Portugal, still the de jure authority in East Timor, strongly opposed the Indonesian occupation. It cut diplomatic ties with Jakarta and brought the East Timor issue to the UN Security Council. In 1975 and 1976, the Security Council passed two resolutions condemning the invasion and calling for self-determination.[9] Although the UN General Assembly adopted resolutions with similar condemnations each year until 1982, voting patterns showed that international support for self-determination was dwindling (see Figure 4.2). After the near defeat of Resolution 37/30 in 1982, Portugal and FRETILIN's diplomatic wing[10] focused their efforts on the UN Special Committee on Decolonization and helped galvanize support for Timorese independence in the European Union.

East Timor became embroiled in Cold War politics, with Western states repeatedly opposing self-determination and the Eastern bloc favoring it. After pro-Western regimes fell in Cambodia and Laos, FRETILIN's Marxist ideology alarmed the United States and deterred it from supporting East Timor's independence. President Gerald Ford expressed support for the annexation of East Timor during a visit to Jakarta and moved to quadruple arms sales to Indonesia between 1974

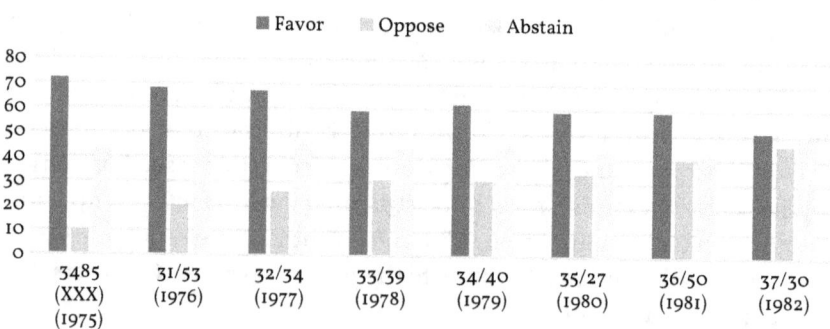

Figure 4.2. East Timor UN Voting

Note: UN General Assembly Resolutions calling for Timor-Leste's self-determination and the withdrawal of Indonesian troops (1975–1982).
Source: https://etan.org/etun/UNvotes.htm.

and 1977.[11] Although the administration of President Jimmy Carter drew attention to human rights violations in East Timor, the United States maintained its pro-Indonesian policy course until President Bill Clinton's administration.

Ensuring a stable relationship with Indonesia was central to Australia's regional engagement efforts. Australia feared having a potential "Cuba" on its doorstep and became one of the few countries that de jure recognized Indonesia's annexation of East Timor in 1976.[12] Australia's interest in oil reserves in the Timor Sea also contributed to its pro-Indonesian stance. In 1989, it signed an agreement on joint exploration and production with Indonesia. Until 1998, Australia repeatedly blocked motions on self-determination at the United Nations.

The Vatican, and by extension the Catholic Church, contributed considerably to the struggle for independence. The Church served as a refuge for those in need and kept meticulous records of human rights violations. In keeping the Dili Diocese separate from the Indonesian Catholic Church, the mostly East Timorese priests were less susceptible to interference from Jakarta. They served as conduits of information to the outside world, which greatly contributed to the efforts of the resistance's diplomatic wing.[13] This support also strengthened legitimacy of the Church inside occupied East Timor.

Indonesia's *Pancasila* philosophy required adherence to one of five monotheistic religions, and the Catholic community increased from 28 percent of the population in 1973 to over 90 percent in 2000.[14] The proliferation of Catholicism helped synthesize a distinct East Timorese identity, even among competing resistance factions. In 1983, the Church began holding mass in Tetum, which gradually came to resemble a lingua franca.

Pope John Paul II's much-publicized visit to Dili in 1989 invigorated previously splintered resistance cells. Clandestine networks that had infiltrated Indonesian education institutions sparked civil disobedience, which attracted international attention. The wave of protests that followed the pope's visit culminated in the Santa Cruz massacre in 1991, where ABRI opened fire at peaceful demonstrators, leaving up to 270 dead.[15] After these events were broadcast around the world, transnational activist networks in over 20 countries started pressuring their governments to support independence. They consisted of civil society organizations that had been active in promoting the Timorese cause since the onset of the occupation. Frequently they were spearheaded by members of the diaspora, particularly in Portugal, Australia, and Indonesia, which hosted the largest communities of Timorese refugees.[16] The massacre helped mobilize the diaspora, amplifying the diplomatic wing's international hearts and minds campaign. The armed resistance gained international support for its 1992 Peace Plan outlining its commitment to democracy and human rights, and which included provisions for disarmament, the establishment of a Portuguese-led transitional administration, and democratic elections.

The Santa Cruz massacre coincided with major geopolitical shifts at the end of the Cold War. Indonesia lost its pivotal role in counteracting the spread of communism in Southeast Asia and, as Security Council members recalibrated long-held positions on East Timor, the balance shifted toward independence. Under increased pressure from activist networks, the changing U.S. stance was particularly consequential. After visiting East Timor in 1993, the U.S. ambassador to Indonesia reported grave human rights violations and called for increased autonomy. Later that year, the UN Commission on Human Rights adopted a landmark resolution that condemned human rights violations in East Timor. Both Australia and the United States supported the resolution. When José Ramos-Horta and Bishop Belo won the Nobel Peace Prize in 1996 for their work in East Timor, pressure on Indonesia increased further.

The Clinton administration began to condition military aid to Indonesia on its human rights performance in East Timor, while the Netherlands, Denmark, and Canada cut aid to Indonesia.[17] Jakarta eventually agreed to resume tripartite talks with Portugal. Although autonomy was not discussed, the negotiations brought different resistance factions and nonpolitical organizations to the table and contributed to the emergence of a national unity body, the Timorese National Resistance Council (CNRT).[18]

Economic pressure on Indonesia was also mounting. The Asian financial crisis of 1997 resulted in Indonesia's economy contracting by 14 points, bank closures, and a significant drop in living standards.[19] Amid widespread violence and allegations of corruption and nepotism, President Suharto of Indonesia stepped down May 20, 1998, and was replaced by B. J. Habibie.

East Timor was increasingly viewed as a considerable burden on the Indonesian economy, and the incoming Habibie administration also was cognizant of a major shift in international opinion regarding East Timor. A few weeks after taking office, Habibie announced his support for a referendum on wide-ranging autonomy.

On May 5, 1999, Indonesia and Portugal agreed to hold a popular consultation in East Timor, which contained a provision that the rejection of autonomy would lead to independence. The agreement became the centerpiece of UN Security Council Resolution 1246, under which the United Nations Mission in East Timor (UNAMET) was deployed to the island to administer the referendum. Despite intimidation campaigns by ABRI-backed militias, on August 30, 1999, an overwhelming 78.5 percent of Timorese rejected special autonomy, opening the door for independence.[20] In response, pro-Jakarta militias went on a bloody rampage, using scorched-earth tactics as retribution for the vote, marking the beginning of yet another crisis.

THE REALITIES OF INDEPENDENCE

Post-referendum violence plunged the emergent nation into a severe humanitarian crisis. Mobs of pro-autonomy militia freely roamed the country, killing over a thousand people, with UNAMET lacking both the mandate and the military capacity to quell the unrest. Over two-thirds of the population were driven from their homes. Many were evacuated to West Timor.[21] A critical shortfall of labor in the agricultural sector diminished food production. An exodus of Indonesian civilian personnel—over 8,000 senior civil servants, including 81 percent of all physicians and 80 percent of secondary school teachers, lawyers, and police officers—further accelerated the collapse of the civilian administration.[22]

In addition to the displacement crisis, the use of scorched-earth tactics resulted in catastrophic damage. Two-thirds of administrative buildings, including schools, clinics, and doctors' offices, were damaged or destroyed, and housing was decimated.[23] Timor-Leste was born one of the poorest countries on earth.[24] A remark from the inbound UN Transitional Administrator Sérgio Vieira de Mello encapsulated the monumental challenges ahead: "We are starting from scratch."[25]

To evaluate the post-independence success of Timor-Leste, immediate state-building interventions can be assessed through the prism of three dimensions of statehood—authority, capacity, and legitimacy.[26]

Authority

On September 15, 1999, the UN Security Council unanimously passed Resolution 1264, which authorized deployment of the International Forces for East Timor (INTERFET) to restore peace and security, protect UNAMET, and facilitate humanitarian assistance. Two weeks later, 12,600 Australian-led troops descended on Dili and ABRI withdrew. Meanwhile, a negotiated and upheld cantonment of the armed resistance provided INTERFET with the authority to protect the population, rather than serve as a neutral peacekeeping force. INTERFET troops raided militia bases and confiscated weapons. Within three months, the security situation in Timor-Leste was normalized.

The UN Transitional Administration of East Timor (UNTAET) was granted a degree of authority unprecedented in the history of the United Nations, assuming full sovereign authority and preventing a power vacuum. The Transitional Administration set forward provisions that vested executive, legislative, and judiciary authorities in the transitional administrator. At its peak, the UNTAET security sector consisted of 8,000 troops, assisted by 1,500 civilian police (CIVPOL).[27] The sheer number of forces in proportion to the size of the population allowed them to quell violent uprisings and maintain stability.

Most security challenges that UNTAET, and subsequently Timor-Leste, faced stemmed from domestic actors and organized groups on the opposing side of Timor-Leste's western border. Although INTERFET was able to impose relative stability, Timor-Leste experienced a staggering increase in organized crime.[28] Thousands of militia members remained stationed near the border for several years, increasing tensions in refugee camps and border townships.[29] Furthermore, historic grievances, calls for peace dividends, and poor socioeconomic conditions led domestic groups to participate in violent demonstrations and commit acts of arson, intimidation, and murder. Because these groups had close alliances with members of the political elite, political disagreements had the potential to return the country to mayhem.

Returning refugees also proved a serious challenge to state-building efforts. Repatriation became a central political objective of the Transitional Administration, in part to ensure the legitimacy of upcoming elections. UNHCR and IOM provided humanitarian assistance and cooperated with local leaders and the Church to facilitate reconciliation efforts once refugees returned to their communities.

UNTAET and subsequent UN missions encountered significant challenges in developing Timor-Leste's security capacities. In 2001, vocal demands from the Timorese elite led UNTAET to bring a new Timorese security force, the Timorese Defense Force (F-FDTL), into existence. The F-FDTL was tasked with the defense of territorial integrity and natural disaster management. Attempting to minimize political infighting, Xanana Gusmão was permitted to handle recruitment.[30] He filled the F-FDTL with his allies and competitively recruited officers, to the great displeasure of the FRETILIN elite, his nascent political rival. Due to a critical shortfall of employment opportunities, former guerrilla fighters who were not conscripted gravitated toward fringe groups that rejected UNTAET's authority.

Establishing a Timorese civilian police force received renewed international attention and resources. CIVPOL, however, struggled to implement its mandate. International officers lacked the linguistic skills and cultural knowledge to interact with the local population effectively.[31] CIVPOL quickly established a curriculum for basic police training and started to recruit potential officers to the East Timor Police Service (PNTL). Capacity shortfalls led to the disastrous decision to rely on some former members of the Indonesian National Police. The inclusion of Indonesian police in the PNTL significantly damaged its legitimacy. Indonesian police, after all, had been held responsible for many atrocities during the occupation.

Like the new military, the police force would fall victim to political rivalries. After the handover of the PNTL to the Timorese government in 2004, Minister of the Interior Rogerio Lobato quickly filled the force with his loyalists, in part to counteract Xanana Gusmão's influence in F-FDTL.[32] A confrontation between F-FDTL and PNTL officers in 2004 served as a precursor to the breakdown of the security sector in 2006.

UNTAET established constitutionally mandated judicial institutions. In practice, the judiciary relied heavily on foreign judicial staff well beyond the transitional period. Joint government, donor, and civil society programs gradually built local expertise, but the judiciary remains the weakest branch of government, in part because the Portuguese legal system was adopted, even though most Timorese were trained in Indonesian law.

Bodies created by the United Nations were not solely responsible for the new state's ability to maintain order. A much more influential, yet often neglected, component of state authority has existed underneath the formal nexus of the emergent security apparatus—customary law and governance. These codes were closely linked to complex local laws (*lisan*) that regulate social norms, morality, and rituals. Village elites use these practices to enforce peace and reconciliation by facilitating and mediating dialogue. For this reason, deficiencies in the police and judicial systems did not completely undermine efforts to establish state authority. Customary practices have allowed local leaders to maintain communal order and resolve crimes that went underreported in the formal system.[33] This system also explains the success of interventions that built on this hybrid political order. For example, the UN-established all-Timorese Commission for Reception, Truth, and Reconciliation (CAVR) was able to process 1,371 militia leaders and their followers by using *lisan* reconciliation processes, considerably improving village cohesion.[34]

Capacity

The broad national consensus on the transition to independence, the success of UN peacekeepers in maintaining relative stability, and the quick institutionalization of a governing authority in the form of UNTAET created a favorable environment for building the new state's administrative and economic capacity.

International donors heavily financed the development of the state bureaucracy, introducing mechanisms that allowed for greater coordination and evaluation. Indeed, Timor-Leste received some of the highest levels of annual aid per capita among post-conflict states.[35] Twenty-five international donors and 25 representatives of different sections of Timorese society carried out comprehensive needs assessments early, which helped mobilize international funds from a diverse set of donor countries.[36] Donors' biannual conferences, monthly meetings, and joint missions allowed them to target efforts, maintain momentum in resolving the humanitarian crisis, track sectorial progress, and develop multiyear budgets. Unfortunately, at times, donors' programs undermined local ownership and became diluted once donors transitioned from humanitarian aid to sustainable development interventions.

The Transitional Administration gradually built the executive and legislative branches of government. UNTAET established a consultative body, allocating seats to CNRT and a few pro-autonomy factions. This body was granted increasing legislative and executive authorities until it transformed into proto-executive and proto-legislative structures that ultimately transferred to Timorese control. Rapidly approaching the end of its mandate, UNTAET set in motion provisions for democratic elections of a Constituent Assembly tasked with drafting a constitution, authorizing its transition into the first parliament of the independent Timor-Leste. FRETILIN decisively won the elections and controlled a solid majority in the Constituent Assembly. Upon recommendation of the Constituent Assembly, FRETILIN leader Mari Alkatiri became chief minister and subsequently prime minister of the first constitutional government. After Xanana Gusmão's overwhelming victory in UNTAET-facilitated presidential elections, the main poles of power were established, and May 20, 2002, marked the beginning of the Democratic Republic of Timor-Leste.

Both the Transitional Administration and international donors promoted programs and policies to ensure the emergence of a liberal democratic political system, a market economy, and a lean government. Parts of the executive continued to rely heavily on international advisers after the transitional period, while severe capacity shortfalls were partially mediated by returning members of the diaspora, who brought vital skills and resources to the country.[37]

Greater institutional performance was achieved when preexisting nongovernmental actors were incorporated into the nascent administrative complex, instead of creating entirely new structures. The rapid expansion in health coverage is in part explained by using this approach.[38] Early handover of middle and upper management positions to Timorese nationals and the gradual transition from organizational and regulatory simplicity to increased complexity also helped achieve these objectives. The introduction of international best practices and heavy investments in capacity-building at the crux of increased complexity further amplified institutional performance. This approach was particularly pronounced during the creation of the Central Bank.[39]

ECONOMIC CAPACITY

Timor-Leste's economic sustainability largely depended on the careful management of its oil resources. The Timorese government recognized that offshore oil deposits would constitute a considerable share of government revenues and would thus require prudent management to avoid the resource curse.[40] The World Bank, International Monetary Fund, and other donors were heavily involved in drafting legislation for the Petroleum fund. Provisions were implemented to assist in public consultations and ensure unanimous political support in the parliament. Experts from the Norwegian oil fund played an important role in transmitting best practices, adding stricter accountability and transparency provisions.[41]

Timor-Leste has become one of the most oil-dependent countries in the world, with 97 percent of government revenues stemming from the petroleum sector, accounting for 76 percent of its GDP.[42] After donors scaled down activities following the transitional period, Timor-Leste's GDP contracted and only began to revive once oil revenues began to flow in 2005.[43] The return to violence in 2006 further contracted the economy, but significant increases in oil production and public expenditure allowed for solid economic performance, which has been maintained ever since.

Economic contraction contributed to an increase in poverty—from 41.5 percent immediately after independence to 43 percent two years later. Family planning policies reduced the staggering fertility rate of 8.3 in 2002 to 5.7 in 2014, but it still outpaces other countries in Southeast Asia and has adverse effects on service delivery and the economy.[44] The demographic bulge has resulted in heavy competition for essential public services, as well as high youth unemployment. Meanwhile, the small middle class, consisting of government contractors and civil servants, remains largely urbanized and contributes to regional inequality.

An array of factors has hampered private sector development and foreign direct investment (FDI). Private sector companies have been in direct competition with the expanding public sector for skilled personnel, with the government able to offer higher wages. Poor infrastructure, a lack of key legislation, and largely inefficient judiciary have undermined the business environment. These factors, along with the small market size, low productivity levels, and higher wages than in other parts of the region, have prevented a considerable inflow of FDI, leaving the economy poorly diversified. Consequently, two-thirds of the population continue to be employed in the agricultural sector.

The ability to diversify the economy amid rapidly dwindling oil receipts in recent years and to boost the productivity of the agrarian sector will likely determine the long-term economic survival of Timor-Leste.

Legitimacy

INTERNAL LEGITIMACY

The widespread use of violence throughout the occupation contributed to a shared sense of trauma. Increases in conversions to Catholicism and the uptake of Tetum strengthened a pancommunal identity. Timor-Leste's new government's legitimacy essentially grew out of the resistance architecture, which had nurtured social and political organization. The resistance network consisted of a hierarchical paramilitary guerrilla front and took other forms (including the FRETILIN party apparatus and clandestine networks), and so transcended the village (*suku*) level, which historically had served as the constituent dimension of governance. The inclusion of clandestine leaders (*nurep*) in the broader resistance network allowed the extension of authority across genealogical lines, as *nurep* frequently held customary leadership roles in their respective *sukus*. The confluence of these forms of social organization contributed to cohesion and introduced a semblance of vertical accountability between the general populace and the resistance leadership.[45] The creation of CNRT helped consolidate the different factions and clans, while also establishing a shared vision of Timorese statehood in the 1998 CNRT Magna Carta. The inclusion of CNRT into UNTAET's proto-government structures and the exodus of a number of pro-autonomy factions to West Timor further increased the legitimacy of the state-building efforts.[46]

The referendum gave the new state democratic legitimacy and instilled a strong democratic undercurrent in Timor-Leste that continues to hold a symbolic value. This is evident in the persistently high voter participation rates, which have averaged 78 percent since independence.[47]

The nascent political elite mostly consists of the 1975 generation of resistance leaders, who share long historic ties and established themselves during the short decolonization period. Xanana Gusmão, Mari Alkatiri, and José Ramos-Horta are the most recognizable and have featured prominently in the political arena since 2002. Historic feuds, power struggles, and ideological differences among the elite continued to affect Timor-Leste's political stability.[48] Alkatiri and Horta are part of a sizable cadre of exiled political elites who returned to Timor-Leste after the referendum. Their membership in the Timorese diaspora has, at times, undermined their legitimacy in parts of the society and has sparked tensions with elite who remained in East Timor during the occupation.

Unsurprisingly, CNRT began to disintegrate during the transitional period, as diverging interests of pluralistic constituencies, pressures to deliver peace dividends, and competition for resources and authority began to mount. Regional and generational fault lines emerged that affected intra-elite relations and had broader repercussions for state-society relations. These divisions contributed to increased competition in the political arena. Many new parties formed alongside FRETILIN and UDT, and mostly operated within the established political environment, allowing rivalries to be settled in a regulated setting.[49] The sovereign authority of UNTAET during the transitional period allowed it to play an important role in enabling this environment.

Xanana Gusmão is arguably the charismatic leader of Timor-Leste, having held a number of top government posts, including prime minister and president. His background as a resistance leader and his capture by the Indonesian forces in 1992 transformed him into an archetypal martyr of the Timorese self-determination movement. He enjoys broad public support, and the military maintains a deep loyalty to him. He initially operated outside of party structures but morphed into a political kingmaker. His endorsement of candidates has significantly influenced election outcomes. His leadership style has, at times, been described as overbearing, even borderline authoritarian.[50] Paradoxically, he has been a vocal supporter of democratic principles and has demonstrated the ability to unify competing factions of the population.

Until an eventual rapprochement in 2013, FRETILIN's secretary general, Mari Alkatiri, was a bitter rival to Gusmão's dominance. His political standing largely originates from his leadership role in the historic resistance party, FRETILIN, rather than actual military credentials. He spent the occupation period in Angola and Mozambique, a fact aggressively exploited by Gusmão.[51] Nonetheless, Alkatiri was able to transition into power after FRETILIN detached from CNRT and won an outright majority in the first parliamentary elections. He has benefited from well-established FRETILIN networks and has maintained power ever since.

Timor-Leste established a semi-presidential system with an elected president and parliament that increased the government's democratic legitimacy. This system contributed to the resolution of conflicts within institutional boundaries, as the constitution bestows the presidency with strong oversight functions over the prime minister, who runs the far more powerful executive. The president reserves the right to dismiss the parliament as well as the prime minister on political and institutional grounds. A nonpartisan president was elected in three subsequent presidential election cycles, which allowed the office to serve as a politically impartial check on the executive and as a moderator of political differences.[52]

Corruption increasingly is a problem and undermines the legitimacy of the state. The culture of gift-giving as an expression of gratitude is deeply entrenched in traditional norms. As many former resistance leaders without educational qualifications transitioned into leadership roles in the public administration, corrupt patronage networks, particularly in public procurement, have become increasingly common. Several high-profile corruption cases, such as the conviction of the minister of justice in 2012, show that political leaders are not immune to prosecution, but such cases usually have strong political undertones.[53]

Religious minorities, particularly the Protestant community, have reported denial of services by local authorities and intimidation at the communal level. These incidents are sporadic, and top religious leaders maintain cordial relations. The first prime minister, Mari Alkatiri, hails from the small Muslim community of Timor-Leste. Allegations of discrimination against western Timorese (*loromono*) led to the 2006 crisis, but these have more of a regional and historic identity rather than an ethnic minority, as *loromono* consist of several distinct ethnic groups.

EXTERNAL LEGITIMACY

The UN General Assembly's unanimous decision to recognize Timor-Leste bestowed external legitimacy and all the privileges of a sovereign state. Yet post-independence success has been heavily affected by the external environment.

As a small state wedged between two G-20 nations, Timor-Leste has had to deal with complex and, at times, constraining geopolitical realities.

While recognizing the legitimacy of Timorese independence, Indonesia and Australia have approached their new neighbor with caution. Both control strategically important levers that raise their bargaining power in achieving favorable policy objectives, as well as ensuring Timor-Leste's territorial integrity.[54] Australia, in particular, has demonstrated the capability and inclination to deploy troops to the island to prevent the emergence of an "arc of instability" in its immediate neighborhood. The deployment of Australian troops contributed to an undercurrent of distrust between Indonesia and Australia. Since the two countries share strategic interests and engage in various dialogue platforms, Timor-Leste lacks the leverage to play them against each other and risks being sidelined in important geopolitical decisions. Timorese policymakers have sought to overcome these constraints through careful diplomatic maneuvering, occasionally at the expense of national interests.

After the transitional period, Timor-Leste embarked on a conciliatory and pragmatic foreign policy course with Jakarta, carefully managing relations with its leaders. Indonesia demanded assurances that Timor-Leste would not seek international human rights trials for the atrocities committed during the occupation.[55] Instead, partial reconciliation was achieved through the bilateral Commission for Truth and Friendship (CTF) backed by presidents of both countries. Historic familial, business, and cultural linkages between the nations, especially between East and West Timorese, have further contributed to reconciliatory efforts and normalization of relations.[56]

Timor-Leste has sought to reduce its dependence on neighboring states by balancing with rising China. China has been actively engaged in Timor-Leste since independence, contributing forces to the UN police and providing increasing amounts of foreign assistance.[57] Growing Sino-American competition in the Asia-Pacific region also motivated China to foster closer military ties with Timor-Leste. Beijing's interest in hydrocarbon reserves and its burgeoning economic presence has provided Timorese leaders with some leverage in the heated maritime border negotiations with Australia and allowed it to garner support for its quest to join ASEAN, which serves as a counterweight to Chinese influence in the region.[58]

Timor-Leste has sought to solidify its independence, seek defense assurances and foreign assistance, and consolidate a distinct identity through its accession to regional and international organizations. It promulgated constitutional provisions mandating development of privileged ties with Portuguese-speaking states and joined the Community of Portuguese Language Countries (CPLP). These moves have underlined its cultural disparity from its neighbors and allowed it to forge links with the European Union and other regional powers, such as Brazil.[59] The accession to ASEAN has been one of Timor-Leste's long-standing policy objectives, largely motivated by its founding principles of noninterference in internal affairs. Timor-Leste has not achieved this objective. Despite Indonesian and Australian backing, members remain concerned about the fragile state of Timor-Leste institutions, which could prevent the formation of a single market.[60] Timorese leadership roles in other intergovernmental groups, such as the G-7+, and participation in the Melanesian Spearhead group and Pacific Islands Forum, have helped in diversifying its regional reach and international profile.

RESOLUTION OF THE 2006 CRISIS

The 2006 crisis occurred because of a convergence of historic[61] and economic factors:[62] the failure to build resilient and legitimate security sector institutions,[63] a lack of reconciliation, and the politically motivated manipulation of communal rivalries. UN peacekeepers neglected to develop civilian oversight bodies, instead focusing on developing security sector forces and quelling threats that undermined the stability of the state.[64] After peacekeepers withdrew, Timor-Leste inherited a military cadre largely consisting of former guerrilla fighters, disproportionally from eastern districts, and a police force with occupation-era Indonesian police officers and politically appointed western recruits. Confrontations between the poorly demarcated security sector institutions ensued, culminating in a nationwide crisis in 2006.

The crisis began when military officers sent a petition to political leaders alleging poor conditions in F-FDTL and discrimination against western Timorese (*loromono*). Following unsuccessful reconciliation efforts with the government and military leaders, 591 soldiers (42 percent of F-FDTL) were dismissed. The petitioners staged a demonstration, emboldened by a fiery speech from President Xanana Gusmão, who denounced the dismissal. It transformed into a full-scale anti-government protest that grew violent and spread across the capital and nearby districts. Without consulting the president, the Alkatiri government deployed military forces consisting of remaining eastern Timorese (*lorosae*) soldiers to assist the police, killing protesters in the process. A spiral of revenge attacks ensued, and command lines gradually disintegrated. The military and police began to suffer widespread defections. Factions mobilized based on regional and political identities that used their respective forces' arms. The crisis culminated with F-FDTL assaulting the PNTL headquarters and gunning down nine police officers. These attacks led to the displacement of about 150,000 civilians.[65]

Losing control over the security forces, the Alkatiri government requested military assistance from Australia, Malaysia, Portugal, and New Zealand. International forces arrived in Dili within 48 hours, followed later by the return of UN police, who assumed command over PNTL. The peacekeepers had a deterring effect on the conflicting parties, contributing to an immediate reduction in violence. Even with this intervention, certain groups remained at large, scattered around mountainous regions of the country, and posed major security threats for the next two years.[66]

The crisis institutionalized regionally distinct political allegiances and ushered in an era of coalition governments. After significant pressure from President Gusmão, Alkatiri resigned. Subsequent elections led to a rearrangement of the political elite. FRETILIN suffered a humiliating defeat during the heavily monitored parliamentary elections, failing to secure a majority. Other parties proved unwilling to cooperate with the former power, leading to a prolonged stalemate, broken only when the newly elected president, Horta, appointed Gusmão to form a majority government (AMP). This action prompted violence and claims of constitutional violations, but international recognition and support from the Catholic Church helped legitimize the new government.

The AMP government used a whole-of-government approach to resolve the crisis. Donor agencies also adhered to the National Recovery Plan. The immediate response to the crisis was the consolidation of police and military command under the command of Xanana Gusmão, and the disarming of PNTL officers, who were subject to review before being allowed to return to the force. Government expenditures nearly quadrupled in the five years following the crisis, stemming from increased oil proceeds, leading to sustained double-digit GDP growth rates, and increased access to basic services.

The government introduced a number of social protection mechanisms that targeted irritants to stability—petitioners received grants to demobilize and disarm ($8,500 each), IDPs received generous return subsidies ($4,000), veterans began receiving generous pensions, and safety nets were expanded to vulnerable members of the public.[67] These policies distributed peace dividends to core pressure groups, buying time for broader reforms. They were also considerable factors contributing to the resolution of the IDP crisis within just two years. Mirroring the CAVR 1999 reconciliation efforts, the government oversaw locally led traditional conflict resolution sessions. These utilized traditional and religious leaders to assist in the resettling of IDPs and petitioners into their communities while addressing broader grievances against the state.

The resolution of the 2006 crisis saw a more assertive political leadership that relied on institutionalized mechanisms to detach them from donors' agendas and to introduce local solutions. These measures allowed Timor-Leste to transition into an era of sustainable development.

CONCLUSION

As the sole Portuguese colony in the archipelago, East Timor stood out among other regions of Indonesia. The Indonesian occupation was tolerated by global powers, particularly in the West, due to Indonesia's strategic importance during the Cold War and broader economic interests. FRETILIN's unilateral declaration of independence in 1975 was not recognized by the international community, leaving a politically weakened Portugal as the de jure administrator, constitutionally bound to decolonization. After the fall of the Berlin wall, Indonesia lost its strategic leverage over the West. Human rights violations in East Timor were difficult to ignore after the widely televised events of 1991, the awarding of the Nobel Peace Prize to José Ramos-Horta and Bishop Belo, sustained advocacy, and diplomatic efforts by the resistance, Portugal, and a growing number of other states. With Suharto's resignation, economic instability, and shifting international sentiments, Indonesia succumbed to international pressure to hold a UN-supervised referendum on independence, falsely believing it would fail. Voters' overwhelming preference for independence was internationally recognized. Pressure from nearly 50 nations and multilateral organizations forced Jakarta to respect the referendum's outcome along with the subsequent deployment of Australian-led peacekeeping troops to quell postelection violence.

The success of the Timorese struggle for self-determination also rested on a few leaders' ability to craft an identity and an organizational framework that could transcend an ethnically and politically fractured society. It built on symbols of resistance, Tetum and Catholicism, and resistance factions' strong political identities, which were linked to customary hierarchies, all underpinned by a shared experience of persecution. This identity filtered through the different wings of the resistance movement, coalescing military, clandestine, and diplomatic efforts aided by a transnational network of activist groups all bearing testament to the incredible resilience of the Timorese people. Furthermore, depoliticization of the resistance, endemic corruption, and protracted violence within the occupying administration tilted allegiances of actors who could have benefited from integration with Indonesia. The national unity body, CNRT, incorporated most pro-independence factions and enjoyed legitimacy among the population as it transitioned into new government institutions.

The UN Transitional Administration established core branches of government and supervised the election of the Constituent Assembly, which drafted a constitution establishing a semi-presidential system. In the long term, this system facilitated the settlement of competing parties' disputes. International donors contributed significant funds to develop institutions, forge policies, and build the capacity of local staff across all sectors. This aid was measured against predetermined benchmarks, which helped ensure coordination while maintaining de facto control over certain functions that lacked local capacity to ensure proper functioning in post-independence times. Interventions that linked traditional practices with the formal institutional framework were more successful in achieving their objectives, as were institutions that experienced the earlier handover of middle and upper management authority to Timorese staff. Challengers to authority were initially deterred by an overwhelming presence of international troops. The premature withdrawal of these forces before civilian oversight structures were in place led to renewed conflict.

The establishment of a sovereign wealth fund provided the government with sufficient domestic resources to solve the 2006 crisis with homegrown approaches. Civil strife opened deep fractures that had existed within the society before. A more comprehensive reconciliation process between security forces, the state, and society in general was needed. Timor-Leste redistributed oil wealth to the population through a variety of means. However, this may prove to be only a short-term solution since oil funds will soon be depleted. Underlying problems of poverty and inequality—the primary culprits in the crisis—remain unresolved and nonoil revenues continue to ebb. On the positive side, Timor-Leste has avoided a repetition of large-scale violence since 2006, and presidents and parliaments have transitioned in and out of office. This progress has ushered in an era of stability and development, allowing a national focus on the building of a just and sovereign nation for which the resistance had fought so hard.

NOTES

1. Derived by comparing the Economist Intelligence Unit's Democracy Index among Southeast Asian nations in 2016, https://infographics.economist.com/2017/Democracy Index/.

2. World War II also illustrated diverging *liurai* political preferences and the absence of a cohesive national identity, as some *liurai* sided with the Japanese, while others sided with Allied forces. Comissão de Acolhimento, Verdade e Reconciliação de Timor Leste (CAVR), *Chega! The Final Report of the Timor-Leste Commission for Reception, Truth, and Reconciliation* (Dili: CAVR, 2013), 149–150.

3. Primary and secondary school enrollment increased from 3,249 in 1950 to 57,500 in 1970. That was still a low figure considering the population of about 650,000. CAVR, *Chega!*, 151–152.

4. The conservative Timorese Democratic Union (UDT) favored a federation with Portugal, the Popular Democratic Association (APODETI) called for integration with Indonesia, while the left-wing Timorese Social Democratic Association (ASDT) favored independence. Other minor parties favoring associations with Australia or the creation of customary kingdoms also emerged. CAVR, *Chega!*, 155–156.

5. See Parliament of Australia, "East Timor: Final Report of the Senate Foreign Affairs, Defence, and Trade References Committee" (December 2000), Chapter 7.

6. Irena Cristalis, *East Timor: A Nation's Bitter Dawn* (London: Zed Books, 2009), 110–126.

7. Cristalis, *East Timor*.

8. The Commission for Reception, Truth and Reconciliation in East Timor (CAVR) found that the armed resistance movement was also complicit in human rights violations. According to some estimates, about 25 percent of illegal killings and 10 percent of all violations were committed by FRETILIN troops during the early years of occupation. CAVR, *Chega!*, 1126.

9. These included UN Security Council resolution 384 (1975) and 389 (1976).

10. A splinter cell of the FRETILIN Central Committee left East Timor three days before the invasion. It was led by José Ramos-Horta, Mari Alkatiri, and other leaders, who worked through diplomatic channels to lobby for self-determination for the duration of the occupation. José Ramos-Horta was accepted by the UN as the spokesman for the East Timorese people in 1975. CAVR, *Chega!*, 203–213.

11. From 1975 to 1995, U.S. arms transfers to Indonesia totaled at an estimated $1.118 billion. William D. Hartung, "U.S. Arms Transfers to Indonesia 1975–1997: Who's Influencing Whom?" World Policy Institute, March 1997, 17.

12. Peter Chalk, *Australian Foreign and Defense Policy in the Wake of the 1999/2000 East Timor Intervention* (Santa Monica, CA: RAND, 2001), 29–46.

13. CAVR, *Chega!*, 246–248.

14. Curt Gabrielson, "The Church in East Timor," Institute of Current World Affairs, August 1, 2001, 2–5.

15. East Timor Action Network (ETAN), "Santa Cruz Massacre," fact sheet, November 2016.

16. Indonesia hosted the majority of roughly a quarter of a million Timorese refugees who had fled occupation, while at its peak only 20,000 settled in Australia and 10,000 in Portugal. CAVR, *Chega!*, 703–706.

17. ETAN, "Santa Cruz Massacre."

18. Attempts to depoliticize the resistance movement and create a national unity body began in 1980s, when Gusmão moved to abandon Marxism and withdraw the military wing of the resistance from the FRETILIN party apparatus. He eventually resigned from FRETILIN himself, to the great displeasure of the remaining party elite. International Crisis Group, *Resolving Timor-Leste's Crisis*, Asia Report No. 120 (Brussels: International Crisis Group, October 2006), 2–6. CNRT included UDT, FRETILIN, the Catholic Church, and CNRM, as well as other smaller factions. The latter emerged after Xanana Gusmão separated the armed forces from the FRETILIN party in late 1980s. CAVR, *Chega!*, 698–702.

19. Steven Radelet, "Indonesia: Long Road to Recovery," Harvard Institute for International Development, 1999, 1–6.

20. CAVR, *Chega!*, 286–299.

21. UN High Commissioner for Refugees (UNHCR), *Evaluation of UNHCR's Repatriation and Reintegration Programme in East Timor, 1999–2003* (Geneva: UNHCR, 2004), 1–10. There are diverging accounts of the extent of the displacement crisis, as other sources claim that nearly 90 percent of the population was displaced. James Dobbins et al., *The UN's Role in Nation-Building: From the Congo to Iraq* (Santa Monica, CA: RAND, 2005), 153.

22. Dobbins et al., *The UN's Role in Nation-Building*, 153–158.

23. Over half of all power stations (13 out of 23) were in urgent need of repairs, hampering power supply. Transmission towers had suffered extensive damage affecting the telecommunications network. Furthermore, the already scarce access to water supply systems was further damaged, exposing the remaining population to the risk of illness. World Bank, *East Timor: Building a Nation: Joint Assessment Mission* (Washington, DC: World Bank, November 1999), 1–13.

24. Timor-Leste's Human Development Index (HDI) score was 0.396 in the immediate aftermath of the violence—the lowest score in Asia. The average Timorese life expectancy was 57, while per capita income was an estimated $337 in 1999, the lowest among 162 countries surveyed. UN Development Programme, *Ukun Rasik A'an: The Way Ahead*, East Timor Human Development Report (New York: UNDP, 2002), 1–3.

25. This statement eventually characterized the brief UNTAET rule over East Timor, as the incoming donor community often lacked local knowledge and moved to import international best practices and institutions that only partially coalesced with local governance structures, resulting in institutional and legislative hybridity. Lee Jones, "(Post-)Colonial Statebuilding and State Failure in East Timor: Bringing Social Conflict Back In," *Conflict, Security & Development* 10, no. 4 (2010): 547–575.

26. The official name of the country under the constitution is the Democratic Republic of Timor-Leste. The term Timor-Leste will be used henceforth when referring to the state post-referendum.

27. Dobbins et al., *The UN's Role in Nation-Building*, 179–180.

28. UN Security Council, "Report of the Secretary-General on the United Nations Transitional Administration," United Nations, April 17, 2000, 4–7.

29. Michael Brown et al., "Conflict Assessment: East Timor," U.S. Agency for International Development, 2004, 5–17.

30. Jones, "(Post-)Colonial Statebuilding and State Failure in East Timor," 547–575.

31. Eva Svoboda and Eleanor Davey, *The Search for Common Ground: Police, Protection, and Coordination in Timor-Leste* (London: Overseas Development Institute, December 2013), 13–17.

32. International Crisis Group, *Resolving Timor-Leste's Crisis*, 2–6.

33. Todd Wassel, *Institutionalising Community Policing in Timor-Leste* (San Francisco: Asia Foundation/Overseas Development Institute, March 2014), 9–12.

34. John Braithwaite, "Evaluating the Timor-Leste Peace Operation," *Journal of International Peacekeeping* 16, no. 3–4 (2012): 291–300.

35. Only Bosnia and Herzegovina and the West Bank and Gaza have recorded higher per capita aid disbursements ($247 and $213, respectively). Note that the United Nations assesses the total contribution budget at roughly $1.28 billion between 1999 and 2002, which also includes the costs of peacekeeping troops and civilian staff. This would increase the per capita figure to $533, more than twice that of the highest recorded expenditure in Bosnia and Herzegovina. Klaus Rohland and Sarah Cliffe, *The East Timor Reconstruction Program: Successes, Problems and Tradeoffs*, Working Paper No. 2 (Washington, DC: World Bank, November 2002), 6–9.

36. Rohland and Cliffe, *The East Timor Reconstruction Program*, 3–5. Arguably, as did political pressure from transnational activist groups. Andrew Rosser and Sharna Bremmer, "The World Bank's Health Projects in Timor-Leste: The Political Economy of Effective Aid," in *Development Assistance for Peacebuilding*, ed. Rachel M. Gisselquist (Abingdon, UK: Routledge, 2017), 442.

37. Kimberly Hamilton, "East Timor: Old Migration Challenges in the World's Newest Country," Migration Policy Institute, May 1, 2004.

38. The health sector saw a rapid expansion in coverage, from near destruction in 1999 to 87 percent in 2004. The Interim Health Authority signed memoranda of understanding with over 100 local nonstate health providers and began directly financing them. Nonstate actors also played a crucial role in hosting international health professionals, largely provided by Cuba, while locally recruited medical staff received training abroad. International medics had a crucial role in recruiting grassroots counterparts and building their capacities. These actors were gradually incorporated into the nascent Ministry of Health. Catherine Anderson, "Timor Leste Case Study: Ministry of Health," in *Institutions Taking Root: Building State Capacity in Challenging Contexts*, ed. Naazneen Barma, Elisabeth Huybens, and Lorena Vinuela (Washington, DC: World Bank, 2014), 303–343.

39. The Central Bank went through three iterations of institutional development. An organizational framework with core intended functions emerged early, allowing easy addition of specialized departments once the mandate became more complex. While international advisers initially held all managerial responsibilities, the Banking and Payments Authority that became the Central Bank was among the first institutions to have an all-Timorese leadership. The World Bank and IMF invested heavily in capacity building and linked the institution with regional counterparts, while promulgating regulations that ensured the leadership cycle would remain separate from the political cycle—thus increasing its autonomy. Lorena Vinuela, "Timor-Leste Case Study: The Central Bank of Timor-Leste," in *Institutions Taking Root*, ed. Barma, Huybens, and Vinuela, 347–371. Similar approaches were used in the creation of the Ministry of Social Solidarity and Ministry of Health.

40. East Timor Planning Commission, *East Timor National Development Plan* (Dili: East Timor Planning Commission, 2002), 89–90.

41. The Central Bank, rather than the executive, is charged with operational management of the fund that absorbs all receipts from oil exports. These are invested in capital markets. There is a ceiling on withdrawals, called the Estimated Sustainable Income (ESI) that demands that only the interest component on the sum of assets can be withdrawn each year, and any excesses require parliamentary approval, which increases transparency. La'o Hamutuk, "Timor-Leste's Petroleum Fund," *La'o Hamutuk Bulletin* 8, no. 1 (March 2007).

42. Extractive Industries Transparency Initiative (EITI), "Timor-Leste," 2014.

43. World Bank, "World Development Indicators: Timor-Leste—GDP Growth (Annual Percent)."

44. Mats Lundahl and Fredrik Sjöholm, *Economic Development in Timor-Leste 2000–2005* (Stockholm: SIDA, June 2006), 16–17; World Bank, "World Development Indicators: Timor-Leste—Fertility Rate (Births per Woman)."

45. The nascent political elite originated from the resistance hierarchy (e.g., Xanana Gusmão, Taur Matan Ruak, and other members of the armed and clandestine resistance), in which leaders of local sacred houses were also incorporated. Thus, families belonging to the sacred houses were indirectly linked to the political elite through the head of their own sacred house.

46. The remaining pro-autonomy groups faced serious difficulties reintegrating into their respective villages. They were targeted and, in certain cases, executed by martial arts groups or their respective communities. Since they do not represent a specific minority group per se and the justice system was slow to prosecute these atrocities, it contributed to increased tensions, suspicions, and violence among the general population. UNTAET established the seats for these groups in consultative bodies.

47. International Foundation for Electoral Systems (IFES), "Election Guide: Democracy Assistance & Election News," http://www.electionguide.org/countries/id/63/.

48. A popular belief in Timor-Leste is that the country is only stable when there is understanding between Gusmão, Alkatiri, and Horta.

49. Rui Graca Feijo, "Semi-Presidentialism and the Consolidation of Democracy," in *The Politics of Timor-Leste*, ed. Michael Leach and Damien Kingsbury (Ithaca, NY: Cornell University Press, 2012), 45–68. There are distinct parties and pressure groups such as CPD-RDTL, Sagrada Familia, Konselho Revolucionário Maubere, and others that have largely operated outside of this setting and have organized several violent protests against the government. James Scambary, "Informal Security Groups and Social Movements," in *The Politics of Timor-Leste*, ed. Leach and Kingsbury, 197–214.

50. Dennis Shoesmith, "Political Parties," in *The Politics of Timor-Leste*, ed. Leach and Kingsbury, 121–144; Angie Baxley and Maj Nygaard-Christensen, "The Lost Leadership of Timor Leste," *New Mandela*, November 7, 2014.

51. Institute for Policy Analysis of Conflict, "Timor-Leste After Xanana Gusmao," July 16, 2014, 9–12.

52. These effects were more pronounced after the coalition governments began to form (after the 2006 crisis). During the first election cycle, differences between the president and the prime minister had a destabilizing effect.

53. Francesco Bosso, "Timor-Leste: Overview of Corruption and Anti-Corruption," Transparency International, February 20, 2015, 2–4.

54. Australia is Timor-Leste's leading donor, providing a total of $1.5 billion in development assistance from 1999 to 2013. These funds played a critical role in the early years of independence, due to a lack of internal revenue streams. Office of Development Effectiveness, *Evaluation of Australian Aid to Timor-Leste* (Canberra: Department of Foreign Affairs and Trade, 2014), 1–6. Once oil production began, oil revenues replaced foreign aid as the

prime source of government revenues. Thus, the economic sustainability of Timor-Leste has hinged on reaching an agreement with Australia on maritime boundaries in the Timor Sea, which holds the hydrocarbon deposits. Indonesia, meanwhile, controls access to the Timorese enclave of Oecussi, and is a major importer of fuel and other vital goods, while the Indonesian military maintains close relations with former militia members that could undercut the internal stability of Timor-Leste. David Willis, "Timor-Leste's Complex Geopolitics," in *Timor-Leste: The Local, the Regional, and the Global*, vol. 1, ed. Sarah Smith et al. (Dili: Timor Leste Studies Association, 2015), 237–243.

55. While this decision sparked domestic and international criticism, Timorese leaders have noted that the pursuit of these trials also posed the risk of antagonizing Indonesian military leaders who still held political authority, as the incoming Reformasi government was still in the process of consolidating power.

56. Since 2002, the two have actively engaged on a diplomatic level with respective embassies operating in both capitals, exchanged military information, and cooperated economically, including in the banking sector. The Indonesian state-owned Mandiri bank has a network of branches in Dili and they continue student exchanges. In 2014, the prime minister of Timor-Leste, Xanana Gusmão, received the Bintang Adipura, Indonesia's highest medal of honor. Gordon Peake, Lia Kent, Andrey Damaledo, and Pyone Myat Thu, "Influences and Echoes of Indonesia in Timor-Leste," *In Brief* 2014/60, Australian National University, 2014.

57. China contributed 55 policemen to CIVPOL—its first contribution of law enforcement officers to a foreign mission. While Chinese aid flows to Timor-Leste gradually increased, these have been vastly overshadowed by foreign aid flows from Australia, Japan, the United States, and Portugal, which remain the largest donors to Timor-Leste. Loro Horta, "Timor-Leste. The Dragon's Newest Friend," Discussion Paper No. 4, Research Institute on Contemporary Southeast Asia, Bangkok, May 2009, 2–9.

58. Selver B. Sahin, "Timor-Leste's Foreign Policy: Securing State Identity in the Post-Independence Period," *Journal of Current Southeast Asian Affairs* 33, no. 2 (2014), 4–21.

59. Selver B. Sahin, "Timor-Leste: A More Confident or Overconfident Foreign Policy Actor?" *Southeast Asian Affairs* 39 (2012): 341–358.

60. Willis, "Timor-Leste's Complex Geopolitics," 237–243.

61. Past feuds between political leaders (e.g., the detachment of FALANTIL forces from FRETILIN in the 1980s), as well as the heterogeneous intensity of armed resistance and the fallout of Indonesian transmigrants and militia in the western districts that contributed to the perception among *lorosae* that *loromono* were Indonesian collaborators or did not sufficiently contribute to the struggle for independence, contributed to the crisis.

62. Stagnating growth in the non-oil sector, high youth unemployment, and increasing rates of poverty in the first years after independence fueled economic grievances. UN Security Council, "Report of the Secretary-General on Timor-Leste Pursuant to Security Council Resolution 1690," United Nations, August 8, 2006, 7–9.

63. There were large gaps in security sector policies and the legislative framework (e.g., lack of procedures for addressing grievances, distribution of arms to the reserve, etc.), and civilian oversight was minimal. Meanwhile, distinct groupings based on identities emerged in the police (ex-Indonesian police, ex-resistance, ex-Indonesian students) that coalesced around senior commanders. In practice, police had several parallel command structures, where the minister bypassed commanders, resulting in increased factionalism, further reinforced by disparities in police training offered by CIVPOL advisers from different nations. Both security arms also had weak coordination mechanisms. Braithwaite, "Evaluating the Timor-Leste Peace Operation"; UN Security Council, "Report of the Secretary-General on Timor-Leste Pursuant to Security Council Resolution 1690," 7–9; UN Independent Special Commission of Inquiry for Timor-Leste (UNISCITL), *Report of the United*

Nations Independent Special Commission of Inquiry for Timor-Leste (Dili: UNISCITL, 2006), 22–101.

64. Sarah Dewhurst and Lindsey Greising, *The Gradual Emergence of Second Generation Security Sector Reform in Timor-Leste* (Kitchener, ON: Centre for Security Governance, January 2017), 13–15.

65. UNISCITL, *Report of the United Nations Independent Special Commission of Inquiry for Timor-Leste*, 22–101.

66. The most notable of these groups was under the command of the former military police commander, Major Reinado, who became a vocal advocate of the *loromono* cause. After two years of repeated attacks on Timorese security forces and unsuccessful negotiations, the group led an assassination attempt on the president and prime minister in 2008, critically wounding José Ramos-Horta.

67. Timor-Leste maintains one of the highest social protection expenditures among developing countries (9 percent), while about 60 percent of these funds are awarded to veterans. World Bank, *Timor-Leste Social Assistance Public Expenditure and Program Performance Report* (Washington, DC: World Bank, June 2013), 1–5.

5. KOSOVO: AN UNLIKELY SUCCESS STILL IN THE MAKING

Daniel Serwer

TIMELINE

1389	Battle of Kosovo Polje
1878	Serbs attempt to deport Albanians to areas now part of Kosovo
1912–1913	Balkan War
1913	Most of Kosovo is incorporated into Kingdom of Serbia
1918	Kosovo incorporated into Kingdom of Yugoslavia
1941	Axis invasion of Yugoslavia; Albania is assigned control over most of Kosovo; 250,000 Serbs forcibly expelled from Kosovo
1946	Kosovo is granted status as autonomous province within Serbia
1974	Yugoslav constitution grants Kosovo sweeping powers
August 1987	Slobodan Milosevic meets with Kosovo Serbs in Kosovo
1988–1989	Serbia passes a new constitution that removes Kosovo's autonomy; Serbia sacks and arrests top Kosovo Albanian officials
September 1990	Albanians are fired from government and media positions
1991	Slovenia and Croatia leave Yugoslav Federation
1992	Albanian members of Kosovo parliament declare independence, elect Ibrahim Rugova as president

	of their "Republic of Kosova," and form a government in exile
1995	Dayton Accords
1996–1997	Kosovo Liberation Army (KLA) launches assaults against Serbian police and security forces
February 1998– June 1999	Kosovo War; at least half a million residents of Kosovo are displaced
March 24, 1999	NATO intervenes
June 10, 1999	Serbian and Yugoslav governments sign Kumanovo agreement; UNSC 1244 establishes UNMIK
June 11, 1999	The Kosovo Force (KFOR) enters Kosovo
May 2000	UNMIK establishes the Joint Interim Administrative Structure
2001	UN establishes Provisional Insitutions of Self-Government (PISG)
March 2004	Ethnic rioting by both Serbs and Albanians
2006	UN report concludes that status quo is unsustainable
2007	UN special envoy Martti Ahtisaari puts forward the Comprehensive Proposal for the Kosovo Status Settlement
February 17, 2008	Kosovo's parliament declares independence

The modern Kosovo state is a product of Albanian nonviolent and violent rebellion, Serbian repression, the dissolution of socialist Yugoslavia, state collapse in Albania, NATO intervention, U.S. and EU support, Russian weakness, and UN administration. Without one or another of these ingredients, it might never have occurred, and certainly not in the surprising way that it did.

ORIGINS OF THE MOVEMENT

Serbs and Albanians living in Kosovo have distinct identities. Albanians define themselves principally by their Indo-European language of possibly ancient but uncertain origins. Today, most are nominally Muslim, though nonbelievers are common, especially in Kosovo. Some Albanians are Catholic. Mother Teresa was an Albanian born in what is today Mace-

Figure 5.1. Map of Kosovo

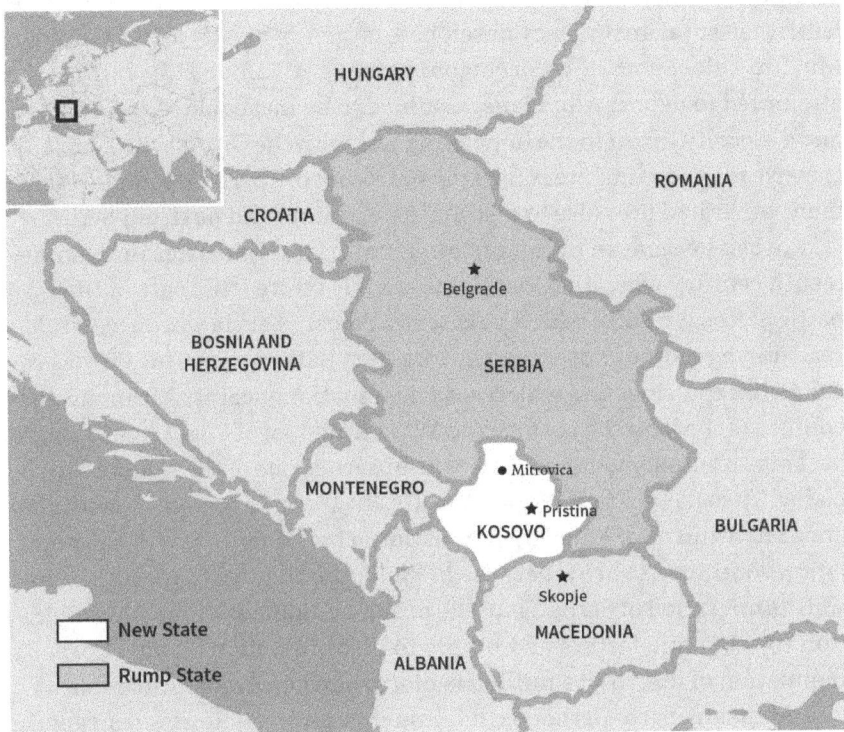

donia. In Albania, but generally not in Kosovo, some Albanians are Orthodox.

By contrast, Serbs view themselves more as an Orthodox religious group, though there are many nonbelievers among them as well. Most Serbs regard their Orthodox church, including its history and property in Kosovo, as the vital locus and carrier of national identity. Orthodoxy distinguishes Serbs from Catholic Croats and Muslim Bosniaks. All speak Slavic languages that are mutually comprehensible (and regarded in the past as a single language, Serbo-Croatian, with regional rather than ethnic variations).

Kosovo was the seat of the medieval Serbian state, which was lost to the Ottomans after the Battle of Kosovo Polje in 1389. Though there were frictions, Serbs and Albanians coexisted in Kosovo both before and under the Ottomans without major violence. That coexistence began to change in the early nineteenth century. With the rise of Serb nationalism, a violent, often rural, insurgency developed, targeting mostly urban Ottoman Muslim rule. Some of its protagonists were Albanians.[1] In 1878, Serbs attempted to deport Albanians, assumed to be incapable of assimilation and a security threat in the impending war with the Ottomans. Ironically, they were exiled into areas now part of Kosovo. There, Albanian resentment generated pressure to discriminate against and push out Serbs.

Kosovo became an object of Serb territorial claims later in the nineteenth century when the poet Vuk Karadzic wrote stirringly of the 1389 battle at Kosovo Polje, which he cast as a defeat.[2] Serbia was successful in reacquiring most of Kosovo in the 1912–1913 Balkan War. This victory resulted in expulsions and widespread depredations against Albanians that continued through the post–World War I Kingdom of Yugoslavia. Kosovo became an autonomous province within Serbia, one of six republics in socialist Yugoslavia after World War II.[3] By then, Albanians constituted about two-thirds of Kosovo's population. Their dominance in the population continued to grow because of higher birth rates than the Serbs as well as migration of Serbs out of the province. Some attribute this migration to economic factors and others to discrimination. Today, Kosovo's population of less than 2 million is more than 90 percent Albanian.

Important Serb Orthodox monuments and religious sites remain throughout Kosovo, which Serbs refer to as "Kosovo and Metohija," the latter term referring to church lands. Some consider it the "Serb Jerusalem," attributing the same significance to Serbs that Jerusalem has to Jews, along with willingness to sacrifice to hold on to it. Some Serbs today express resentment of the presumed privileged role of Muslim Albanians in the Ottoman Empire. At the same time, they also may refer to Albanians as ill-educated and uncivilized. Albanians can be no less prejudiced and resentful of Serb privileges and behavior. The stereotypes are remarkably symmetrical.

Albanians in Kosovo during most of the socialist period aspired for Kosovo to become a full-fledged republic within the Socialist Federal Republic of Yugoslavia (SFRY). At that time, independence was not an issue. The province had acquired substantial powers in the Yugoslav constitution of 1974: a parliament, police force, educational system, courts, and a representative on the collective presidency of the Yugoslav Federation.[4] The Albanian political elite were well-integrated in the Yugoslav League of Communists. All educated Kosovo Albanians spoke Serbian as well as their mother tongue.

Grievances in Kosovo were, in part, economic. Post–World War II, Kosovo was the poorest and least developed section of Yugoslavia, heavily dependent on state-owned enterprises and government jobs. Demonstrations over economic issues were sometimes violent, but Kosovo legally remained a province within Serbia. The territory lacked full-fledged republic status, presumed in socialist Yugoslavia to entail the right of secession. Whether Kosovo had that right is still mooted.

Slobodan Milosevic, until then a communist apparatchik, unintentionally initiated the independence process when he discovered at a 1987 meeting with Kosovo Serbs at Kosovo Polje—site of the 1389 battle with the Ottomans—that he could generate genuine political enthusiasm by promising to protect them from Albanians. He appealed above all to the Serb sense of victimhood. Albanians, he declared, would not be allowed to beat Serbs or chase them out of the province. By 1989, he was a convert to Serbian nationalism and managed to deprive Kosovo of its autonomous status by dubious legislative means. Soon after, he expelled Albanians from the province's state institutions, generating an Albanian nationalist reaction.[5] Albanians' dependence on the state was reduced, many went abroad, and numerous small family businesses emerged, more involved in trade than production.

Once Slovenia and then Croatia left the Yugoslav Federation in 1991, most Kosovo Albanians considered it unthinkable to remain in a truncated federation dominated by Serbia and led by an elected Serb strongman, already using Yugoslav security forces to repress Albanian protests. The main resistance initially was political and nonviolent. Albanian members of the Kosovo parliament met to declare independence, elect Ibrahim Rugova "president" of their "Republic of Kosova," and form a government in exile. No other sovereign state formally recognized the declaration, but by the early 1990s, independence was the goal of virtually all Kosovo Albanians.

THE INDEPENDENCE MOVEMENT

The Kosovo Albanian liberation struggle initially was a movement for human rights, freedom, and a nationalist enterprise, at least for those inside the province if not for the diaspora. The independence movement emerged in a society with democratic forms of governance, even if post-Tito socialist Yugoslavia was not a liberal democracy and Milosevic's post-socialist Yugoslavia was an elected autocracy. Some Kosovo independence protagonists had experience in political parties, elections, parliament, and government, which were pertinent to more democratic rule.

Rugova led an avowedly nonviolent movement (the Democratic League of Kosovo, or LDK) that included the withdrawal of Albanians from Kosovo's Serbian institutions and mass street demonstrations. His government set up "parallel" institutions, including health services provided by a nongovernmental organization, the Mother Teresa Society, as well as a voluntary school system that operated in homes and apartments for the better part of the next decade.

The LDK financed this effort with contributions from the Albanian diaspora, primarily but not exclusively in Europe, who were urged to contribute 3 percent of their income to a Fund for the Republic. This fund collected well over $100 million in the 1990s and transferred an average of $1.3 million per month into Kosovo.[6] Kosovo Albanians also organized a "blood feuds reconciliation" campaign. This effort used the need to confront Serbian authorities to unify the Kosovo Albanian community by ending the long and bloody tradition of intra-Albanian blood feuds, which remain far rarer in Kosovo than in Albania.[7]

Milosevic's efforts to withdraw Kosovo autonomy and repress the nonviolent and later the violent insurgency poisoned what had been an increasingly free political environment. Some violent resistance to Serbian rule was initiated in the early 1990s with small-scale attacks against Serb officials. The violent rebellion became more popular and prominent only after the 1995 Dayton Accords, which ended the war in Bosnia and Herzegovina. Albanian disillusion with the failure of the international community to deal with Kosovo issues at Dayton boosted the advocates of violent rebellion about the same time that massive quantities of Kalashnikovs and other arms became available because of state collapse in Albania. Chaos reigned in Albania due to the government's inability to make good on pyramid schemes it had sponsored. The arms were brought over the mountains from Albania with little hindrance from Albanian or Serbian authorities, both preoccupied with internal security.

The nonviolent movement against Serbia and in favor of independence might have succeeded, but the evolution of events in Kosovo made violence the main driver of independence.⁸ The Kosovo Liberation Army (KLA) knew it could not defeat the far more powerful Serbian forces, but Kosovo forces were creating serious difficulties for Serb authorities by attacking Serbian police and other security forces from 1996 to 1997. With Tirana's consent, the KLA used Albania as a base of operations and supply for these missions. The KLA controlled territory at times, but Serbian forces could snatch it back when they wanted and often did so.

Albanian forces next went underground, melting into the local population rather than retreating. Dispersion proved the better approach, as it spread Serbian forces thin and made them easier targets for guerrilla-style attacks. The KLA also sought to create situations that provoked Serbian overreaction, including more than one mass murder. These atrocities attracted international attention and eventual intervention. This was the KLA's goal: to provoke Milosevic into repressive action that would appall the international community and gain the kind of attention that Bosnia's war had gained from 1992 to 1995.

Not to be left on the sidelines, the LDK government in exile covertly formed and financed a second insurgent force called the Armed Forces of the Republic of Kosovo (FARK), but it never gained the traction of the KLA. The principal target of violence by the KLA and the FARK was the Serbian security forces, especially police. While they occasionally directed violence at each other, the main internecine violence occurred after Serbian withdrawal.

Just as the LDK relied on the diaspora for funding, so too did the KLA. A major financing and recruitment effort, "Homeland Calling," drew thousands of young cadres from many different parts of the world and unknown (and unaccounted for) tens of millions in contributions to the KLA.⁹ The diaspora, mainly from Switzerland, Germany, and the United States, also helped ensure political, and hence diplomatic, support for Kosovo in those key countries.

INTERNATIONAL INTERVENTION[10]

The Balkan region was not strategically important to the United States after the Cold War. Secretary of State James A. Baker had declared during the breakup of socialist Yugoslavia that Washington had "no dog in that fight." However, Kosovo's self-determination occurred in a post–Cold War context in which the United States thought of itself as the defender of liberal democracy and had the military, political, and economic predominance needed to act as the "world's policeman"—a role then regarded in a positive light.

Kosovo Albanians' lobbying efforts costing about $10 million in the United States focused on Congress, where Republican Representative Joseph Dioguardi succeeded in interesting human rights advocates such as Representative Tom Lantos and Senator Robert Dole in the Kosovo cause. Until the late 1990s, the State Department and White House were reluctant to focus on Kosovo and prioritized dealing with the far more deadly and intense conflict in Bosnia and Herzegovina. Managing that conflict required Milosevic's cooperation, which would have been more difficult to get if he had been pressed on Kosovo as well.

President Bill Clinton ultimately decided, as he had in Bosnia in 1995, that the United States needed to intervene to stop the ethnic cleansing and to uphold universal human rights norms in the post–Cold War era. The UN Security Council–authorized NATO bombing of Serbs in Bosnia in 1995 had succeeded in bringing an end to the war, so Clinton decided to try again in Kosovo in 1999, believing Milosevic would respond only to the use of military might. The United Nations was not politically or militarily capable of the required intervention. Russia blocked Security Council action, and the United Nations intervenes only with the consent of the host government, which Belgrade would never have provided.

NATO was ready and willing to take action, as the disappearance of the Soviet Union left it without any apparent strategic purpose. After an unsuccessful effort to negotiate a political settlement at Rambouillet, France, in early 1999, NATO bombed Serbia (including Kosovo) for 78 days. Ultimately, Belgrade agreed to a military/technical agreement (reached at Kumanovo, Macedonia) to withdraw its security forces from Kosovo.[11] Milosevic yielded when the damage to dual-use infrastructure in Serbia proper risked becoming irreversible.[12] Russia remained allied with Serbia throughout. It tried to seize the airport in Pristina at the end of the NATO/Yugoslavia war, but Boris Yeltsin's Russia was still weak in the aftermath of the collapse of the Soviet Union. The United States blocked Moscow from gaining overflight permission for planes carrying supplies and additional forces to the Pristina airport and eventually negotiated Russian withdrawal to a U.S.-controlled sector in southeastern Kosovo.

The "CNN effect" of conflict broadcast in real time was still novel. NATO's air intervention in 1999 caused Milosevic to double down on efforts to chase Albanians out of Kosovo, thus attracting even more CNN footage and international concern. At least half a million Albanians became refugees in neighboring countries. Some in Europe and the United States were concerned that their presence might destabilize Macedonia. There the ethnic balance between Albanians and Macedonians was a delicate one and might lead to intervention by Greece and possibly Bulgaria.

Neighboring states played both unintentional and intentional roles. Serbian repression generated Albanian enthusiasm for independence. Albania and Macedonia, the former happily and the latter grumpily, as well as Montenegro, sheltered hundreds of thousands of refugees during the NATO intervention. Kosovo Albanians returned with redoubled determination to be rid of Serbian rule forever.

Only after NATO forces liberated Kosovo in 1999 did Albanians control most of Kosovo's territory. Fifteen percent of the country north of the Ibar River and some Serb enclaves in the south, where most of the Serb population still lives, remained. Serb municipalities north of the Ibar are still not fully reintegrated with the rest of Kosovo. Most of the Kosovo movement's protagonists renounced irredentist ambitions toward the territory of Albanian populations in other states: Montenegro and Serbia (which have small Albanian populations, mostly contiguous with Kosovo), Macedonia (whose population was more than 20 percent Albanian, much of it contiguous with Kosovo), and Albania. The Kosovo constitution, at the insistence of the international community, would later include a prohibition on union with any other state or part of another state.

This was the West's quid pro quo for Kosovo's self-determination. The United States and most of Europe were prepared to recognize changes in the status of internal boundaries to international borders, as had been done with the independence of Slovenia, Croatia, Bosnia, and Macedonia (and would eventually do so with Montenegro as well). But Washington and Brussels did not want to move the lines to accommodate ethnic differences, fearing that would open Pandora's box and lead to a violent paroxysm aimed at redrawing the borders (or moving populations) not only of Kosovo but also of Bosnia, Croatia, Macedonia, and even in Serbia proper.

BUILDING THE NEW STATE

After Milosevic's forces withdrew, NATO-led forces—denominated KFOR—occupied Kosovo's territory. KFOR was authorized by UN Security Council Resolution 1244, which constituted a post facto legalization of the NATO/Yugoslavia war and tasked the international civilian presence (later known as the UN Mission in Kosovo, or UNMIK) with a strong mandate to establish locally led and democratic Provisional Institutions of Self-Government (PISG) that would gradually take over administration of Kosovo and transfer authority to "institutions established under a political settlement."[13]

To govern effectively, the UN mission needed to dissolve parallel structures the LDK had created during the previous decade and to displace Serb governing institutions. Also needed was the establishment of consultative institutions with Kosovar participation, accomplished by late 1999 in the Joint Interim Administrative Structure. This included a 35-member Kosovo Transitional Council to advise on legislation, an Interim Administrative Council, and 20 administrative departments, headed jointly by internationals and Kosovars. The KLA in the immediate aftermath of the NATO intervention appointed mayors to replace those the LDK appointed before the war. That proved to be a mistake. They were largely swept away in the first UNMIK-organized municipal elections in 2000 in favor of LDK leaders, though some have returned to power since.

While Kosovars returned quickly from exile in Macedonia, Albania, and Montenegro, the initial period after the NATO intervention was tumultuous for Serbs and allied minorities. Some Albanians sought violent revenge. Fearful, many Serbs and Roma fled their homes. Kosovo Albanians are alleged to have kidnapped and killed some Serbs for their organs at facilities in northern Albania, an allegation still under investigation.[14] There was Albanian-on-Albanian political violence as well, with fear of a civil war between the KLA and Rugova's LDK.

UNMIK, on paper, held virtually dictatorial executive, legislative, and judicial powers under Resolution 1244: it could promulgate legislation, provide services, hire and fire at will, as well as administer justice, with support from KFOR. It was also given authority to "control the implementation of the international civil presence" and "to coordinate closely with the international security presence to ensure that both presences operate towards the same goals and in a mutually supportive manner." This mandate was much stronger than that civilians had been given in Bosnia and Herzegovina and much clearer direction to coordinate with the NATO-led forces.

The KLA was demilitarized and partly transformed into the Kosovo Protection Corps (KPC), a civilian emergency reaction cadre, with assistance from the International Organization for Migration.[15] Some fighters joined the newly established Kosovo Police Service, recruited and trained by the Organization for Cooperation and Security in Europe (OSCE).[16] It eventually became the most respected institution in Kosovo and remains a model, even if far from perfect, of successful institution-building in a postwar environment.[17]

UNMIK and other international organizations acting under its umbrella administered Kosovo with increasing participation and decision-making authority delegated to the PISG, established in 2001 by a UN-dictated "constitutional framework."[18] In addition to police training, the OSCE played a significant role in building democratic institutions, especially parliament and the electoral process. An EU rule of law mission (EULEX) has nurtured the judicial sector. Many other intergovernmental and nongovernmental international organizations have been involved, including WHO, UNESCO, IOM, and UNHCR.[19] The World Health Organization, for example, drove the reestablishment of the health care system, which proved difficult because of lack of capacity to implement its theoretically well-designed scheme.[20] Meanwhile, UNESCO played a similar role in the reestablishment of the education system.[21] Net official development assistance and official aid received amounted to upwards of $4 billion from 2009 to 2015, more than other countries in the region on a per capita basis.[22]

Gradually, ministry by ministry, the PISG took over from UNMIK, despite Russian and Serb protests. This deliberate process of building institutions and transferring governing authority to them generated controversy. Albanians wanted the transfer of power to accelerate, while Serbs preferred delay or even a halt.[23] The process was successful in building a viable and generally democratic state within a decade, one that managed to endure with international help. That evolution occurred even as a prime minister accused of war crimes was shipped to The Hague for trial at the International Criminal Tribunal for the former Yugoslavia (he was twice acquitted) and even though two presidents were removed from office due to Constitutional Court rulings. With a lot of international support, Kosovo's institutions have weathered some challenging moments.

In March 2004, ethnic rioting involving both Serbs and Albanians raised questions about UNMIK's and KFOR's capabilities and the durability of local patience.[24] A UN report concluded in 2006 that the political status quo was not sustainable.[25] It was no longer possible to postpone the final political settlement foreseen in UNSC Resolution 1244.

The UN secretary general appointed former Finnish president Martti Ahtisaari to negotiate the future political status of Kosovo.[26] With support from the European Union and the United States, he put forward a plan in 2007 that met extensive Serb demands for protection while recommending that Kosovo become a sovereign state, a demand of Albanians.[27] In coordination with the United States and major European powers, independence was declared in 2008. Kosovo authorities pledged to implement the Ahtisaari Plan despite the failure of Belgrade to recognize the new state.[28] In an advisory opinion sought by Serbia, the International Court of Justice found in 2010 that the declaration of independence breached no international law or other obligations.[29]

All of Kosovo's immediate neighbors except Serbia recognized the newly declared state quickly, as arranged in advance with the United States and the European Union. Russia had agreed to UNSC Resolution 1244, which made lack of UNSC authorization for the NATO attack on Yugoslavia irrelevant. But Resolution 1244 also asserted Yugoslav sovereignty in its preamble. Moscow has continued since to block Kosovo's UN membership by threatening to use its veto in the Security Council and is directly responsible for this aspect of incomplete sovereignty.

An International Civilian Office (ICO) oversaw implementation of the Ahtisaari Plan for several years. It provided protection for Serbs and other minorities in the newly independent state, including reserved seats in parliament and the need for a double-qualified majority (two-thirds of both Albanian and minority parliamentarians) to approve constitutional amendments.[30] Most Albanians and non-Serb minorities accepted the sovereignty and territorial integrity of the new state. Most Serbs rejected them, particularly those living in the four majority-Serb municipalities north of the Ibar River, contiguous with Serbia. Serbs who live south of the Ibar generally accept the de facto authority of the Kosovo state, even if they continue to view it as an autonomous subnational unit of the Serbian state.

For the past several years, reintegration of Serb-majority municipalities north of the Ibar and other issues have been the subject of technical and political dialogues between Belgrade and Kosovo authorities, held under EU auspices. Belgrade has accepted the validity of the Kosovo constitution on its entire territory, but has not explicitly endorsed its independence and sovereignty. Yet it has agreed that Serbia and Kosovo will qualify for and enter the EU separately, something only sovereign states can do.[31] Kosovo has agreed in principle to the establishment of an association of Serb municipalities, which will need to comply with requirements of the Kosovo constitution, as clarified by the Constitutional Court.[32]

Kosovo now has a parliamentary system with an indirectly elected president, prime minister, and all the usual ministries, a parliament (the Kosovo Assembly), Constitutional Court, police, and a judicial system. Municipalities govern at the local level. Monoethnic political parties compete for power in elections that the international community has either administered or supervised (six times since 1999). The press, by Balkan standards, is relatively free, as is the economy. Working mainly with (now declining) international resources, civil society is reasonably vibrant: Kosovar think tanks devoted to security and development are among the better ones in the Balkans, and its watchdog organizations try to track corruption, trafficking, rule of law, and human rights.

Many Albanian military leaders became political leaders, including two who currently dominate Kosovo politics: President Hashim Thaci, political leader of the KLA, former head of the Democratic Party of Kosovo (PDK), and prime minister (2008 to 2014); and Prime Minister Ramush Haradinaj (who previously served in that position from December 2004 to March 2005), one of the independence fighters and founder of the Alliance for the Future of Kosovo (AAK). Now in coalition, their political parties competed until recently, leaving the LDK more room to maneuver and far more opportunities to exercise power than if the KLA had remained united. LDK leader Isa Mustafa, prime minister from 2014 to 2017, was the treasurer of the Fund for the Republic that financed Kosovo's parallel Albanian institutions in the 1990s.

Thaci has played a major role in the Brussels dialogue with Belgrade, which Haradinaj opposed. The Self-Determination Movement, led by

Albin Kurti, a leader of nonviolent demonstrations in the 1990s, also opposes dialogue with Belgrade and supports union with Albania. The LDK has supported dialogue. Thus, the split between the nonviolent and violent rebellions continues, but heirs to those two traditions have not agreed on one of the most important current political challenges: how to deal with Serbia and its opposition to Kosovo's sovereignty and territorial integrity.

Many other KLA veterans still serve in parliament, local administrations, and Kosovo institutions. KLA military commander Agim Ceku led the Kosovo Protection Force (the demilitarized version of the KLA) and served as minister of the Kosovo Security Force, the lightly armed cadres that are slated to become Kosovo's army, and as prime minister (2006–2008). Current speaker of the Kosovo Assembly Kadri Veseli headed the clandestine intelligence service associated with the KLA during the war.

Ibrahim Rugova remained the mostly uncontested charismatic leader of the Kosovo Albanians until his death in 2006. But his political engagement was limited and his management style distant. He presided but rarely exercised power, especially after an ill-fated effort at reconciliation with Milosevic in 1999. The exile prime minister and government he appointed in 1991 never gained much support inside Kosovo, though they were instrumental in raising funds and lobbying on Kosovo's behalf. The shadowy figures who formed the KLA became heroes at the end of the war.

The Serb community in Kosovo has not had stable leadership, as it often reflects those in power in Belgrade. In the aftermath of the NATO intervention, Serbs remained largely under Milosevic's thumb, but that changed with his electoral defeat in 2000. Subsequent Serbian presidents each have had favorites in Kosovo. At present, the "Serbian List," closely allied with Serbian President Vucic, is dominant.

ONGOING CHALLENGES

Kosovo's sovereignty remains incomplete. NATO-led foreign forces—not the lightly armed Kosovo Security Forces—guarantee territorial integrity. International prosecutors and judges are included in its judicial system at least until 2018 (mainly for interethnic crimes), and a Kosovo court staffed by internationals has been established in The Hague to try some postwar criminal cases. Parts of Serb-majority northern Kosovo do not fall entirely within the authority of the Pristina government. Russia has also continued to block Kosovo's membership in the United Nations, which requires a recommendation of the Security Council. It has not been recognized by Serbia, five European Union members, and four NATO members despite recognition by well over a hundred other sovereign states.

Nonrecognition remains a serious impediment to Kosovo's ambitions, which include EU, NATO, and UN membership, as well as inclusion in international organizations that require UN membership as a prerequisite. Despite Washington's affections for Kosovo, it was only recently accepted as eligible for (U.S.) Millennium Challenge Corporation funding, because it had been unable to produce data normally collected and processed by UN specialized agencies.

The European Union footed much of the international bill for Kosovo for many years and will continue to do so as Kosovo tries to qualify for candidacy and, eventually, membership. Kosovo's economic growth since 1999 has been relatively strong, with only a single year (2002) of negative growth despite the global financial crisis and Europe's slow recovery. At purchasing power parity, it has narrowed the gap with Serbia significantly.[33] Much of the population continues to be disappointed with the economic results of independence, due largely to the high official unemployment rate and the perception of widespread corruption, especially in government procurement and hiring.[34] Kosovo has used the euro as its currency since 2002, even though it is not officially within the euro zone. This has ensured macroeconomic stability: devaluation is impossible, inflation is at low European levels, and government debt is low. Foreign assistance, as well as the presence of foreign troops and civilians, has contributed significant economic stimulus.

Kosovo's independence occurred as financial crisis struck the world economy, and full recovery still eludes Europe. Foreign direct investment in Kosovo has declined from a peak of 12.5 percent of GDP in 2007 to 5.4 percent in 2015, when it amounted to $470 million and went primarily to real estate, financial services, and construction.[35] There are more stable and better-connected places in the Balkans, and beyond, with lower levels of perceived corruption. Major corporations can invest there without the political uncertainty arising from Kosovo's still incomplete sovereignty. Serbia proper has been far more successful in attracting major foreign industrial investments.

Almost half of Kosovo's population is still poor. The middle class is larger today than in the Yugoslav period, but the economic elite remains disproportionately small. Many Kosovars continue to depend for at least a portion of their livelihoods on remittances, which make up 14 percent of GDP.[36]

Kosovo has large mineral deposits, especially lead, zinc, and other base metals, but they are of dubious economic viability. Ownership of Trepca, a large former Yugoslav mining complex, remains disputed between Pristina and Belgrade. Both think its resources are worth more than the market does. Kosovo's more economically viable rock quarries have attracted some foreign investment. It has no exploitable oil and gas but does contain vast quantities of lignite, a solid hydrocarbon fuel used to generate electricity. Unfortunately, that fuel produces prodigious quantities of pollution responsible for poisoning Pristina's air each winter A new, cleaner power plant is slated to come online in 2023.

CONCLUSION

Kosovo remains a work in progress because its sovereignty is incomplete. Integration of its Serb citizens, especially in the north, is unfinished business. On the plus side, Kosovo can now boast of democratically legitimized governing institutions that function normally on most days, even if internationals still play vital roles in security, justice, and financing.

The country faces significant economic and political challenges. Among these are dependence on remittances from Albanians living abroad and unsustainably high unemployment, especially among youth. Productive foreign direct investment is minimal, and perceived levels of corruption are at the high end of the regional spectrum. Politics are fractious. A hung parliament (one lacking a clear majority coalition) was elected in June 2017. A new coalition government was formed only three months later. Two strong and diametrically opposed, extraconstitutional political movements are important factions inside the Kosovo Assembly: the Albanian Self-Determination Movement, which wants to conduct a referendum on union with Albania prohibited by the constitution, and the Serbian List, which does not accept Kosovo's sovereignty and independence.

Circumstances were uniquely favorable to international intervention in Kosovo: the end of the Cold War left the United States as the sole remaining superpower and generated enormous enthusiasm for democracy and international human rights norms. The Kosovo Albanians sought a democratic outcome. Their adversary was elected, but was an autocrat. With the Soviet Union gone, NATO was in search of a strategic role. Russia was too weak to protect its Serbian favorite. Real-time video broadcasting of the conflict, vital to gaining international attention during the Bosnian war, continued to arouse public condemnation of Milosevic's behavior.

This relative success depended on a truly unusual, even unlikely, sequence of events: the breakup of socialist Yugoslavia; Milosevic's removal of autonomy and repression of the nonviolent movement; failure of the international community to deal with the Kosovo problem at Dayton; state collapse in Albania; the rise of the KLA; NATO armed intervention; Russian weakness; a strong UN mandate; and the willingness of the European Union, OSCE, and other international organizations to spend time and resources in a small country of no great geostrategic significance. The effort has cost per capita far more than UN efforts in Africa and elsewhere. Though the population remains poor and sovereignty incomplete, Kosovo is a case of nonviolent failure, successful violent insurgency with international support, followed by partly successful, luxury state building with enormous international care, attention, and mentorship.

The main lesson learned in Kosovo is that massive international intervention can produce an economically viable democratic transition in a newly created state. This works only if sustained over a decade or more. Even then, the outcome may be less than fully satisfactory. All those who contemplate military intervention should include in their calculations a sustained postwar political and economic commitment.

NOTES

1. Djordje Stefanovic, "Seeing the Albanians through Serbian Eyes: The Inventors of the Tradition of Intolerance and Their Critics, 1804–1939," *European History Quarterly* 35, no. 3 (2005): 465–492.
2. Michael Sells, *The Bridge Betrayed: Religion and Genocide in Bosnia* (Berkeley: University of California Press, 1998).
3. Noel Malcolm, *Kosovo: A Short History* (New York: HarperCollins, 1999).
4. The Constitution of the Socialist Federal Republic of Yugoslavia, 1974, http://www.cnj.it/documentazione/Cost63.htm.
5. Lenard J. Cohen, *Serpent in the Bosom: The Rise and Fall of Slobodan Milosevic* (Boulder, CO: Westview, 2002), 106–152.
6. Paul Hockenos, *Homeland Calling: Exile Patriotism and the Balkan Wars* (Ithaca, NY: Cornell University Press, 2003), 202–237.

7. Oral History Kosovo, "Blood Feuds and Reconciliation," http://oralhistorykosovo.org/research/blood-feuds-reconciliations/.

8. Shkelzen Maliqi, *Why Nonviolent Resistance in Kosovo Failed* (Pristina: Kolana MM, 2011).

9. Hockenos, *Homeland Calling*, 254.

10. For a detailed account of the various, mostly unsuccessful, diplomatic efforts in Kosovo, see "Kosovo," Chapter 6 of Sinisa Vuković, *International Multiparty Mediation and Conflict Management: Challenges of cooperation and coordination* (New York: Routledge, 2016), 114–146.

11. The Military Technical Agreement between the International Security Force (KFOR) and the governments of the Federal Republic of Yugoslavia and the Republic of Serbia, June 9, 1999, http://www.nato.int/kosovo/docu/a990609a.htm.

12. Stephen Hosmer, *The Conflict over Kosovo: Why Milosevic Decided to Settle When He Did* (Santa Monica, CA: RAND, 2001).

13. UN Security Council Resolution 1244 on the situation relating Kosovo, S/RES/1244/99, June 10, 1999.

14. Dick Marty, "Inhuman Treatment of People and Illicit Trafficking in Human Organs in Kosovo," Council of Europe Committee on Legal Affairs and Human Rights, January 7, 2011.

15. Ramadan Qehaja, Kosum Kosumi, and Florian Qehaja, "The Process of Demobilization and Integration of Former Kosovo Liberation Army Members—Kosovo's Perspective," Kosovar Centre for Security Studies, n.d.

16. Michael Dziedzic, Laura Mercean, and Elton Skendaj, "Kosovo: The Kosovo Liberation Army," in *Criminalized Power Structures: The Overlooked Enemies of Peace*, ed. Michael Dziedzic (Lanham, MD: Rowman & Littlefield, 2016), 155–201.

17. Morgan Greene, Jonathan Friedman, and Richard Bennett, "Rebuilding the Police in Kosovo," *Foreign Policy*, July 18, 2012.

18. Constitutional Framework for Provisional Self-Government in Kosovo, 2001.

19. Balkan Analysis, "International Organizations: Kosovo," http://www.balkanalysis.com/kosovo/international-organizations/.

20. Valerie Percival and Egbert, "A Case Study of Health Sector Reform in Kosovo," *Conflict and Health* 4, no. 7 (2010).

21. Marc Sommers and Peter Buckland, *Parallel Worlds: Rebuilding the Education System in Kosovo* (Paris: International Institute for Education Planning, 2004).

22. World Bank, "Net Official Development Assistance and Official Aid Received," https://data.worldbank.org/indicator/DT.ODA.ALLD.CD?contextual=region&end=2015&locations=XK&start=2009&view=chart.

23. Kosovar Center for Security Studies, *Re-Establishment and Reform of the Justice System in Kosovo 1999–2011* (Pristina: Kosovar Center for Security Studies, 2011).

24. UN Security Council, "Report of the Secretary-General on the United Nations Interim Administration Mission in Kosovo, S/2004/348," April 30, 2004.

25. Letter dated October 7, 2005 from the Secretary-General addressed to the President of the Security Council, S/2005/635, October 7, 2005.

26. United Nations, "Secretary-General Appoints Former President Martti Ahtisaari of Finland as Special Envoy for Future Status Process for Kosovo," November 15, 2005.

27. UN Security Council, "Comprehensive Proposal for the Kosovo Status Settlement," S/2007/168/Add.1, March 26, 2007.

28. Kosovo Declaration of Independence, February 17, 2008, https://www.assembly-kosova.org/common/docs/Dek_Pav_e.pdf.

29. International Court of Justice, "Accordance with International Law of The Unilateral Declaration of Independence in Respect of Kosovo (Request for Advisory Opinion)," 2010 I.C.J.141 (July 22, 2010).

30. International Civilian Office (ICO), *State Building and Exit: The International Civilian Office and Kosovo's Supervised Independence, 2008–2012* (Pristina: ICO, December 2012).

31. First Agreement of Principles Governing the Normalisation of Relations, April 19, 2013, http://www.kryeministri-ks.net/repository/docs/FIRST_AGREEMENT_OF _PRINCIPLES_GOVERNING_THE_NORMALIZATION_OF_RELATIONS,_APRIL_19, _2013_BRUSSELS_en.pdf.

32. Constitutional Court of Kosovo, "Judgment in Case No. KO130/15," December 23, 2015.

33. Franjo Stiblar, *Economic Growth and Development in Post Yugoslav Countries* (Washington, DC: Wilson Center, June 2013).

34. Kosova Democratic Institute and Transparency International Kosova, *Assessment of Institutional Integrity: Kosova 2011* (Pristina: Kosova Democratic Institute and Transparency International Kosova, 2011).

35. World Bank, "Foreign Direct Investment, Net Flows (Percent of GDP)," http://data.worldbank.org/indicator/BX.KLT.DINV.WD.GD.ZS?locations=XK.

36. World Bank, "Personal Remittances, Received (Percent of GDP)," http://data.worldbank.org/indicator/BX.TRF.PWKR.DT.GD.ZS.

6. SOUTH SUDAN: THE PAINFUL RISE AND RAPID DESCENT OF THE WORLD'S NEWEST NATION

Richard Downie

TIMELINE

1955	Beginning of the First Civil War between northern and southern Sudan
1956	Sudan gains independence from Anglo-Egyptian rule
1969	Gaafar Nimeiri takes power in a coup and begins talks with the southern rebels
1972	The Addis Ababa Agreement ends the First Civil War and grants the south greater autonomy
1983	Nimeiri declares Sudan an Islamic state and ends southern autonomy; the Sudan People's Liberation Movement/Army (SPLM/A) is formed and the Second Civil War begins
January 2005	The Intergovernmental Authority on Development (IGAD) and partners including the United Nations, African Union, and "Troika" countries negotiate the Comprehensive Peace Agreement, ending the Second Civil War
July 2005	John Garang, the leader of the SPLM/A, dies in a helicopter crash; Salva Kiir succeeds him
April 2010	Sudan holds general elections; the SPLM wins overwhelmingly in the south
January 2011	Referendum on South Sudan's independence

July 2011	South Sudan declares independence
April 2012	South Sudan occupies Sudanese oil fields following a dispute over the excessive fees demanded by Khartoum to use its export pipeline
July 2013	President Kiir fires Vice President Machar and his cabinet
Dec. 2013	Violence between armed factions loyal to Kiir and Machar begins
August 2015	Kiir and Machar sign the Agreement on the Resolution of the Conflict in the Republic of South Sudan (ARCSS), establishing the Transitional Government of National Unity (TGoNU) and a power-sharing deal between the two men
April 2016	The TGoNU takes office, but implementation of the ARCSS is incomplete
July 2016	Fighting between the different factions resumes; Kiir removes Machar as vice president

On July 5, 2011, tens of thousands of people gathered in the furious heat of Juba to witness a moment many thought would never occur in their lifetimes: the entry of South Sudan into the community of nations. The event capped five decades of struggle—including 39 years of war—that began before Sudan, the nation from which the new state seceded, achieved its own independence. After signing South Sudan's interim constitution, the country's new president, Salva Kiir, addressed the jubilant crowds: "We have waited more than 56 years for this. It is a dream come true."[1]

Within two and a half years, that dream lay in ruins. In December 2013, fighting erupted between army factions loyal to Kiir and supporters of the man he had ousted as his deputy, Riek Machar. The fighting escalated into mass killings, the renewal of old enmities, and the outbreak of a civil war that quickly pitted the nation's main ethnic groups against each other.

How did South Sudan, which entered independence on a wave of international support—including the steadfast backing of the United States—fail so fast? Warning signs were present from the outset for anyone who looked past the facile narrative advanced by U.S. advocacy groups and congressional allies that depicted the civil war as a clash

Figure 6.1. Map of Sudan and South Sudan

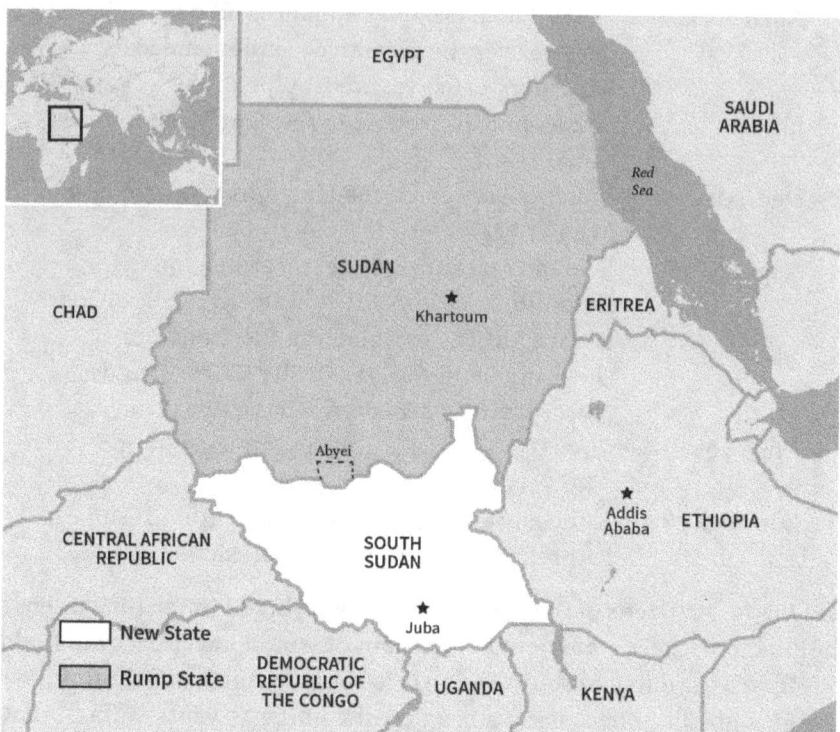

between virtuous (mainly Christian) liberation heroes in the south and malevolent (mainly Muslim) oppressors in the north.

The new nation faced sobering challenges, and few serious preparations were made to overcome them during the critical period leading to independence. South Sudan had virtually no infrastructure, limited human capital, an economy overwhelmingly reliant upon oil, and a hostile neighbor on its yet-to-be-demarcated northern border. These hurdles were not insurmountable, but required enlightened, accountable leadership and consistent support from international partners. Unfortunately, neither was present. Instead, the government of the Sudan People's Liberation Movement (SPLM) mimicked the governance model of its erstwhile oppressors in Khartoum, establishing a regime based on exclusion, venality, and repression. The United States had played an instrumental role in sustaining South Sudan during the final decade of its civil war and supported the negotiations of the peace settlement that paved the way to statehood. But the United States was distracted at critical moments and failed to confront the new country's leaders about their governance failures until it was too late.

CIVIL WARS AND THE ILLUSION OF A NATIONAL IDENTITY

The South Sudanese independence movement was forged in the face of ferocious, sustained oppression that predated Sudan's own independence in 1956 and an even longer history of accumulated grievances. Colonial powers that ruled Sudan since the early nineteenth century exploited the south's resources and people: from 1820, the Turco-Egyptian empire used the south as a vast reserve for slave raids. The "internal colonialism"[2] of the Islamic Mahdist state (1883-1898) continued the plunder. The Anglo-Egyptian condominium (1899-1955) waged a protracted campaign of pacification in the south, even as Sudanese in the north were integrated into the civil administration. With the expulsion of the Egyptian army in the 1920s, the British ruled the south indirectly, relying upon indigenous structures. Their intention was to keep the south separate and isolated from the north, which was directly governed along "Arab" rather than "African" lines and where most commercial activity was clustered. The effect was to retard development and keep southern populations at arm's length from political power. The sense of alienation and separateness entrenched in the colonial period only grew after independence in 1956 as successive regimes in Khartoum attempted to impose centralized rule and a narrow Arab, Islamic identity on southerners, who were denied political power and access to resources, and who were terrorized by state and paramilitary forces when they resisted.

The south's emerging national identity relied on the existence of outside threats and remained a fragile concept throughout the civil wars (1955-1972 and 1983-2005) that dominated Sudan's post-independence era. The wars launched against successive regimes in Khartoum sought primarily to win greater autonomy and representation for the south. More ambitious political objectives were not embraced until much later, when the 2005 Comprehensive Peace Agreement (CPA) made full independence a viable possibility.

The first major southern rebellion of the modern era erupted on the eve of Sudan's independence, when the Equatoria Corps mutinied in 1955, partly out of fears that they would be marginalized by northerners in the new nation. The Anyanya insurgency, which came to be known as the First Civil War, grew from the seeds of this uprising, demanding southern self-determination and provoking a ferocious response from northern forces. The fortunes of the Anyanya movement improved over time, as it secured military support from Ethiopia, Uganda, and Israel and capitalized on the presence of a weak government in Khartoum following the coup d'état that brought Gaafar Nimeiri to power in 1969. Peace talks began, ending in the Addis Ababa Agreement of 1972, which granted regional autonomy to the south.

When the Addis Ababa agreement unraveled following Nimeiri's decision to impose Shari'a law nationwide in 1983, southern forces launched the Second Sudanese Civil War under the leadership of John Garang, whose Sudan People's Liberation Movement/Army (SPLM/A) became the most powerful of several armed resistance groups. Garang portrayed himself as a national, rather than a southern leader, embracing the loftier ambition of reforming governance and addressing underdevelopment in all of Sudan. Achieving independence for South Sudan was not a stated goal.

Garang personified the promise and limitations of the resistance movement in the south. Charismatic and visionary, he was committed to building a "New Sudan," an inclusive, well-governed polity that could accommodate its diverse peoples. He was also an unabashed authoritarian who brooked no dissent and had scant regard for human rights.

The discovery of significant oil deposits in Sudan after the signing of the Addis Ababa Agreement added an important dimension to the conflicts between north and south. While most of the oil was in the south, Khartoum signed agreements with Chevron and Total to exploit the resources without consulting the southern regional government. These actions fed existing southern grievances about economic exploitation. The oil fields, most located near the north–south border, became important battlegrounds during the Second Civil War. The beginning of commercial production in 1999 brought new international actors onto the scene as Sudan's government established joint ventures with companies from China, India, and Malaysia. U.S. companies were locked out of the industry in 1997 when Washington imposed sanctions on doing business with the regime in Khartoum. The loss of an economic stake in Sudan weakened U.S. influence over Khartoum and—eventually—over Juba, after South Sudan achieved independence.[3]

International alliances and geopolitical dynamics drove important momentum shifts during the Second Civil War and ultimately tilted the battlefield advantage away from Khartoum. The outcome was a stalemate that eventually brought the warring parties to the negotiating table, enabling the SPLM/A to negotiate on equal terms with the government of Sudan. During the early years of the war, the United States considered Sudan within its broader Cold War calculus. Washington saw Nimeiri's government as an ally against the Soviet-backed regime of Mengistu Haile Mariam in neighboring Ethiopia and was unfriendly toward the SPLA, which relied upon Ethiopian support and drew ideological inspiration from Marxism. The situation transformed when Mengistu was ousted in 1991 by an alliance of armed liberation groups.

Ethiopia's new government, which benefited from Khartoum's military support, was initially hostile to the SPLA and expelled its forces from the country, depriving it of rear bases. However, the SPLA gradually moved into the U.S. orbit. This process was hastened by the regime in Khartoum, which became more militantly Islamic and whose support for international terrorism—including hosting Osama bin Laden in the early 1990s—made it a pariah state. The SPLM/A cause received the backing of some curious bedfellows in the United States: a mixture of Washington insiders, student groups, Christian activists who painted the civil war in religious terms, and antislavery advocates who accused Khartoum of orchestrating slave raids. Their lobbying efforts in Congress resulted in diplomatic and humanitarian support, as well as security assistance. Ultimately, most of southern Sudan's neighbors—including Ethiopia, Uganda, and Eritrea—provided material support to the SPLA and began to play an important role in the push for peace negotiations.

Southern Sudan united due to the collective trauma of the war years, which claimed an estimated 2 million lives during its second phase, displaced millions more, and deprived successive generations of children of the right to an education. However, the civil war was as much a conflict among South Sudanese as one conducted against a hostile government in the north. The SPLM/A was not universally supported, and the movement was internally divided by competing strategic visions, personal ambitions, and regional and ethnic rivalries that Khartoum was quick to exploit. Antagonisms that presaged the SPLM/A fracture in 1991 into Garang's wing and the so-called Nasir faction, led by Riek Machar and Lam Akol, never disappeared. Instead, memories of their bloody confrontations were buried just below the surface, only to violently reemerge in 2013 with many of the same protagonists at the helm.

The fragility of southern Sudanese unity, and the speed with which it unraveled after independence, is better understood by taking account of this history. The territory that became South Sudan is notable for its diversity and the frequency—and ferocity—of internal conflicts. Political contests widened the traditional fault line between the largest ethnic group, the Dinka, and other groups, including the second-largest, the Nuer. Perceived Dinka dominance of the political and security affairs of the south has been a constant source of discord. However, it is not accurate to portray the South Sudanese as locked in a dualist battle between Dinka and Nuer, with other groups forced to pick sides. First, there are important intra-ethnic divisions within each group. Furthermore, ethnicity is not the only identity marker for South Sudanese, who embrace multiple, often overlapping labels related to region, language, religion, and lifestyle. One such divide is between settled farmers and pastoralists. Forging a united nation among these diverse, often antipathetic peoples was no easy task.

THE COMPREHENSIVE PEACE AGREEMENT AND THE ROAD TO INDEPENDENCE

The Comprehensive Peace Agreement (CPA), signed in January 2005, officially ended the civil war and—contrary to the intentions of its authors—placed the south on the road to outright independence. The agreement was the culmination of two and a half years of negotiations led by East Africa's regional body, the Intergovernmental Authority on Development (IGAD), with support from the African Union (AU), United Nations (UN), and a "Troika," consisting of the United States, the United Kingdom, and Norway. The CPA instituted power- and wealth-sharing agreements between the former warring parties and established joint security arrangements in an attempt to promote national unity. The SPLM was given representation in the national government in Khartoum and a semi-autonomous Government of Southern Sudan was established in Juba.

One of the agreement's shortcomings was that it distilled Africa's longest civil war into a contest between the government of Sudan and leaders of the SPLM. The CPA, by conferring privileged status on the

SPLM, gave it sole authority to determine the south's destiny. Garang's death in a helicopter crash, just six months after the peace agreement was signed, altered the course of that destiny. Garang's personal commitment to making Sudan's unity attractive was abandoned in favor of an all-out dash toward independence. The SPLM pursued this goal by exploiting a fateful compromise at the heart of the CPA. In exchange for accepting the continuation of Shari'a rule in the north, the SPLM was offered a referendum on self-determination at the end of a six-year interim period.[4] Mediators of the peace deal dangled the referendum prospect in an attempt to cajole the SPLA to the negotiating table. Intended to act as an insurance policy, it was a means to compel the north to abide by the agreement. For the south, Garang's vision of a New Sudan died with him, and the referendum on independence became the ultimate objective. Both sides sat out the interim period and made little attempt to transform Sudan in the ways envisaged by the CPA.

During this critical period, the attention of the United States and other key partners was diverted by the intensifying conflict in Darfur. No one applied consistent pressure, and their inaction made full independence for the south increasingly likely. Intermittent efforts were made by the United States to make the peace deal work, but its main focus was ramping up development in the south. While a worthwhile objective, this strategy fostered an unhealthy patron–client relationship and a culture of expectation among the SPLM, which, fixated on its goal of independence, took none of the necessary steps to prepare for government or lay the foundations for peace and stability. Notably, it dodged the critical task of security sector reform by simply integrating other armed groups into the already swollen ranks of the SPLA, including militias that had fought on the side of Khartoum. Pragmatists argued that the "big tent" approach, while unpalatable and expensive, was a price worth paying for stability. Yet that stability was a mirage, for it gave spoilers the opportunity to haggle for their continued loyalty and spawned a legion of conflict entrepreneurs who continually threatened the peace and drained the coffers of South Sudan.

The independence referendum, held in the opening days of 2011, was a fleeting moment of optimism and euphoria in southern Sudan. Among those who voted, 98.8 percent opted for independence. The referendum process ran smoothly and the result was accepted by the government in Khartoum. In many ways, the results of Sudan's final elections as a unified nation, held the previous year, were a more accurate harbinger of the governance direction the south was taking. The SPLM won a crushing victory, receiving almost 93 percent of the vote in a contest marred by fraud and intimidation that sparked armed revolts by defeated candidates. The clear message to the South Sudanese was that Salva Kiir's position was unassailable. The international community was content to turn a blind eye to irregularities in the south, viewing Sudan's first multiparty elections in more than two decades as a distraction from—and potential risk to—the forthcoming referendum.

REALITY STRIKES: SOUTH SUDAN'S SHORT HONEYMOON

The jubilation that greeted South Sudan's independence in July 2011 was almost immediately tempered by a realization of the vast social, economic, governance, and security challenges that lay ahead. South Sudan was woefully underdeveloped, with fewer than 250 miles of paved roads at independence.[5] Generations of southern Sudanese had missed out on education, leaving a skills vacuum. Meanwhile, many members of the diaspora, who would be expected to play a central role in plugging these personnel gaps, played a wait-and-see role. Those who did return were often viewed with suspicion and resentment by their compatriots who had remained home throughout the conflict.

Added to these internal challenges were the external threats that resulted from South Sudan's failure to negotiate the terms of its separation from the north. Five sections of the 1,300-mile international border between Sudan and South Sudan were disputed and discussions on the status of Abyei, a contested enclave straddling the north and south, were deadlocked. Meanwhile, the costs of failing to resolve the status of South Kordofan and Blue Nile, states in the north where the SPLM had a strong presence, immediately became apparent when civil war erupted within Sudan, poisoning relations between Khartoum and Juba.

Most damaging was the inability of the two governments to agree on equitable sharing of oil revenues. There were strong reasons for Sudan and South Sudan to cooperate; after all, the south produced 75 percent of the oil within the former Sudan but relied entirely upon the north's export pipeline to generate revenue. Yet within months of independence, South Sudan's exasperation at Sudan's refusal to charge a fair price for use of its pipeline prompted it to take the drastic step of shutting down its production in protest, severing its economic lifeline to the outside world and leaving the state virtually bankrupt. It compounded its folly by occupying Sudan's most productive oil field in April 2012, until international pressure forced it to withdraw. The oil shutdown was ruinous for South Sudan's economy and damaged the new country's reputation as a reliable partner. A foretaste of things to follow, this episode also illuminated the SPLM government's failure to take serious steps toward diversifying the economy.

In mid-2013, South Sudan tumbled into a governance crisis from which it has never recovered. The tipping point was Kiir's decision to fire Vice President Machar and his cabinet, a move that reflected a steady descent into autocratic rule based on a narrow, mainly Dinka clique of the SPLM. When rival factions of the presidential guard respectively aligned with Kiir and Machar clashed in Juba, the fighting quickly escalated into a series of massacres along ethnic lines. Within days, Machar formally announced his intention to take up arms under the banner of the SPLM in Opposition (SPLM-IO) to force Kiir from power. The country descended into a civil war that continues to the present day. In the process, nearly 2 million South Sudanese have been internally displaced and another 2 million have fled the country.[6] Food shortages have left an estimated 6 million people—two-thirds of South Sudan's population—in need of emergency assistance.[7]

ACCOUNTING FOR SOUTH SUDAN'S FAILURE

South Sudan faced immense challenges at independence, and the international community was guilty of wishful thinking about the new government's ability to cope. South Sudan possessed few tools to prepare for independence, and its leaders made repeated mistakes that led the country into war within three years.

Why did South Sudan fail so quickly?

First, the long history of conflict and brutality in southern Sudan proved to be an insurmountable barrier. Bitter memories of civil wars, grievances, and the repeated failure to bring perpetrators of violence to justice created a volatile mix that boiled over at the first sign of provocation. The urgent task of national reconciliation was postponed at independence and was taken up by President Kiir only in late 2016, when the civil war had already raged for three years. Even then, civil society criticized the national dialogue as hollow and unrepresentative.

The return to violence was not inevitable, but South Sudan's leaders failed to take steps to avoid it, fanning the flames instead.

One important mistake was the failure to provide a compelling and unifying national vision. Like all nation-states, South Sudan is an artificial creation. Therefore, it was incumbent on its leaders to explain to the people why they should set aside divisions and embrace the concept of being South Sudanese, in addition to being Dinka, Nuer, or Shilluk. Few attempts were made to develop national symbols and institutions. The only institutions with national scope, the SPLM and SPLA, were not inclusive and were viewed as Dinka-dominated. Collective opposition to Khartoum during the war years created the illusion of unity. Once the common enemy receded from view, old divisions quickly resurfaced, to be exploited by self-interested individuals.

Meanwhile, the SPLM squandered the independence dividend, the outpouring of goodwill—both national and international—that accompanied South Sudan's new nationhood. South Sudan's citizens were optimistic about independence but also impatient for improvements in their lives after years of war. They also had unrealistic expectations about the economic benefits their country's oil wealth would deliver. South Sudan's development needs were pressing at independence: nearly one in every five children failed to live beyond their first birthday, only a quarter of people had access to clean water, barely a tenth had sanitation, literacy stood at just 15 percent, and only one in 50 children completed primary school.[8] Yet little effort was made to provide essential services that would improve people's lives and strengthen the legitimacy of the government. Instead, the government was content to entrust responsibilities for service provision—and the associated costs—to international development partners. South Sudan's rash decision to shut down oil production in 2012 was taken without consultation with international partners; the government simply assumed that donors would fill the budget gap.[9]

The extended oil shutdown also revealed the absence of a plan for broad-based economic development. No serious effort was made to lessen South Sudan's fatal dependence on oil, which accounted for 98 percent of government revenue on the eve of independence.[10] There was no development of other promising sectors of the economy, such as agribusiness, that could provide jobs for demobilized soldiers and youth. Instead, the SPLM elite, centered in Juba, devoted their attention to collecting oil rents, accumulating enormous wealth at the expense of the population. In 2016, U.S. advocacy groups documented how senior leaders of the government, including President Kiir and his then-chief of staff of the SPLA, General Paul Malong Awan, had looted the country's wealth and used corrupt business connections in the oil, mining, and financial sectors to amass vast fortunes that were mostly laundered overseas.[11]

The rampant corruption that rapidly took hold under SPLM rule was responsible more than perhaps any other factor for the erosion of public faith in the government and growing disillusionment with the new nation. No steps were taken to stop the rot. In 2012, President Kiir claimed that 75 current and former officials had collectively stolen $4 billion from the treasury. Citizens waited in vain for prosecutions.[12]

The president led the march toward South Sudan's collapse with his venal, predatory, and unimaginative leadership. Salva Kiir is a dour, divisive, military man who failed to adapt to civilian life and never felt secure enough to refrain from repressive actions against perceived rivals. His governance style became increasingly autocratic, narrow, and exclusive, mirroring failures of the regime in Khartoum that he fought against for so long. His emphasis has been on extracting loyalty and obedience to the state, wielding power through informal patronage networks, and co-opting opponents. He has alienated political rivals and hurtled down a path of ethnic chauvinism. Kiir and Machar allowed their personal rivalry to drag people back into conflict. At no point has either man shown any empathy for, or interest in, his own people.

By basing governance around personalities and patronage ties, South Sudan has neglected the building of strong, accountable, and independent institutions. Power has remained highly concentrated in Juba, despite a policy commitment to decentralized government. While the SPLM/A are strong, they are far from accountable and have failed to transition from liberation movement/rebel militia to accountable, democratic government/national army. The SPLM has become the state in South Sudan. It refuses to share the political stage with other parties, which have not been allowed to develop beyond a few personality-driven groupings, despite the efforts of international development partners. The pattern established in the 2010 elections, which amounted to a coronation for the SPLM, continued into the independence era.

Democratic development within the SPLM has also foundered. Following independence, President Kiir circumvented SPLM internal processes, making full use of the overly broad powers accorded to the executive in the interim constitution. In July 2013, Kiir fired his cabinet, setting off a political crisis that culminated in the outbreak of fighting and the fragmentation of the SPLA into warring factions. The Agreement on the Resolution of the Conflict in the Republic of South Sudan (ARCSS), signed—under duress—by Kiir and Machar in 2015, imposed power sharing and established the Transitional Government of National Unity (TGoNU), which took office in April 2016. President Kiir, however, made no serious attempt to implement the agreement. When fighting broke out two months later, he quickly seized the military and political advantage, reconfiguring the TGoNU in his favor, replacing Machar as first vice president, and installing a former Machar ally, Taban Deng Gai, in his place. A panel of experts set up by the UN Security Council cites evidence that Kiir has established a "shadow government" packed with Dinka allies.[13]

The absence of political pluralism in South Sudan underlined the need for strong, independent voices outside government. But civil society has been harassed and stymied by the government. All nongovernmental organizations are required to register with authorities. Those that do not comply face intimidation and the seizure of their assets. The media is considered a threat to be monitored or silenced, especially since the civil war began, when journalists were reminded that their first responsibility is loyalty to the state. South Sudan's internal intelligence agency, the National Security Service (NSS), modeled on its feared counterpart in the north, routinely intimidates and arrests journalists, shuts down media outlets, and conducts surveillance on perceived opponents of the SPLM.

Perhaps the most consequential institutional failure of South Sudan's independence era has been the failure to establish a truly national, professional army. Instead of modernizing the SPLA, the army remained an unwieldy patronage machine, a place to house the men with guns for fear of what they might do if they were turned out of their barracks. The events of December 2013 exposed the failure of South Sudan and its security partners—led by the United States—to undertake security sector reform. The breakdown of discipline that occurred and the splintering of the SPLA into ethnic factions exposed the shallowness of the reform effort.

While South Sudan's leaders bear ultimate responsibility for the collapse of their nation, the international community failed to avert the catastrophe through its inattentiveness, ineffectiveness, and lack of unity. No major donor conditioned support on advances in governance, accountability, or basic competence. South Sudan's government quickly realized there were no consequences for bad behavior, even when its abject performance created humanitarian crises. Since the civil war began in 2013, the international community has been hopelessly divided, and that reality convinced the warring parties that they need not take the peace process seriously. Instead, they agreed to a series of flimsy cease-fires with no intention of complying, even if they had the ability to enforce them upon the patchwork of militia groups they lead in name only.

The United States has been inconsistent in its dealings with Sudan and South Sudan—highly engaged at times but inattentive during critical periods. Washington allowed itself to become too close to the southern leadership during the Second Civil War as relations with Khartoum grew hostile under the Clinton administration. For the SPLM, the knowledge that its powerful ally "had its back" partly explained its reluctance to enter peace negotiations even though it had long been clear that a decisive victory on the battlefield was increasingly unlikely. The George W. Bush administration invested heavily in the peace process that led to the CPA, but attention wandered again after its signing. The United States' lack of engagement resulted in the south's drift toward self-determination. Following independence, Washington did not acknowledge the SPLM's slide toward autocratic rule until it was too late. Rather than using its influence to promote responsible governance, some of its words and actions had the contrary effect. In one example, a former U.S. envoy to Sudan urged the United States to provide anti-aircraft systems to South Sudan just a month after it launched military incursions into Sudan's main oil field.[14] The United States belatedly discarded the simplistic view that the north was bad, the south good, and began to take a tougher line with the Kiir government. This shift drew a hostile counterreaction that poisoned relations and prompted South Sudan's friends in Washington to walk away in self-defeatist frustration.

Since the civil war began in 2013, the ability of the United States to influence Juba's conduct has ebbed, despite an inflow of more than $11 billion in U.S. humanitarian and development assistance between 2005 and

2016.¹⁵ Instead of changing the calculus of the warring parties in favor of peace, Washington's policy has been largely reactive and has had the unintended consequence of strengthening President Kiir's military position. This, in turn, has made him less willing to make compromises that would increase the chances of a lasting settlement. Although U.S. diplomats worked hard to impose the ARCSS on the reluctant parties in 2015, they failed to hold either Kiir or Machar to their commitments when they proceeded to flout the agreement. While the AU and South Sudan's neighbors condemned Kiir's decision to reconfigure the TGoNU in the wake of the July 2016 fighting, their objections to this clear breach of the ARCSS were undercut by the United States, which quickly accepted the new political reality. The failed U.S. effort at the UN Security Council to impose an arms embargo on South Sudan summed up the paucity of effective policy options, the lack of consensus on meaningful responses, and the inability to corral allies in the region.¹⁶ U.S. policy toward South Sudan has reverted to little more than providing humanitarian operations, for which its aid workers are attacked and harassed by Kiir's government.

South Sudan's neighbors also failed to demonstrate the leadership and unity necessary to stem the crisis, taking opposing sides in the conflict. Sudan's default position has been to weaken and undermine its southern neighbor, providing active support for Machar's SPLM-IO during the initial phases of the conflict.¹⁷ Uganda has provided equally robust military support to Salva Kiir. These divisions have undermined efforts by IGAD to negotiate an end to the fighting. President Kiir has skillfully manipulated divisions among his regional neighbors. He won important military support from Egypt, for example, by siding with Cairo in its dispute with Ethiopia over water rights in the Nile basin.

The United States compounded diplomatic mistakes in South Sudan by its muddled approach toward its neighbors. For example, Uganda's decision to send troops to prop up Kiir during the early days of the conflict was instrumental in saving his regime. Even after withdrawing, Uganda continued to transfer weapons to South Sudan, helping prolong the conflict.¹⁸ At the same time, Uganda is the United States' largest beneficiary of security assistance in sub-Saharan Africa. The United States, however, failed to use this leverage and poured humanitarian assistance into Uganda to support the flood of approximately 1 million South Sudanese refugees that Kampala's own military adventurism has aggravated.¹⁹

CONCLUSION: WHAT CAN BE DONE?

The quest by the diverse peoples of South Sudan for greater autonomy and ultimately independence has been a slow and painful process that has cost millions of lives. For most of the almost four decades of conflict, full independence was neither an objective nor a feasible possibility. When nationhood became a realistic prospect after the signing of the CPA, the SPLM was offered an interim period to serve its apprenticeship at the head of a civilian government in the south and prepare for the ultimate prize of full independence. It had the benefit of powerful support from the international community and plentiful natural resources. As independence dawned, the mood was optimistic, despite the unfinished business of negotiating relations with an unpredictable and hostile northern neighbor. That South Sudan collapsed into civil war within three years of achieving statehood is a damning indictment of its leaders, who squandered the opportunity to build a nation their citizens could believe in. Instead, they left the responsibilities of governing to over-compliant donors while they concentrated on getting rich and settling scores.

As South Sudan descended into yet another conflict that shows no sign of ending, the mounting frustration of the international community has generated a collective sense of desperation mixed with cynicism. This despondent mood has led to some creative but far-fetched solutions being floated, including the imposition of an international trusteeship on South Sudan,[20] something neither Kiir nor the AU is ever likely to approve. Going forward, the international community—starting with IGAD and the AU, but also including the United States—must consistently engage in the peace process and be prepared to take tough actions when the warring parties make no progress. A priority must be to find a political solution that sidelines Kiir, just as Machar appears to have been. Beyond that, inclusive peace and security talks are needed that engage ordinary South Sudanese for the first time. A critical part of that process will be to address the culture of impunity that has defeated previous national reconciliation efforts, by agreeing on transitional justice arrangements and by holding the worst perpetrators of violence to account through an AU hybrid court. Only then can begin the arduous task of regaining citizens' trust in the national project and fashioning truly national institutions.

NOTES

1. Jeffrey Gettleman, "After Years of Struggle, South Sudan Becomes a Nation," *New York Times*, July 9, 2011.
2. Douglas H. Johnson, *The Root Causes of Sudan's Civil Wars* (Bloomington: Indiana University Press, 2007), 6.
3. This situation endured until January 2017, when the Obama administration suspended most of the economic and trade sanctions against Sudan, pending a review of Khartoum's progress in five areas. In October 2017, the Trump administration determined that sufficient progress had been achieved and made the suspension permanent.
4. International Crisis Group, "The Khartoum-SPLM Agreement: Sudan's Uncertain Peace," July 25, 2005, 2.
5. U.S. Department of State, "2013 Investment Climate Statement, South Sudan," February 2013, https://www.state.gov/e/eb/rls/othr/ics/2013/204855.htm.
6. UN High Commissioner for Refugees (UNHCR), "Operational Update—Dadaab, Kenya, 1–15 September 2017," https://reliefweb.int/report/kenya/unhcr-operational-update-dadaab-kenya-1-15-september-2017.
7. World Food Programme, "South Sudan Emergency," http://www1.wfp.org/emergencies/south-sudan-emergency.
8. Richard Downie, *Statebuilding in Situations of Fragility and Conflict: Relevance for U.S. Policies and Programs* (Washington, DC: USAID, February 2011).
9. Richard Downie, *The State of Public Health in South Sudan: Critical Condition* (Washington, DC: CSIS, November 2012).
10. Justin Willis et al., "Land and Water," in *The Sudan Handbook*, ed. John Ryle et al. (Suffolk, UK: James Currey, 2012), 56.
11. Sentry, *War Crimes Shouldn't Pay: Stopping the Looting and Destruction in South Sudan* (Washington, DC: Sentry, September 2016).
12. Hereward Holland, "South Sudan Officials Have Stolen $4 Billion: President," Reuters, June 4, 2012.
13. UN Security Council, "Final Report of the Panel of Experts on South Sudan," S/2017/326, April 13, 2017, 8.
14. Andrew S. Natsios, "To Stop the War in South Sudan, the U.S. Should Send Weapons," *Washington Post*, May 11, 2012.
15. Kate Almquist-Knopf and Princeton Lyman, "To Save South Sudan, Put It on Life Support," U.S. Institute of Peace, July 20, 2016.
16. U.S. policymakers were divided among themselves for much of 2015 and 2016 over the efficacy of an arms embargo. Supporters of an embargo, including then secretary of state John Kerry and U.S. ambassador to the United Nations Samantha Power spent many months overcoming the opposition of National Security Adviser Susan Rice. See Colum Lynch, "Inside the White House Fight over the Slaughter in South Sudan," *Foreign Policy*, January 26, 2015.
17. Washington eventually persuaded Sudan to drop its support for Machar and other anti-Kiir elements as part of the set of conditions for ending most of its economic and trade sanctions against Khartoum. This had the inadvertent effect of strengthening Kiir's position on the battlefield, which increased his intransigence toward the United States.
18. See evidence cited in UN Security Council, "Final Report of the Panel of Experts on South Sudan," S/2016/70, 39.
19. UNHCR, "Dashboard: South Sudan Refugee Crisis (as of 31 August 2017)," September 13, 2017, https://reliefweb.int/map/uganda/dashboard-south-sudan-refugee-crisis-31-august-2017.
20. See, for example, Almquist-Knopf and Lyman, "To Save South Sudan, Put It on Life Support."

7. THE IMPORTANCE OF BEING BALANCED: LESSONS FROM NEGOTIATED SETTLEMENTS TO SELF-DETERMINATION MOVEMENTS IN BOSNIA, MACEDONIA, AND KOSOVO

Erin Jenne and Beáta Huszka

On every continent, self-determination movements have challenged state governments for statehood, yielding a proliferation of de jure and de facto states extending from the former socialist republics of Yugoslavia, the Soviet Union, and Czechoslovakia to South Sudan, Eritrea, and East Timor. Elsewhere they have produced "quasi-states" with limited international recognition, including South Ossetia and Abkhazia in Georgia; Northern Cyprus; Nagorno-Karabakh in Azerbaijan; Somaliland; and Transnistria in Moldova.[1] Today separatists the world over press for greater political independence from existing state governments—sometimes through violence, other times through popular referenda. Examples of the former include Kurds in northern Iraq and Russians in eastern Ukraine; examples of the latter include Scots in the United Kingdom, Québécois in Canada, and most recently Catalans of Spain. Once activated, movements for self-determination often recur periodically in tandem with regime transition and other institutional changes.

Self-determination movements are potent sources of political destabilization, leading in extreme cases to violent conflict when the majority and minority fail to find a compromise that each would prefer to taking up arms.[2] The preferred solution of the United Nations and other peacemaking organizations is complex power-sharing agreements from which no party prefers to defect unilaterally. This means successful settlements must at a minimum achieve an acceptable division of political power between majority and minority groups in the state while laying the foundation for a functional state over the entire territory.

The international community favors negotiated solutions to such conflicts for a number of reasons. First, cooperative solutions avoid the moral hazard of rewarding secessionist organizations with statehood while forestalling further fragmentation. Second, inducing a compromise agreement is believed to be the best way of protecting vulnerable minorities against retaliation by a hostile government or ethnic majority. Third, negotiated solutions are consistent with the Westphalian norm of sovereignty, increasing the legitimacy of the solution in the eyes of the target state population. Finally, cooperative agreements represent a relatively cost-effective method of settling territorial wars at least risk and cost to the interveners. To be successful, such settlements should be based on minority autonomy, either through devolution or decentralization.[3]

Critics warn, however, that immediate benefits of negotiated settlements can obscure long-term costs. Although satisfying minority demands for autonomy, the conferral of such institutions may inadvertently reinforce separatist impulses while giving secessionist organizations the material and symbolic resources needed to mobilize for independence down the road.[4] Research indicates that minorities with a history of territorial autonomy are more likely to mobilize for independence than those without.[5] A recent analysis suggests these effects are probably overstated, but also shows that territorial autonomy alone is unlikely to achieve success unless the minority also has a stake in the center.[6] Achieving a balance between "power-dividing" elements (such as territorial self-government) and "power-sharing" elements (such as a grand coalition in the central government) lies at the heart of *consociational* models of conflict management.[7]

The West Balkan region presents a natural laboratory with which to illustrate this simple principle. Despite their common origins, different settlement logics were used to resolve the violent self-determination struggles in Bosnia and Herzegovina (Bosnia), Macedonia, and Kosovo. Their common origins are clear. All three states once were part of Yugoslavia. Each conflict was resolved with the intervention of NATO and Western powers, which sought an acceptable division of power between rival groups that would also stabilize state institutions. None is a resounding success, but each post-conflict trajectory is a predictable consequence of each settlement's design.

We argue that while scholars have long recognized the importance of achieving a balance between competing interests at the domestic level, *they often underestimate the impact that regional conflict dynamics can have on the fate of such settlements.* Peacemakers must consider whether sufficient safeguards are built into institutions to protect against regional destabilization of fragile ethnic settlements, a problem compounded in chronically unstable neighborhoods.

OVERVIEW OF WEST BALKAN SETTLEMENTS

In 1991–1992, the Slovene, Croatian, Bosnian-Herzegovinian, and Macedonian republics declared independence from the Socialist Federal Republic of Yugoslavia (SFRY); in 2008, Kosovo declared independence from Serbia. Internal fragmentation plagued the newly independent states, as Serbs and Croats sought to secede from Bosnia; Serbs launched a violent bid for independence from Croatia and sought to separate from postwar Kosovo; and ethnic Albanians mobilized violently against the Former Yugoslav Republic of Macedonia (FYROM, hereafter Macedonia). In three of four conflicts—Bosnia, Kosovo, and Macedonia—the international community used negotiated settlements to rebuild peaceful multiethnic states.

Bosnia

The Yugoslav Republic of Bosnia and Herzegovina was highly ethnically integrated; there was no outright majority in 80 percent of its municipalities.[8] Yet it was the site of the bloodiest war of postcommunist Europe. Like the other five republics, the republic had its own independent parliament, which consistently voted with the League of Communists of Yugoslavia. As the party lost power in the waning days of the Cold War, divisions emerged between Muslims, Serbs, and Croats in parliament. When the Muslim-dominated assembly declared independence for Bosnia and Herzegovina, Serb delegates indicated that they would boycott the referendum with the aim of forming an independent Bosnian Serb state.[9] With Belgrade and Zagreb intervening on the side of their

Figure 7.1. Map of Western Balkans

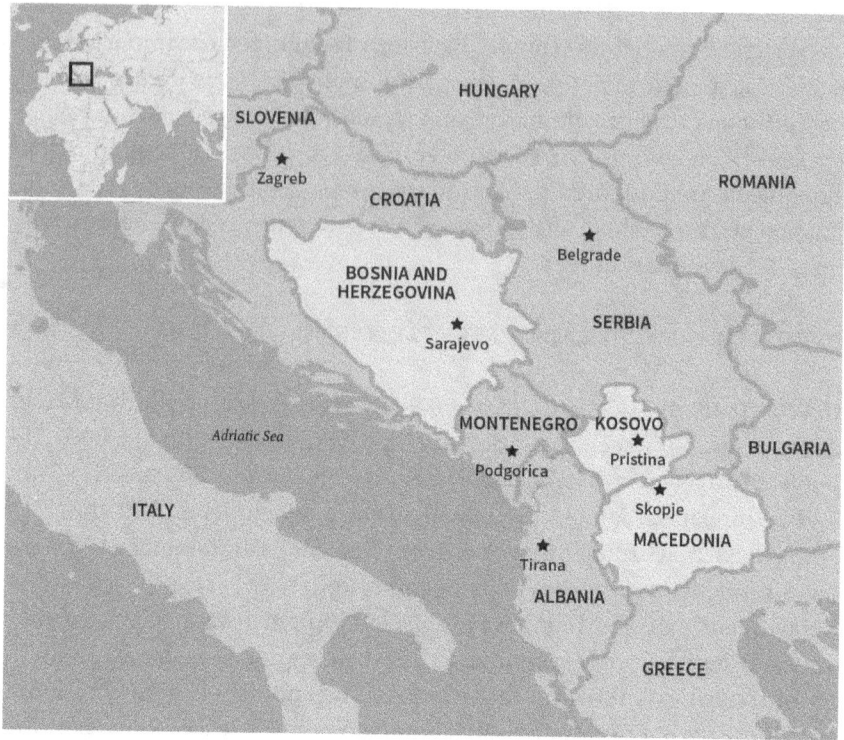

respective coethnics, escalating hostilities led to a three-year war among the three groups. About 100,000 people died, and a million more were displaced[10] before NATO bombing of Bosnian Serbs induced the three constituent groups, together with the Serbian and Croatian governments, to agree to a U.S.-brokered negotiated settlement in Dayton, Ohio, in 1995. Annex 4 of the Dayton Peace Agreement (DPA) established a constitution following principles of consociationalism. The settlement was designed to alleviate concerns of the Serb and Croat minorities (33 percent and 17 percent, respectively) that Bosniak Muslims (44 percent) would establish a unitary state.

The settlement included a three-member Bosnian presidency as well as radical autonomy for two entities—the federation (for Bosniak Muslims and Croats) and Republika Srpska (RS) for Serbs. Within the federation, the Croats and Bosniaks were given significant territorial autonomy through a system of 10 cantons, which functioned as mini-states, each with its own government, parliament, courts, and police.[11] Serbs and Croats were permitted special relationships with Serbia and Croatia, respectively. It was hoped that the DPA represented the right balance of centripetalism (with the three-member presidency and minority vetoes in the parliament) and centrifugalism (with extensive canton- and entity-level authorities and mutual ethnic vetoes) to forge a lasting peace. The United Nations Peace Implementation Council appointed a high representative (HR) to oversee "the implementation of the civilian aspects of the peace settlement."[12] They placed the fledgling state under international tutelage with a range of IOs in charge of implementing the terms of Dayton. Thousands of NATO troops were installed to enforce the settlement.

Macedonia

Although the war in Macedonia was relatively short and yielded far fewer casualties, prewar ethnic tolerance was significantly lower there than in Bosnia or in Yugoslavia as a whole.[13] Macedonia declared its independence from the SFRY in 1991 following a successful referendum. The vote was boycotted by the Albanian minority, on the grounds that the preamble of the new state constitution was ethnically exclusive.[14] At the heart of the struggle was the status reversal between majority Macedonians and minority Albanians, who had once been a titular nation under federal Yugoslavia but who now sought equal status within the new Macedonian state. Albanian separatists organized their own referendum on the territorial autonomy of Western Macedonia in 1992, declaring an autonomous republic of Ilirida.[15] Demonstrations were held in the name of Albanian language and education rights, cultural autonomy, and territorial autonomy—a period marked by episodic violence.[16] Despite these disruptions, most scholars believe ethnic harmony improved throughout the 1990s, with the government agreeing to extensive minority concessions in order to secure accession to NATO and the EU.

In 2001, former fighters from the Kosovo conflict fomented a low-intensity war in the border region under the moniker of the Albanian National Liberation Army (NLA) and quickly gained the support of many Albanians. Escalating hostilities between rebels and Macedonian security forces nearly reached Skopje, leading to dozens of casualties on both sides. More than 170,000 civilians were displaced. The war ended when NATO and U.S. representatives pressured rebel forces and Macedonian leadership to sign separate cease-fire agreements with NATO. The NATO-negotiated Ohrid Framework Agreement (OFA) was signed in mid-2001 by the two largest Macedonian and Albanian parties. The settlement attempted to satisfy Albanian demands for self-determination by giving them de facto, if not de jure, political power, in contrast to the consociational Bosnian peace agreement. To enforce the deal, 3,500 NATO peacekeepers were installed in the tiny country and the EU appointed a special representative to oversee implementation.[17]

Minority autonomy in Macedonia was achieved through *decentralization*. Groups with over 20 percent of the local population were given language and educational rights in their mother tongue. In principle, any sizable minority can exercise this right, but in practice this applied only to Albanians. Consequently, Albanian was introduced as a second official language in municipalities where Albanians made up more than 20 percent of the population—principally in the northwest. The OFA also contained provisions for education in minority languages, addressing long-standing demands for higher education in the Albanian language. Mutual vetoes were introduced through double-majority voting (requiring support of a majority of delegates of both ethnic groups) on laws concerning culture, language, education, personal IDs, and the use of symbols.[18] An Interethnic Council was created in parliament to resolve interethnic disputes. There were centripetalist elements in the OFA as well, such as minority quotas in state administration. Although these quotas may have contributed to the growth of ethnic patronage, the OFA has generally been regarded as a success.[19]

Kosovo

Both during and after Yugoslav times, Kosovo had an overwhelming Albanian ethnic majority and a small Serbian minority (roughly 10 percent, according to the 1991 census). Although only an autonomous province in the Yugoslav Republic of Serbia, it enjoyed extensive autonomy—including a provincial assembly, mother tongue language, educational rights, and an Albanian language university. By the mid-1980s, the tide had shifted as Serbian politicians and pundits began to rally the Serbian public around the perceived oppression of Serbs in Kosovo. This culminated in the abolition of provincial autonomy in 1989 and a purge of Albanians from schools, hospitals, and other state institutions.[20] In the 1990s, the Kosovo Liberation Army (KLA) launched a guerrilla war against Yugoslav forces. A NATO air campaign induced Belgrade to withdraw from the province in 1999. UNSC Resolution 1244 set up a UN-administered transitional authority in Kosovo, with NATO-led international peacekeepers to enforce the arrangement.

At the end of the war, a large proportion of Kosovo Serbs fled to Serbia proper. Kosovo's Ibar River became the de facto dividing line between Serbs living in the northern breakaway territory and the southern part where Albanians lived. Serbs and Albanians now live on either side of the Ibar River, which bisects the segregated town of Mitrovica; traffic has never flowed freely across the bridge. Today, there is a Serbian enclave in the north (for many years controlled by the Serbian Interior Ministry) and scattered Serbian enclaves in the south.[21] Serbs number approximately 120,000 or 6 percent of the Kosovo population.[22] Although Serbian is an official language in Kosovo, public information and institutions are rarely accessible in Serbian.[23]

To address these problems, the international community resolved to build a peaceful multiethnic state through a negotiated settlement, culminating in the so-called Ahtisaari Plan. This accord called for devolving state powers to municipalities (giving Serb enclaves de facto control over local affairs) and reserving seats for minorities in parliament. Stalled for many years by the Kosovo government, progress was finally made once Belgrade and Pristina started an EU-mediated dialogue to decide the status of Kosovo.[24] The Brussels Agreement of April 2013 attempted to integrate the breakaway northern territory into the Kosovo state. A further agreement in August 2015 established the Community of Serbian Municipalities in Kosovo, and mandated unification of the divided town of Mitrovica and integration of energy and telecommunications between the north and south.[25]

Despite many advances in this direction, the settlement is not considered a success. Still today, the Serb and Albanian communities live parallel lives, with limited contact. In the south, Serbs are largely confined to ethnic enclaves; in the north, ethnic interaction is even rarer because of almost complete separation. Ethnic accommodation has been absent from Kosovo for decades.[26]

COMPARING WEST BALKAN SETTLEMENTS

The three West Balkan settlements represent different mixes of centrifugalism and centripetalism, demonstrating the trade-off between satisfying minority demands and creating a functional state.

The **Bosnian settlement** tilted toward minority empowerment at the expense of state integrity. The agreement weakened the central government by devolving extensive state powers to the entities (which, in the beginning, even had their own armies) and, to a lesser extent, the cantons. The DPA also gave Bosnian Croats and Serbs the right to form special relations with their respective kin states, weakening their commitment to the central government.

On the other end of the spectrum, the **Kosovo settlement** favored state integrity at the expense of minority rights. Following costly engagements in Bosnia and Croatia, the international community had little stomach for another lengthy commitment in the Balkans. As a consequence, neither KFOR nor the UN Mission to Kosovo (UNMIK) intervened to protect Serbs from forced migration after the war in 1999 or from anti-Serb riots in 2004. They further failed to ensure the return and property restitution of Serb minority refugees and allowed former KLA fighters to integrate seamlessly into the state army—reinforcing Serb perceptions that the government was tilted against the minority.

Tilted neither in one direction nor the other, the **Macedonian settlement** struck an even balance between minority empowerment and state functionality. The plan included a mix of consociational principles, such as increasing minority representation in state institutions and the 2008 law mandating that the government include the strongest Albanian party in every ruling coalition.[27] By decentralizing the state along nonethnic lines, the settlement met Albanian minority aspirations without creating ethno-territorial autonomy. The notable benefit was that the Albanian minority remained strongly committed to remaining in the Macedonian state (in contrast to aggrieved minorities in Kosovo and Bosnia). This can be attributed, at least in part, to the balance the OFA struck between minority empowerment and state integrity. Key contributing factors were the international community's stabilization of the regional environment and effective management of the Macedonian government.

Figure 7.2. Comparing the Negotiated Settlements*

	Kosovo (Ahtisaari Plan)	Macedonia (Ohrid Framework Agreement)	Bosnia (Dayton Peace Agreement)
Power-sharing at the central level	No formal requirement.	A formal requirement since 2008, although practiced informally since 1992.	Strict rules of power-sharing among the three constitutive nations in the presidency, government, and both houses of parliament.
Reserved minority seats in parliament	Ten guaranteed seats for Serbs, 10 for other minorities (out of 120 seats).	No guaranteed seats; Albanian parties usually have around 20% of votes (i.e., 15–20 seats out of 123).	Five for each ethnic group in the upper house of 15 members.
Ethnic quotas in the public sector	Key institutions, such as the courts, police, and state-owned companies were to introduce quotas for Serbs and other minorities, but this has not been implemented.[a]	Flexible provision: the OFA mandated increased minority representation in public administration proportionate to their population share (partially implemented, improvements in some areas).	Public institutions must grant proportional representation to all constituent peoples corresponding to their prewar population share.
Minority veto	Double-majority requirement for changing the constitution and adopting laws of vital minority interest (not practiced).	Double-majority requirement was introduced in parliament on a set of issues.[b]	Double mechanism: entity veto and vital interests veto at the state and entity level.

(continued)

Figure 7.2. *continued*

Territorial autonomy	Formally not granted; minority autonomy is exercised indirectly, through the municipalities.	Formally not granted; minority autonomy exercised indirectly at the local level through decentralization.	Granted to Bosnian Serbs through the RS and de facto to Croats through cantons.
Institutionalized ties with homeland state	Kosovo Serbs have the right to receive funding from Serbia and to cooperate with Serbian institutions.	None.	RS has the right to form special relations with Serbia.
External guarantor	UN (UNMIK) International Steering Group for Kosovo (ISG), NATO (KFOR), EU (EULEX).	NATO and the EU; NATO implemented the peace agreement, while the EU appointed a special representative to oversee its implementation.	United Nations Peace Implementation Council, Office of the High Representative (OHR), EU (EUSR), U.S., NATO.

*Darker shadings indicate a relative tilt toward minority empowerment.

[a] Directorate-General for External Policies of the Union, Directorate B, Policy Department, "Mainstreaming Human and Minority Rights in the EU Enlargement with the Western Balkans" (European Parliament, December 2012), 54, http://www.europarl.europa.eu/RegData/etudes/etudes/join/2012/457114/EXPO-DROI_ET(2012)457114_EN.pdf.

[b] "[C]onstitutional amendments and other laws that involve local administration, territorial division, use of languages, flags and symbols and protection of cultural identity can be changed only with a double majority that includes approval of the parliamentary representatives of the smaller ethnic communities." International Crisis Group, "Macedonia: Ten Years after the Conflict," Europe Report No. 212 (August 11, 2011), 3, https://d2071andvip0wj.cloudfront.net/212-macedonia-ten-years-after-the-conflict.pdf.

DANGERS OF MINORITY EMPOWERMENT:
TERRITORIAL AUTONOMY, POWER-SHARING,
MINORITY VETOES, "HOMELAND" STATE INVOLVEMENT

This brief comparison suggests that negotiated settlements should limit autonomy or veto power to separatist minorities as this may weaken or even break up the state.

Settlements that mandate extensive power-sharing or minority vetoes can incapacitate legislative bodies and grind the gears of government to a halt. Giving minorities territorial autonomy can create proto-states that may mobilize for secession at a later date. Permitting these units to conduct independent foreign policy with their kin states can further undermine state integrity by giving hostile neighbors license to intervene in the state's domestic affairs to "protect" their compatriots.

Bosnia presents a textbook case on the dangers of minority empowerment. The DPA is highly imbalanced in favor of ethnic minorities at the expense of the state (see the dark-shaded cells in Figure 7.2). Each entity and most cantons have a titular minority that enjoys disproportionate political power over that jurisdiction—sometimes to the exclusion of other groups. Carl Bildt, the first international representative in Bosnia, declared that despite its flaws, the DPA "is based on the hope that over time the imperative of integration in the country and the region will be the dominant factor."[28] However, the settlement has instead served to prevent the development of statewide political formations, producing a de facto partitioned state along divisions institutionalized by the peace agreement.[29]

The Republika Srpska (RS), in particular, has functioned as a proto-state, and a number of RS leaders have amassed wealth and power through an ethnic spoils system that emerged during the war.[30] The RS lost little time forging ties to Serbia, an arrangement permitted under the DPA. Since then, RS leaders have continually used their veto power to obstruct efforts by the international community to strengthen the state. When the OHR tried to create a unified national Bosnian police force across ethnic lines and entity borders, the implementation was blocked by Serb leaders.[31] RS delegates have stymied numerous legislative reforms, such as an amendment of the witness protection law in 2008, which was part of Bosnia's European Partnership agenda. They also obstructed modification of the law on confidential information in 2009 that would have harmonized Bosnian law with EU and NATO standards. Bosnian Serb leaders, in general, have slowed down accession to the EU. The settlement permits Bosnian leaders to profit from the state by establishing personalized control over the public sector, allowing them to extract rents from utilities, state-owned banks, privatization, public tenders, and "other sources of revenue and patronage."[32] Networks of party patronage now permeate the state. Most jobs depend on officials' favors, and public institutions serve party interests.[33]

When Serbia assumed a more moderate stance following its defeat in the Kosovo war, Bosnian Serb leaders followed a more conciliatory policy—currying favor with international actors to increase leverage within the state. But with the resurgence of nationalism in Serbia in the 2000s, RS leaders resumed their obstructionism. Milorad Dodik came to power in 2006 on a tide of demonstrations for RS secession. On his watch, the republic began to block efforts to reinforce Bosnia's state government and institutions. Dodik repeatedly challenged Bosnia's Office of the High Representative (OHR), threatening to declare RS independence.[34] Mutual vetoes have produced chronic legislative gridlock in the Bosnian parliament.

Bosnia signed its Stabilization and Association Agreement (SAA) with the EU in 2008, but ratification was delayed until 2015 due to disagreement on how to bring the constitution in line with an important court ruling. According to the ICG, a key problem is that Bosnian politicians have remained largely unaccountable to their constituents due to the state's protectorate status; they could readily blame failures on the OHR.[35] In this way, international actors inadvertently undermined the Bosnian state.[36]

Meanwhile, ethnic quotas have led to discrimination against nonconstituent ethnic groups as well as against Serbs, Bosniaks, and Croats who reside outside their designated entities or cantons. Segmenting the state in this way has allowed ethnic parties to control the distribution of benefits to their ethnic constituents. According to the ICG, Bosnia's ethnic parties consistently field candidates who serve party rather than constituent interests, producing descriptive, but not substantive, representation of minorities.[37]

Macedonia offers lessons in how to satisfy minority separatism without undermining the state. The OFA implemented minority autonomy on a nonethnic basis rather than creating ethno-territorial carve-outs. Despite concerns that Macedonian decentralization would lead to separatism, the OFA did not split the state along ethno-territorial lines, but instead created crosscutting "local versus central" political cleavages and a shared identity among local elites.[38]

Not all OFA actions have been curative. Education reforms extending the scope of teaching in Albanian has led to increased ethnic segregation in schools and a growing ethnic distance and intolerance among the youth.[39] Another unintended effect has been empowerment of political parties at the expense of rule of law, as well as a preference for informal practices such as coalition deals. This has paved the way for growing clientelism, nepotism, and corruption, which has undermined the legitimacy of the settlement.[40]

DANGERS OF MAJORITY EMPOWERMENT: WEAK MINORITY RIGHTS, WEAK EXTERNAL OVERSIGHT, CENTRALIZED STATE

Our comparison further suggests that the lack of external checks on the majority-controlled government can endanger vulnerable minorities.

In contrast to the Bosnian case, Kosovo's settlement illustrates the dangers of majority empowerment. The lack of adequate external monitoring and enforcement in Kosovo has created a permissive environment for minority discrimination, fueled Serbian separatism, and perpetuated ethnic tensions nearly two decades after the Kosovo conflict.

After the war, UNSC Resolution 1244 installed UNMIK in Pristina to implement the terms of the settlement. UNMIK counseled Kosovo leadership that fulfilling conditions of the settlement would be deemed an essential condition for Kosovo independence. "Standards before Status" was UNMIK's official policy. This included protection of human and minority rights, implementing effective mechanisms in response to human rights violations, and implementing the Council of Europe's Framework Convention for the Protection of National Minorities.[41] The NATO-led Kosovo Force (KFOR) was established to enforce the agreement.

Peacekeepers, however, failed to prevent forced migration of Serbs at the end of the war. They did not intervene to halt the 2004 anti-Serb riots. Nineteen people died and thousands were displaced. Orthodox churches and shrines were destroyed. This sent a strong signal to the Serbian minority that UNMIK was a biased, rather than neutral, enforcer of the peace agreement. Serbs fled urban centers for ethnic enclaves in the north and the south; others relocated to Serbia. This was a defensive response to a hostile Albanian majority in the context of weak external security guarantees.

The Ahtisaari Plan endeavored to address problems of majority empowerment by providing Serbs with a degree of segmental autonomy and representation in the central government. Talks commenced in Vienna between Pristina and Belgrade over the final status of Kosovo in 2006. UN special envoy Martti Ahtisaari facilitated the negotiations. The talks led nowhere due to the diametrically opposing stances of the parties. Ahtisaari presented his settlement plan to the UNSC in 2007, and Russia effectively vetoed it. Ultimately, elements of the Ahtisaari Plan were incorporated into the constitution in return for Western recognition of Kosovo statehood.[42] However, the key provisions of the agreement remained unimplemented for many years due to governmental obstructionism.[43]

The value of external enforcement can be seen in Bosnia after 1997. That is when the UNSC gave the OHR so-called Bonn powers to force local authorities to accept minority returns and property restitution. What followed was a notable upsurge of minority returnees.[44] In Macedonia, too, international pressure was crucial for implementing minority concessions. The EU, in particular, has played a key role in keeping the government honest. In early 2001, the Macedonian government signed the Stabilization and Association Agreement with the EU—the first step on the country's path to EU membership. Macedonia became an EU candidate in 2005. The European Commission in 2009 recommended opening accession negotiations. Macedonian authorities were notified that accession to NATO and EU hinged on increasing minority representation in state institutions. Available evidence suggests that this has had some success. Prior to the agreement, Albanians remained significantly underrepresented in the public sector, especially in security forces and the judiciary. After the OFA, Albanians increased their representation in state institutions, although equal representation has not yet been achieved.[45]

Things took a turn for the worse for Macedonia at a NATO summit in 2009 when Greece threatened to veto Macedonian accession over its ongoing name dispute with Skopje. Unable to offer membership to the country in the near term, the EU and NATO lost influence in the country.

The stalemate led to an upsurge of populist nationalism. Formerly pro-Western, conciliatory Macedonian prime minister Nikola Gruevski adopted more nationalist policies and rhetoric. This shift culminated in the massively pro-Hellenic "antiquitization" public works program. Massive Byzantine structures were erected all over Skopje, greatly antagonizing the Albanian minority. No longer focused on fulfilling standards demanded by these bodies, Macedonia experienced a rapid deterioration of democratic governance and media freedoms.[46] In Kosovo, the trend went in the opposite direction. The beginning of accession talks with Serbia in 2012 led to successive agreements under which Serbia toned down nationalist rhetoric toward Kosovo and has gradually withdrawn its parallel structures, leading to a surge in Serb participation in the Kosovo state. These within-case, over-time fluctuations show that adequate and sustained international pressure must be placed on governments to ensure that minority rights are implemented, both in letter and in spirit.

DANGERS OF AN IMBALANCED EXTERNAL ENVIRONMENT

Finally, our analysis shows that conflict spillover or partisan intervention by outside actors can stall or fatally undermine negotiated settlements. All three West Balkan examples demonstrate the vital importance of a stable external environment for ensuring ongoing success of negotiated settlements.

In Bosnia, RS leaders have consistently relied on signals from their kin state of Serbia to determine how far they can push demands against the Bosnian government. Serbia has played a crucial role in Bosnian Serb politics by providing financial and political support to the RS leadership. According to the ICG, EU integration would render such clientelist arrangements illegal. This unwelcome prospect possibly has incentivized RS leaders to stall the EU integration process.[47]

In Kosovo, too, the wider neighborhood has been a key source of conflict. Kosovo Serbs have consistently followed Belgrade's political lead in talks over Kosovo's status. Soon after the war's end, Serbia reclaimed de facto control over Serbian enclaves in Kosovo, an arrangement the international community tolerated because they were unwilling to risk open conflict with Belgrade-backed secessionists or provoke the ire of Russia.

When Belgrade indicated that it could no longer afford to support parallel structures in the south, Serbs in the south began to vote in Kosovo elections and participate in Kosovo institutions. By contrast, Serbs in the north (where parallel structures remained) continued to hew to a hardline position, rejecting UNMIK and EULEX (the rule of law mission of the EU overseeing the transition). Belgrade finally agreed to dismantle its parallel structures in the north as part of EU accession negotiations in March 2012.[48] Soon after, northern municipalities indicated their willingness to integrate into the Kosovo state. This shows that balancing regional interests is foundational to the success of ethnic settlements.

Ethnic violence has in fact fluctuated in tandem with conflict in the wider environment. Ethnic relations between Serbs and Albanians hit bottom in 2004, the year of anti-Serb riots in Kosovo. There was a significant improvement from that point until June 2007, the period of the Vienna negotiations. Until Kosovo's declaration of independence, a rising number of Serbs thought ethnic relations were getting worse. This negative dynamic turned around in November 2008, a few months after Kosovo proclaimed independence and ethnic relations resumed the trend of improvement until June 2011. During the crisis in Mitrovica (July to November 2011), tensions were high, but declined once Belgrade began to withdraw parallel institutions from Kosovo in conformance with conditions of its SAA.[49]

In Macedonia, ethnic tensions have also fluctuated in response to tensions in the wider neighborhood. In the early 1990s, the tiny republic sought international help managing ethnic tensions and protecting its borders. The United Nations sent a border-monitoring mission, UNPREDEP, to Macedonia in 1995 to prevent ethnic violence and monitor the border. Max van der Stoel, the OSCE high commissioner for national minorities, conducted mediation talks between the government and the Albanian minority during key crisis periods in the 1990s.

Although ethnic relations were fairly harmonious prior to the 2001 conflict, they quickly deteriorated when Albanian guerrillas crossed the border from Kosovo into Macedonia. Episodic violence popped up throughout the 1990s, but resulted in no major conflict. Only after the UN border mission in Macedonia was suddenly withdrawn did guerrilla fighters sneak over the border to foment conflict.[50]

CONCLUSION

The West Balkan settlements offer lessons in squaring the circle of satisfying minority aspirations for self-government while protecting the capacity and territorial integrity of the state.

First, the central government must have adequate power to fulfill basic state functions such as national defense, independent foreign policy, and protection of its citizens. A state's integrity is compromised whenever other countries have a sovereign claim to its territory or citizens, or whenever its subnational units are able to undermine or obstruct any basic functions. Settlements should avoid dividing sovereignty at the domestic and regional level.

Second, successful settlements must satisfy minority self-determination without alienating the majority. While opinions on the settlements in Bosnia and Kosovo are largely divided along ethnic lines,[51] the divide is much less extreme in Macedonia. According to one survey, 57 percent of Albanians thought the OFA was very important for the stability of Macedonia, while only 42 percent of ethnic Macedonians thought the same. The majority of respondents from both groups (52 percent of Albanians and 59 percent of Macedonians) agreed that the OFA primarily served the interests of Albanians. But both minority and majority were on board with the settlement, and public trust in Macedonia's public institutions increased significantly for both groups following the settlement.[52] NATO and EU accession is sufficiently attractive to both Macedonians and Albanians that they are each willing to make serious concessions to accelerate the process.

Finally, a stable regional and international environment is essential for the effectiveness of negotiated settlements to self-determination struggles. Protection from conflict spillover from Kosovo, Serbia, or Albania was a precondition for OFA to keep ethnic peace. By contrast, negative regional dynamics, such as a deadlock in the NATO and EU integration process (Macedonia) or intermittent interventionism by a neighboring state (Serbia in Kosovo), can fuel discrimination against minorities or separatism by minority organizations. Unstable regional environments clearly undermine negotiated settlements.[53]

To succeed, peacemakers must ensure a complex balance between majority and minority empowerment as well as between domestic and external environments, paying close attention to how minorities and kin states interact. Successful settlements must get the institutions right and engage in continual, active recalibration of domestic and external relations as facts change on the ground. Doing this well requires a level of foresight, dedication, and luck that rarely play out in practice. It also entails years, and sometimes decades, of commitment by outside intervenors. Peacemakers should question whether they can reasonably deliver on all fronts before embarking on missions to remake a multiethnic state.

NOTES

1. Tozun Bahcheli, Barry Bartmann, and Henry Srebrnik, *De Facto States: The Quest for Sovereignty* (New York: Routledge, 2004); Robert Jackson, *Quasi-States: Sovereignty, International Relations and the Third World* (Cambridge: Cambridge University Press, 1993). See also Nina Caspersen, *Unrecognized States: The Struggle for Sovereignty in the Modern International System* (Cambridge: Polity, 2013); and Philip G. Roeder, *Where Nation-States Come From: Institutional Change in the Age of Nationalism* (Princeton, NJ: Princeton University Press, 2007).

2. In this chapter, we use "majority" to refer to the dominant group in the state, whether or not it is in the numerical majority. For a formal treatment of the bargaining dynamic, see James D. Fearon, "Rationalist Explanations for War," *International Organization* 49, no. 3 (1995): 379–414; James D. Fearon, "Bargaining, Enforcement, and International Cooperation," *International Organization* 52, no. 2 (1998): 269–305.

3. For example, see Stefan Wolff, "Complex Power-Sharing and the Centrality of Territorial Self-Governance in Contemporary Conflict Settlements," *Ethnopolitics* 8, no. 1 (2009): 27–45; Hurst Hannum, *Autonomy, Sovereignty, and Self-Determination: The Accommodation of Conflicting Rights* (Philadelphia: University of Pennsylvania Press, 1996); Kjell-Åke Nordquist, "Autonomy as a Conflict-Solving Mechanism: An Overview," in *Autonomy: Applications and Implications*, ed. Markku Suksk (The Hague: Kluwer Law International, 1996), 59–77; Ruth Lapidoth, *Autonomy: Flexible Solutions to Ethnic Conflicts* (Washington, DC: U.S. Institute of Peace, 1996); Yash P. Ghai, *Autonomy and Ethnicity: Negotiating Competing Claims in Multi-Ethnic States* (Cambridge: Cambridge University Press, 2000); Arend Lijphart, *Democracy in Plural Societies: A Comparative Exploration* (New Haven, CT: Yale University Press, 1977); and John McGarry and Brendan O'Leary, eds., *The Politics of Ethnic Conflict Regulation:Case Studies of Protracted Ethnic Conflicts* (London: Routledge, 1993).

4. See, for example, Svante E. Cornell, "Autonomy as a Source of Conflict: Caucasian Conflicts in Theoretical Perspective," *World Politics* 54, no. 2 (2002): 245–276; Ronald G. Suny, *The Revenge of the Past: Nationalism, Revolution, and the Collapse of the Soviet Union* (Stanford, CA: Stanford University Press, 1993); Yuri Slezkine, "The USSR as a Communal Apartment, or How a Socialist State Promoted Ethnic Particularism," *Slavic Review* 53, no. 2 (1994): 414–452; Philip G. Roeder, "Soviet Federalism and Ethnic Mobilization," *World Politics* 43, no. 2 (1991): 196–232; Roeder, *Where Nation-States Come From*; Henry E. Hale, "The Parade of Sovereignties: Testing Theories of Secession in the Soviet Setting," *British Journal of Political Science* 30, no. 1 (2000): 31–56; Charles King, "The Benefits of Ethnic War: Understanding Eurasia's Unrecognized States," *World Politics* 53, no. 4 (2001): 524–552; and Dawn Brancati, "Decentralization: Fueling the Fire or Dampening the Flames of Ethnic Conflict and Secessionism?" *International Organization* 60, no. 3 (2006): 651–685.

5. Erin K. Jenne, Stephen S. Saideman, and Will Lowe, "Separatism as a Bargaining Posture: The Role of Leverage in Minority Radicalization," *Journal of Peace Research* 44, no. 5

(2007): 539–558; Stephen M. Saideman and William R. Ayres, "Determining the Causes of Irredentism: Logit Analyses of Minorities at Risk Data for the 1980s and 1990s," *Journal of Politics* 62, no. 4 (2000): 1126–1144; James D. Fearon and David D. Laitin, "Ethnicity, Insurgency, and Civil War," *American Political Science Review* 97, no. 1 (2003): 75–90; Daniel Treisman, "Russia's 'Ethnic Revival': The Separatist Activism of Regional Leaders in a Postcommunist Order," *World Politics* 49, no. 2 (1997): 212–249; Monica D Toft, *The Geography of Ethnic Violence: Identity, Interests, and the Indivisibility of Territory* (Princeton, NJ: Princeton University Press, 2003); and David S. Siroky and John Cuffe, "Lost Autonomy, Nationalism and Separatism," *Comparative Political Studies* 47 (2014): 1738–1765.

6. Lars-Erik Cederman, Simon Hug, Andreas Schädel, and Julian Wucherpfennig, "Territorial Autonomy in the Shadow of Conflict: Too Little, Too Late?" *American Political Science Review* 109, no. 2 (2015): 354–370.

7. Arend Lijphart, the leading authority on consociationalism, has argued that such models can be used to rebuild a multiethnic state after war by combining elements designed to guarantee rights of minorities (through "segmental autonomy" and "mutual vetoes" over areas of sensitive legislation) while giving minorities a stake in the central government (through a "grand coalition" representing all ethnic groups and "proportionate representation" of minorities in state institutions). See especially Lijphart, *Democracy in Plural Societies*; Brendan O'Leary and John McGarry, eds., "State of Truce: Northern Ireland after Twenty-Five Years of War," *Ethnic and Racial Studies*, special issue 18, no. 4 (1995); John McGarry and Brendan O'Leary, "Consociational Theory, Northern Ireland's Conflict, and Its Agreement. Part 1: What Consociationalists Can Learn from Northern Ireland," *Government and Opposition* 41 (2006): 43–63.

8. Sheri P. Rosenberg, "Equality after Genocide: Jurisprudence of the Legal Institutions Established in Dayton's Bosnia," in *Deconstructing the Reconstruction: Human Rights and the Rule of Law in Postwar Bosnia and Herzegovina*, ed. Dina Francesca Haynes (Aldershot, UK: Ashgate, 2008), 119–120.

9. Raju G. C. Thomas and H. Richard Friman, eds., *The South Slav Conflict: History, Religion, Ethnicity, and Nationalism* (New York: Routledge, 2013), 129.

10. "Bosnia War Dead Figure Announced," BBC News, June 21, 2007, http://news.bbc.co.uk/2/hi/europe/6228152.stm; Internal Displacement Monitoring Center, "Bosnia and Herzegovina: Internal Displacement in Brief," December 2013, http://www.internal-displacement.org/europe-the-caucasus-and-central-asia/bosnia-and-herzegovina/summary.

11. Of the 10 cantons, five have a Bosniak majority, three have a Croat majority, and two cantons have a mixed population. International Crisis Group, *Bosnia's Future*, Europe Report No. 232 (Brussels: International Crisis Group, July 2014), 33.

12. Dayton Agreements, Annex 10: Civil Implementation, Article I-1.

13. Cvete Koneska, *After Ethnic Conflict* (Aldershot, UK: Ashgate, 2014), 59–64. The fact that ethnically integrated Bosnia should experience intense conflict while ethnically divided Macedonia had a much less intense war should be a reminder that the occurrence of ethnic violence is poorly predicted by prior ethnic relations.

14. Koneska, *After Ethnic Conflict*, 67; preamble of the constitution.

15. The referendum was declared illegal by the Macedonian authorities. Albanians, lacking external support, abandoned the idea of an autonomous republic. Maria Koinova, "Why Do Ethnonational Conflicts Reach Different Degrees of Violence? Insights from Kosovo, Macedonia, and Bulgaria during the 1990s," *Nationalism and Ethnic Politics* 15, no. 1 (2009): 100.

16. Koinova, "Why Do Ethnonational Conflicts Reach Different Degrees of Violence?"

17. Erin K. Jenne, *Nested Security, Lessons in Conflict Management from the League of Nations and the European Union* (Ithaca, NY: Cornell University Press, 2015), 144.

18. Florian Bieber, "Partial Implementation, Partial Success: The Case of Macedonia," in *Power Sharing: New Challenges for Divided Societies*, ed. Ian O'Flynn and David Russell (London: Pluto, 2005), 116.

19. Koneska, *After Ethnic Conflict*, 70–74.

20. Ian Bache and Andrew Taylor, "The Politics of Policy Resistance: Reconstructing Higher Education in Kosovo," *Journal of Public Policy* 23, no. 3 (2003): 287.

21. Lars Burema, "Reconciliation in Kosovo: A Few Steps Taken, a Long Road Ahead," *Journal of Ethnopolitics and Minority Issues in Europe* 11, no. 4 (2012): 11.

22. W. Benedek et al., "Mainstreaming Human and Minority Rights in the EU Enlargement with the Western Balkans," European Parliament, Directorate-General for External Policies of the Union, 2012, 53.

23. Benedek et al., "Mainstreaming Human and Minority Rights," 18–19.

24. Spyros Economides and James Ker-Lindsay, "'Pre-Accession Europeanization': The Case of Serbia and Kosovo," *JCMS: Journal of Common Market Studies* 53 (2015): 1028.

25. European External Action Service, "Statement by High Representative/Vice-President Federica Mogherini following the Meeting of the EU-Facilitated Dialogue," August 25, 2015, http://eeas.europa.eu/statements-eeas/2015/150825_02_en.htm. The 2015 agreement would give ethnic Serbs territorial autonomy indirectly through the creation of the community, uniting Serb municipalities under a single umbrella. However, this part of the agreement has not yet been implemented because the Kosovo parliament has refused to ratify it.

26. Burema, "Reconciliation in Kosovo," 9.

27. It should be noted that this empowered ethnic parties to distribute spoils of the OFA, which has led to the growth of clientelism and other ill effects documented further below.

28. Carl Bildt, *Peace Journey: The Struggle for Peace in Bosnia* (London: Weidenfeld and Nicolson, 1998), 392, as cited in Samantha Bose, *Bosnia after Dayton: Nationalist Partition and International Intervention* (Oxford: Oxford University Press, 2002).

29. Erin Jenne, "The Paradox of Ethnic Partition: Lessons from De Facto Partition in Bosnia and Kosovo," *Regional & Federal Studies* 19, no. 2 (2009): 273–289.

30. Michael Pugh, "Postwar Political Economy in Bosnia and Herzegovina: The Spoils of Peace," *Global Governance* 8, no. 4 (2002): 467–482.

31. International Crisis Group, *Ensuring Bosnia's Future: A New International Engagement Strategy*, Europe Report No. 180 (Brussels: International Crisis Group, February 2007), 14.

32. International Crisis Group, *Ensuring Bosnia's Future*, 12.

33. International Crisis Group, *Ensuring Bosnia's Future*, 13–14.

34. International Crisis Group, *Bosnia: What Does Republika Srpska Want?*, Europe Report No. 214 (Brussels: International Crisis Group, October 2011), 1–2.

35. Zeljko Komsic is not among them, though he was elected to the presidency twice. See International Crisis Group, *Bosnia's Future*.

36. Author's interview with Adnan Huskic, Friedrich Naumann Foundation, Sarajevo, March 30, 2015.

37. International Crisis Group, *Bosnia's Future*, 21.

38. Koneska, *After Ethnic Conflict*, 97.

39. Koneska, *After Ethnic Conflict*, 137.

40. Transparency International data show corruption in Macedonia was on the decline until 2013 and only began to increase again after 2014, 13 years after the conclusion of the OFA (see Transparency International's CPI index for Macedonia, https://www.transparency.org/cpi2015/). Clientelist arrangements actually predated the OFA in Macedonia by many years. Jessica Giandomenico, "Transformative Power Challenged: EU Membership Conditionality in the Western Balkans Revisited," PhD dissertation, Uppsala University, 2015, 150.

41. Burema, "Reconciliation in Kosovo," 92.

42. Under the Ahtisaari Plan, Kosovo Serbs would be given high-level local autonomy indirectly through decentralization in finance, health care, education, and culture; the right to receive funding from Serbia and to cooperate with Serbian institutions; guaranteed seats in the Kosovo assembly; and veto power over governing coalitions, constitutional amendments, and laws on a number of sensitive issues, such as the use of language, protection of cultural heritage, education, and the use of symbols. Comprehensive Proposal for the Kosovo Status Settlement, Annex I. Article 3.7, http://www.unosek.org/docref/Comprehensive_proposal-english.pdf. Key institutions, such as the courts, Kosovo police, and state-owned companies had to introduce quotas for Serbs and other minorities. Serbian became an official language in Kosovo. International Crisis Group, *Setting Kosovo Free: Remaining Challenges*, Europe Report No. 218 (Brussels: International Crisis Group, September 2012); Judith Brand and Valdete Idrizi, *Grass-Root Approaches to Inter-Ethnic Reconciliation in the Northern Part of Kosovo*, Policy Paper Series 2012/03 (Pristina: Kosovar Institute for Policy Research and Development, February 2012).

43. Helsinki Committee for Human Rights in Serbia, *Serb Community in Kosovo* (Belgrade: Helsinki Committee for Human Rights in Serbia, June 2012), 30; author interview with Shpend Emini, D4D, Pristina, July 11, 2013.

44. Erin Jenne, "Barriers to Reintegration after Ethnic Civil Wars: Lessons from Minority Returns and Restitution in the Balkans," *Civil Wars* 12, no. 4 (2010): 370–394.

45. International Crisis Group, *Macedonia: Ten Years after the Conflict*, Europe Report No. 212 (Brussels: International Crisis Group, August 2011), 15.

46. See Freedom House's "Nations in Transit" indicators.

47. International Crisis Group, *Bosnia's Future*, 15; Vedran Džihić and Angela Wiesler, "Incentives for Democratization? Effects of EU Conditionality on Democracy in Bosnia & Herzegovina," *Europe-Asia Studies* 63, no. 10 (2011): 1803.

48. This was just the beginning of a long process. The last roadblock on the Mitrovica bridge connecting the northern and southern part of the city was removed only in August 2016.

49. Beáta Huszka, "Human Rights on the Losing End of EU Enlargement: The Case of Serbia," *Journal of Common Market Studies* 56, no. 2 (March 2018): 352–367.

50. Jenne, *Nested Security*, 126–129.

51. Serbia and Kosovo Serbs rejected the Ahtisaari Plan primarily because it granted independence to Kosovo, although Serbs in the south participated in its implementation. Albanians resented the decentralization provisions of the Ahtisaari Plan, fearing that it would lead to the federalization of Kosovo along ethnic lines, creating a situation similar to that in Bosnia. See Denisa Kostovicova, "Legitimacy and International Administration: The Ahtisaari Settlement for Kosovo from a Human Security Perspective," *International Peacekeeping* 15, no. 5 (2008): 631–647. In Bosnia, the problem is not whether Serbs accept the DPA (because they do in its original form) but that they are unwilling to cooperate in its overhaul aimed at strengthening Bosnia's central institutions.

52. Marija Aleksovska, "Trust in Changing Institutions: The Ohrid Framework Agreement and Institutional Trust in Macedonia," *East European Quarterly* 43, no. 1 (2016): 55–84.

53. Jenne, *Nested Security*.

8. GENERALIZING THE FINDINGS
Will Todman

The cases in this volume, like most histories, often seemed to hinge on specific individuals and events. While we could draw some conclusions, we did not see a large number of clear and obvious patterns. Part of the challenge was the specificities of the cases themselves. Confoundingly, factors that loomed large over one case were either marginal or absent in others. For example, Kosovo would not likely have gained independence and achieved its current level of stability if not for the vast amount of international support it received, and yet Eritreans managed to win independence and then function as a stable independent state (at least for a time) with remarkably little international involvement. In other instances, factors that had strongly positive effects in one circumstance sometimes seemed negative in another. Natural resource revenues were key to Timor-Leste's post-independence success, for example, but in South Sudan profits from oil fueled the very corruption and violence that ripped the country apart.

Part of the challenge, as well, was sample size. The CSIS project design contained a limited number of case studies to allow their exploration in depth. But with fewer than 10 countries under study, we could be mistaking unusual outcomes for normal occurrences and so have missed strong patterns that would have emerged had our project examined a much larger number of case studies. In order to explore whether a broader approach would tell us things that a case-study approach would miss, CSIS constructed a database of all the countries that have gained independence since 1960 and then analyzed the database to measure statistical correlations between certain variables and new states' relative levels of success.

To our surprise, the statistical analysis of a larger set of countries did not reveal strong associations that had been missing from the case studies.

Even seemingly likely correlations—such as the idea that states born out of violence would be less likely to thrive—did not hold up under our analysis. We did not have complete data for every year for every state under study, and missing data may have influenced the results. In addition, factors that do not lend themselves easily to quantification—such as the quality of leadership a self-determination movement enjoys—may loom large and yet elude this kind of analysis.

We do think it is telling, however, that a broader-scale examination of the factors that lead to thriving societies after independence does not yield clear patterns. It reinforces our belief in the importance of small decisions in the ultimate success of newly independent societies, and underlines the uncertainty that pervades the enterprise of pursuing, winning, and implementing independence.

QUANTITATIVE METHODOLOGY

In order to analyze the experience of a large number of states for its statistical analysis, CSIS sought to ensure that the data it analyzed would have integrity. Only states that gained membership in the United Nations or that had diplomatic relations with two major powers are included, following the convention set by the Correlates of War project. States that had a population of under 500,000 at the date of independence are also excluded, so that very small nations do not skew the results. We ended up with a list of 70 states that gained independence between 1960 and 2016 and that meet these criteria.[1]

Because we wanted to investigate new states' performance in their early years, we collected data for each of these states for the first six years after independence. With six years of data for 70 states, the database includes a maximum of 420 observations for each variable. However, several indicators are missing data because the databases on which we relied did not have complete data. Data were collated from a range of sources including the World Bank's database, the CIA *World Factbook*, the Center for Systemic Peace, and datasets built by academics.

One of the biggest challenges was selecting appropriate variables. The study was restricted by the difficulties of identifying variables that represent opportunities to extend the findings from the case studies, are quantifiable, and have sufficient data available for the full-time frame of the study. Some of the key findings of the case studies are either not quantifiable in a meaningful way or do not have data available for the time frame of the study. These factors include the importance of the new state's population having a shared sense of history and identity, the negative impact of corruption, and the importance of leadership.[2]

Upon reflection, CSIS sought to evaluate the impact of five factors on a new state's success: geostrategic location, the conditions in which the self-determination group gained independence, international aid, international peacekeeping missions, and reliance on revenues from natural resources. These five indicators are not intended to be a comprehensive overview of the factors that influence success, but a range of factors that seem to have a bearing on post-independence success, as revealed by the case studies. These indicators are the independent variables of the study.

Quantifying the concept of success was also challenging. To avoid a normative approach, success would most fairly be judged in terms of the self-determination movement's goals. However, leaders often deliberately make these goals unclear in case things do not work out as hoped, and so this was not feasible. We decided to explore values that are generally accepted indicators of success. Four variables were chosen that cover economic performance, the security situation, and the provision of state services. These are the study's dependent variables:

Annual Change in GDP per Capita

Annual change in gross domestic product (GDP) per capita indicates one aspect of success, as it shows whether a state's economy is on a positive or negative trajectory. As such, it reflects whether the new state is able to create an environment of economic prosperity or not.

However, certain factors could have an outsized impact on economic growth in the period immediately after a state gains independence. States that experience significant economic disruption due to conflict prior to secession may start with such low levels of GDP per capita that they then appear to grow very quickly after independence, even if absolute growth numbers are relatively low. Large injections of international aid into the new state's economy could also provide an artificial sense of economic growth.

This study uses World Bank data, which include one or more observations for 62 countries' annual GDP per capita growth from 1961 to 2016 out of a total of 70 countries in the dataset.

Annual Change in Infant Mortality Rate

Infant mortality is highly sensitive to structural changes and so is an indicator that is often used as a proxy measure of a population's health.[3] General factors that affect a population's health, such as economic development, rates of illness, general living conditions, social well-being, and the quality of the environment affect infant mortality rates. As such, annual changes in infant mortality rates represent another aspect of success as they indicate a government's capacity to improve the quality of services it provides to its citizens.

However, using infant mortality as a proxy for a population's overall health is problematic because it excludes large parts of the population.

This study uses World Bank data, which includes one or more observations for 62 countries' infant mortality rate from 1960 to 2016 out of a total of 70 countries in the dataset.

Change in Displacement

Displacement figures indicate an estimation of the total number of people that were displaced internally (IDPs) or externally (refugees) in a given year. By investigating changes in displacement, we can see if people are being newly displaced or if they are returning to their homes. A combination of security, political, economic, and social factors drive displacement. Broadly speaking, displacement represents citizens' perception that the state is unable to provide adequate services and protection. As such, low displacement figures reflect another aspect of a new state's success.

This study uses data from the Forcibly Displaced Populations dataset, compiled by the Center for Systemic Peace. The dataset covers the period from 1964 to 2008, and there are data for at least some of the years being investigated for 68 of the 70 states investigated in this study.[4]

Large-Scale Violence

Violence that leads to deaths in a new state reflects a state's failure to establish its complete authority over its territory and provide security for its citizens. As such, the intensity of the violence in a new state represents an important element of a state's success.

This study uses data from the Uppsala Conflict Data Program (UCDP) at the Department of Peace and Conflict Research and the Centre for the Study of Civil War at the Peace Research Institute, Oslo (PRIO). Data are available for all 70 countries in the study.

LIMITATIONS OF THE DATA

As described above, there are no data available for certain indicators for all of the states included in the study, or for all of the years under investigation. We cannot assume that missing data are random. In fact, the majority of missing data are for states in sub-Saharan Africa. Data could be missing because the new state's government lacks the institutional capability to collect them or because the government deliberately chooses to limit transparency and accountability. It was beyond the scope of this project to attempt to fill these gaps with original data, and the time period being examined for each new state is too short for statistical software to be used to estimate missing data in a reliable and accurate manner.

The study focuses on a time in history that witnessed rapid decolonization, a unique historical phenomenon. Recognizing that dynamics in states that gained independence from colonial powers may be different from those in secessionist states that did not experience colonial rule, we used former colonies as a control.

DATA ANALYSIS

As the dataset constructed is cross-sectional time series, CSIS used linear regression for analysis of panel data to investigate the relationships between the dependent and independent variables. Because of missing data for international aid and revenues from natural resources, two models of analysis were run. The first (Model 1) includes all of the independent variables, and the second (Model 2) omits international aid and revenues from natural resources. The lowest number of observations included in a regression in Model 1 was 104, while the lowest number in Model 2 was 239. Two full tables of the results of the regressions can be found at the end of the chapter, showing the correlation coefficient, the standard error, the p-value, and R-squared.

ANALYSIS

Geostrategic Location

Geography impacts both self-determination movements' ability to gain statehood and their chances of succeeding post-independence. The location in which a group operates has a bearing on its ability to organize and evade repression from the central state. Jason Sorens finds that geographical separation from the central state and access to the sea are factors that increase the likelihood of secession.[5] East Pakistan's geographical separation from West Pakistan facilitated the mobilization of the Bengali independence movement, as perceptions of economic disparities between the two wings and political exclusion fueled a sense of shared grievances in Pakistan's eastern wing.

Countries with rough terrain are more likely to experience rebellion because the rebel movement is better able to maintain the movement over time, James Fearon and David Laitin argue.[6] Cullen Hendrix expands on this argument, suggesting that rough terrain has indirect negative effects on state capacity, including limiting the state's ability to collect taxes, which in turn ostracizes local communities and makes rebellion more likely.[7] South Sudan's rough terrain and lack of infrastructure meant that large areas were isolated, allowing southern rebels to operate more freely. In Timor-Leste, mountainous terrain in the center of the island served as a safe haven for separatist guerrilla fighters for many years. However, it should be noted that if rough terrain provides access challenges to a central state, the newly independent state will have to overcome those same obstacles when it seeks to provide services to its population.

If a region is rich in natural resources, it increases the incentives for secession and provides a group with the means to fight for it. Paul Collier and Anke Hoeffler argue that the presence of natural resources provides greater opportunities for rebel groups to make money through primary commodity exports, creates more possibilities for corruption, increases the incentives for secession, and raises exposure to shocks, therefore increasing the chances of conflict.[8] Of the case studies selected for this volume, South Sudan and Timor-Leste have the most significant reserves of natural resources. Khartoum exploited the oil deposits in the south without consulting the southern regional government, and it was some time before the south benefited from the proceeds of its natural resources. However, secessionist southern leaders frequently heralded the economic benefits the new country would reap from the country's oil wealth, which stirred expectations among the population of great wealth post-independence. A similar situation existed in East Timor. The people of East Timor did not benefit much from oil deposits because the Indonesian armed forces tightly controlled financial transfers from Indonesia to the island and also monopolized lucrative coffee exports. Therefore, although the island's natural resources did not contribute greatly to secessionists' finances, they also helped create expectations of the wealth that would come when they gained control over the assets.

The region's geostrategic relevance to great powers is critically important. Powerful states' external and domestic interests impact who is admitted into the international community.[9] If recognizing a new state improves regional stability in an area of strategic importance to a great power, or if it helps destabilize a great power's adversaries in the region, recognition is more likely. Western nations feared the destabilizing impact of continuing violence in Europe and were also keen to weaken Russia's influence in the Balkans. As such, Western powers had various incentives to encourage Kosovo's secession from Serbia, a pro-Russian power. Conversely, the United States opposed Bangladeshi independence for many years because it needed to maintain favorable relations with Pakistan, a key player in its strategy to forge better relations with China. India's desire to weaken Pakistan incentivized it to support secessionist Bangladeshis. Both the United States' and India's policies were motivated by the second-order effects Bangladesh's independence would have.

The lack of international attention given to the Eritrean struggle for independence can be explained at least partially by the fact that Eritrea did not occupy a position of critical strategic importance for any great powers. International powers only recognized Eritrea when facts on the ground dictated it. The United States' inaction over rights violations in East Timor further reveals the importance of broader geostrategic factors. It was only at the end of the Cold War, when U.S. calculations about the threat of a new Marxist state emerging dissipated, that the United States supported Timorese self-determination.

Domestic vulnerabilities also play a role in international powers' decisions to recognize a new state or not. Russia's fears over its own domestic secessionist movements are one of its motives for continuing to oppose various self-determination movements around the world, including refusing to recognize Kosovo's independence.[10] The United States' calculations about recognizing new states' independence have not been similarly affected by domestic concerns, not having faced a serious domestic secessionist movement during the period of study.

Great powers' strategic calculations about recognizing new states are critical because international recognition brings various benefits. As well as the political benefits of gaining a seat in the United Nations and the ability to form official diplomatic relations with other states, new states also unlock economic support from the World Bank and other international financial institutions after achieving international recognition. For some self-determination groups that do not occupy a position of geostrategic importance to great powers, but that fulfill most other theoretical standards of statehood, such as Somaliland, international recognition remains elusive.

After a group has gained independence, a great power will not let it fail if it holds a position of critical importance. Western nations are willing to provide continued support to help build Kosovo's state capacity because they can simply not afford a return to large-scale violence in Europe. For Australia, the same is true of Timor-Leste. Canberra's swift deployment of peacekeeping forces to Timor-Leste when violence broke out in 2006 shows its enduring commitment. Eritrea and South Sudan, however, neither occupy key positions in great states' national security strategies nor have any powerful neighbors who are prepared to commit high levels of support to prevent failure.

A new state's neighbors gain important influence over its ability to export goods and develop a prosperous economy if it is landlocked. Sudan maintained a high degree of leverage over South Sudan's oil industry as the south initially relied entirely on the north's export pipeline to generate revenue. When South Sudan decided to shut down oil production in protest against the price of using Sudan's pipeline, South Sudan's economy was ruined and it was left virtually bankrupt. Should the Kurdish Regional Government gain independence from Iraq, it would likely face similar challenges as it would be forced to rely on cooperation with its neighbors to export oil.

Many of these factors cannot be quantified in a meaningful way as great power's geostrategic interests can shift as the international environment changes. However, we can investigate the impact of a new state being landlocked and whether it does reduce its economic opportunities or not.

HYPOTHESIS 1: IF A NEW STATE IS LANDLOCKED, IT WILL BE
LESS SUCCESSFUL POST-INDEPENDENCE

A binary variable for whether a new state is landlocked or not was created. Twenty-six states in the dataset are landlocked and 44 are not:

Landlocked	Frequency	Percent
Not landlocked	264	62.86
Landlocked	156	37.14
Total	420	100.00

When we ran the statistical analysis, neither model showed a strong correlation between a state being landlocked and any of the proxy variables for success. Although we may not have expected any relationship between a state being landlocked and change in infant mortality rates, change in displacement, or levels of violence, it is interesting that it does not appear to have any statistically significant impact on economic performance.[11] The ability to export goods via sea does not appear to be a significant boon to a new state. As such, the data indicate that Hypothesis 1 is incorrect—being landlocked may stifle self-determination groups' ability to gain independence, but it does not make a new state less successful post-independence.

Method of Gaining Independence

While some groups are able to gain independence through a nonviolent campaign or a legislative process, many are forced to take up arms and wage a violent struggle. The violence and destruction wrought by conflict mean that states are often born in incredibly challenging circumstances. Two-thirds of all administrative buildings in the newly independent Timor-Leste were destroyed in the fight for independence, and it was born one of the poorest countries on earth. After the 30-year struggle with Ethiopia, Eritrean leader Isaias Afewerki declared, "when you see such destruction you forget about victory."[12] Meanwhile, the loss to human capital through death and displacement is often severe. The Bangladeshi war for independence resulted in the displacement of approximately 7 million refugees, and conflict in South Sudan displaced over a quarter of the population. Conflict can also stifle economic development as it diverts resources from productive activities to military operations.

However, engaging in an armed struggle for independence may actually benefit a new state in certain respects. Charles Tilly famously wrote that states not only make war, but wars also make states.[13] Groups that successfully wage war must develop the administrative capacity to mobilize resources and extract the revenue they need to fight, and these systems can be incorporated into the new state.[14] For example, the EPLF developed complex systems of administration in territory that it liberated from Ethiopia and these structures became an integral part of independent Eritrea's system of governance. In East Timor, the FRETILIN resistance network combined paramilitary guerrilla groups with local village leaders, coalescing various sources of governance and social organization in a structure that resembled a proto-state. In both cases, the shared experiences of conflict helped unite the population and introduce new forms of administration.

Yet, widespread coverage of violent self-determination struggles belies the fact that secession is generally becoming more peaceful. Just 13 percent of all cases of secession between 1945 and 2016 were violent, as opposed to 78 percent of those that occurred between 1816 and 1945.[15] Many self-determination groups gain greater autonomy or full independence through peaceful negotiations with their rump states. States dealing with separatist groups calculate the concessions they are prepared to make to those groups based on a number of domestic and external factors. If the number of ethnic groups in a country is high, the central state is less likely to make concessions to a group seeking self-determination.[16] If the central state lacks the resources to adopt economic or political policies that provide incentives for the group to remain in the state, secession is more likely.[17] Additionally, if a central state judges that great powers and other foreign states will impose punitive measures if it does not grant a group independence, secession becomes more likely.

HYPOTHESIS 2: IF A STATE IS BORN IN A CONTEXT OF VIOLENCE,
IT WILL BE LESS SUCCESSFUL

This study examines levels of violence at secession to ascertain the context in which independence was achieved. Following the standard convention,

(0) is recorded when secession was not violent (fewer than 25 deaths occurred in the given year); (1) is recorded for low levels of violence (25–999 deaths); and (2) is recorded for high levels of violence (1,000 or more deaths).

This study uses Ryan Griffiths's data from his 2015 article in *International Organization*.[18] Fifty-eight countries recorded no armed conflict; eight countries recorded 25–999 deaths in the year of secession; and four countries recorded more than 1,000 deaths in the year of secession.

Violent Secession	Frequency	Percent
Not violent	348	82.86
Low levels of violence	48	11.43
High levels of violence	24	5.71
Total	420	100.00

The regressions indicate that if secession occurs in a context of high violence, higher levels of violence will continue to plague the new country in the years following independence. Although there is no strong relationship between the two in Model 1, when the higher number of observations was investigated in Model 2, a highly statistically significant relationship emerged.

However, there was no statistically significant relationship between higher levels of violence at secession and GDP per capita growth, change in infant mortality rates, or even change in levels of displacement. The data thus indicate that Hypothesis 2 is incorrect. A state born in a context of violence does not seem to have a negative or positive bearing on most of the indicators of success we investigated. This lack of impact may imply that the positive and negative factors of gaining independence through violence actually cancel each other out, as the academic literature shows.

Peacekeeping Missions

During the late twentieth century, the United Nations came to play an increasingly important peacekeeping role around the world. Peacekeeping missions underwent a shift in the late 1980s, transforming from predominantly military operations to take on more of a peace-building role that included oversight of the implementation of peace settlements. Many of these missions were created to protect and support new states, although their mandates varied significantly. Michael Doyle and Nicholas Sambanis argue that the United Nations should expand its role in launching development projects after civil wars, concluding that economic development is the best way to decrease the risk of renewed violence in the long run.[19]

Scholars have identified a number of factors that make peacekeeping missions more successful. Doyle and Sambanis highlight the necessity of giving peacekeeping missions appropriate authority and adequate resources. Jacques Koko and Essoh Essis argue that longer conflicts typically lead to more successful peacekeeping missions because the United Nations has more time to prepare for its missions.[20] They also find that the greater the number of UN Security Council members involved in the peacekeeping operation, the more successful it is. They highlight U.S. spending on peacekeeping missions as being particularly effective. Finally, they note that the United Nations has enjoyed greater levels of success in interstate conflicts than in intrastate conflicts.

There is no one-size-fits-all model for peacekeeping operations. Lise Morjé-Howard highlights the importance of local context and argues that the principal factor in the success of a peacekeeping mission is when peacekeepers learn and adapt their strategies to their environment instead of imposing preconceived notions.[21] Indeed, if international actors rush to establish democratic governments and punish outgoing leaders, they sometimes cause greater levels of conflict than they avert.[22]

International peacekeeping missions with strong mandates were deployed to both Timor-Leste and Kosovo, with international bodies building state institutions and then gradually transferring them to local administrators. Discussing the case of Timor-Leste, Simon Chesterman emphasizes the importance of choosing local partners carefully and involving them early in the policymaking process.[23] If international administrators do not involve a cross section of local actors, certain sections of society could experience long-term exclusion in the new state. Engaging nonstate actors, and especially armed groups, is key to mitigating the potential for renewed conflict.[24]

The Kosovo experience shows that sustained international attention and a peacekeeping mission with a strong mandate can build a viable and largely democratic state within a decade, although its sovereignty is still not complete, and international actors continue to play key roles in providing security, justice, and financing.

Given that the success of peacekeeping missions is highly dependent on context, investigating whether or not a peacekeeping mission was deployed is not sufficient. We need to explore the authority a mission is given instead.

HYPOTHESIS 3: IF A PEACEKEEPING MISSION WITH A STRONGER MANDATE IS DEPLOYED TO A NEW STATE, IT WILL BE MORE SUCCESSFUL

The data for international peacekeeping missions were taken from a dataset compiled by Mark Mullenbach for Harvard University.[25] Data are available for all 70 countries in the dataset, because when a country was not included in Mullenbach's dataset, it was assumed that no international peacekeeping mission was deployed there.

For international peacekeeping missions, a score of (0) was given to each year in which no third-party peacekeeping mission was deployed to the country in question; (1) was given to each year in which a third-party peacekeeping mission was deployed with a role limited to military observation or monitoring; (2) was given to peacekeeping missions that had a limited military role, including interpositionary deployment or humanitarian protection; and (3) was given to missions that included full-scale military deployment to maintain law and order, protect civilians, or provide security for key installations.

Peacekeeping	Frequency	Percent
No mission	359	85.48
Observation mission	6	1.43
Limited military mission	14	3.33
Full-scale military mission	41	9.76
Total	420	100.00

The data do not show any strong relationships between the strength of the peacekeeping mission and our indicators of success. In Model 1, a statistically significant but weak relationship emerged between annual change in infant mortality rates and the strength of the peacekeeping mandate. The stronger the mandate of the peacekeeping mission, the greater the annual reduction in infant mortality rates. This relationship could be explained by the fact that peacekeeping missions help improve access to health care facilities by providing protection and reducing violence.

It is surprising that there is no relationship between a stronger peacekeeping mission and lower levels of violence or a reduction in overall levels of displacement. The lack of correlation may be explained by the difficulty of separating causation from correlation. Peacekeeping missions with strong mandates are often deployed to countries that already have high levels of violence. However, the lack of correlation between peacekeeping missions and annual change in displacement is harder to explain. It may be that the presence of even the most robust peacekeeping missions is not enough to convince people to return to their homes. Some may also be unable to do so if their homes were destroyed as post-conflict reconstruction is often a lengthy process.

The data indicate that Hypothesis 3 is incorrect. The deployment of peacekeeping missions with stronger mandates is not associated with greater levels of success in the period after a new state gained independence. The benefits of a peacekeeping mission could be felt beyond the time period covered in this study.

International Aid

A lively debate exists about whether high levels of international aid are positive or negative for new states. Some scholars have drawn comparisons between states built through international aid and rentier states. Aid hinders the development of a meaningful social contract between the government and its citizens and also disrupts market efficiency, they argue. Nicolas Lemay-Hébert and Syed Mansoob Murshed examine Kosovo's experience with UNMIK and conclude that the international state-building project provided Kosovo with such a high source of nonproduced income that it left the state less accountable to its people and less interested in or able to develop an internationally competitive productive base.[26] International aid can make new governments more accountable to foreign governments than to their own populations. Although South Sudan received vast amounts of aid after gaining independence, the South Sudanese government was forced to adhere to donors' uncoordinated and at times competing agendas rather than the population's real needs. Furthermore, aid was not delivered according to benchmarks. When the government discovered there were no negative repercussions of not using funds effectively, corruption increased and aid became even less impactful. When aid is not channeled through local institutions, a parallel public sector can emerge that is led by donor staff rather than local bureaucrats.

When aid is provided in a bottom-up manner, building on preexisting informal systems of governance, it can help strengthen new institutions.[27] Indeed, if aid is provided through the formal budget process and runs through domestic institutions, it can serve to bolster their capacity. Assessing the success of USAID state-building operations, Max Boot and Michael Miklaucic conclude that the aid organization should focus on state-building and not on service provision since "successful states are not successful because they provide public goods; they provide public goods because they are successful."[28] They argue that less should be spent on poverty alleviation, global health, biodiversity, and women's empowerment, and more should be spent on building security forces, a professional civil service, and financial mechanisms to raise and spend revenues effectively.

The case studies support the argument that providing large quantities of international aid is not an effective way of ensuring success. South Sudan is testament to this, with severe ongoing humanitarian emergencies despite having received billions of dollars in international aid. Instead, lower levels of aid can be more effective if they are spent in a way that helps buttress preexisting systems of government, helps ensure that the state's security forces monopolize the use of violence, helps develop a professional bureaucracy, and supports the development of the state's revenue-collecting capabilities.

HYPOTHESIS 4: THE GREATER A NEW STATE'S RELIANCE ON
INTERNATIONAL AID, THE LESS SUCCESSFUL IT WILL BE

To investigate a new state's reliance on international aid, this study examines the percentage of official development assistance (ODA) of a state's gross national income (GNI). A score of (0) was given to countries in which less than 5 percent of GNI came from ODA; a score of (1) was given to countries in which 5 to 20 percent of GNI came from ODA; and a score of (2) was given to countries in which over 20 percent of GNI came from ODA. The data for ODA as a percentage of GNI came from the World Bank and are available for at least some years for 51 of the 70 countries in the dataset. Of the 277 observations, a score of (0) was awarded in 173 instances, a score of (1) was awarded in 83 instances, and a score of (2) was awarded in 21 instances.

Index of International Aid	Frequency	Percent	Cumulative
0	173	62.45	62.45
1	83	29.96	92.42
2	21	7.58	100.00
Total	277	100.00	

The relationship between the various indicators of success and the proportion of a new state's GNI coming from official development assistance (ODA) is very weak. The only statistically significant result was a weak relationship between the percentage of ODA in a state's GNI and annual change in displacement. Greater reliance on international aid was associated with a slight reduction in annual displacement. This relationship could be explained by the fact that people believe a new state will be able to support them if they receive a large degree of international assistance, and so are willing to return to their homes.

Given that the literature suggests interventions to reduce infant mortality are a common feature of international aid and that aid can have an artificial impact on economic growth, it is interesting that greater reliance on international aid does not have a statistically significant impact on infant mortality rates or annual GDP per capita growth. The data indicate that if a new state relies more heavily on international aid, there is no consistent positive or negative impact on its performance after independence, meaning that Hypothesis 4 is also incorrect. Although missing data mean fewer observations were able to be tested in this case, this reaffirms the fact that a new state's reliance on aid is not the decisive factor. A state could be highly dependent on aid, but if it is spent in an effective manner, that is not a bad thing. Therefore, this regression shows that how people choose to manage aid is what is most important.

Dependence on Natural Resources

Natural resources provide a new state with revenue that could be used to build state capacity and improve public services. The Timorese government recognized that a considerable proportion of government revenues would come from oil revenues, and so sought advice from Norwegian oil experts when setting up the national petroleum fund to introduce strict accountability and transparency measures. The fund, rather than the executive, absorbs all receipts from oil exports, and revenues are invested in capital markets. Only interest on the assets can be withdrawn.

However, not all new countries have managed their natural resources as well. Rentier state theory suggests that too great a reliance on natural resource rent has a negative impact on a state's development. Without needing to tax its population, the social contract between the government and its people is weaker and the government is less accountable. Governments are usually incentivized to promote economic growth because they can extract more from taxpayers who are prosperous. As such, a government that does not have to tax the population is less incentivized to create conditions for strong economic growth. In addition, states do not need to create complex bureaucratic apparatuses for tax collection if they enjoy high levels of rent.[29] A further negative effect of large natural resource reserves is the opportunities it provides for corruption. Corruption is one of the greatest challenges new states face, as economic and political institutions are often weak and in many cases the state does not have the authority to impose the rule of law. As we have seen, this was a critical factor in South Sudan's descent into chaos and violence.

Even states that manage their resources most prudently are vulnerable to downward shifts in international markets. Timor-Leste may have managed its oil wealth responsibly, but the government is still heavily reliant on oil receipts and falling oil prices threaten the country's long-term economic stability.

Data for levels of corruption are not available for the majority of the countries included in the dataset, but we can investigate the link between a new state's reliance on natural resource rents and its post-independence success. This study uses data from the World Bank showing natural resource revenues as a percentage of a new state's GDP. Data are available for one or more years for 37 of the 70 countries included in the dataset, and there are 175 observations.

HYPOTHESIS 5: THE GREATER A NEW STATE'S RELIANCE ON REVENUES FROM NATURAL RESOURCES, THE LESS SUCCESSFUL IT IS

We may have assumed that Timor-Leste was an outlier in terms of how well it managed its natural resources, but the data do not support this. Instead, they do not show any statistically significant relationships between too great a reliance on natural resources and the indicators we chose to represent a new state's success. It could be that the relationship between a new state's reliance on natural resource revenues and its success is not linear. Too great a reliance on natural resource rent is likely to be detrimental, as discussed above, but also not having any revenues from natural resources could be detrimental to a new state's success as the government lacks a source of funding to finance its state-building activities. Kosovo exemplifies the pitfalls of having no natural resources to rely on. Its economy is still underdeveloped and remains heavily dependent on international support. Finally, it should be noted that many data are missing, and the regression could only be run on 107 observations. Therefore, although the data do not support Hypothesis 5, showing neither a negative nor a positive relationship between greater reliance on natural resource rent, we should be careful not to over interpret this.

RESULTS

Table 8.1. Model 1 Regression Results

	Change in Displacement	Change in Infant Mortality	GDP Annual Growth	Battlefield Deaths
Landlocked	0.01 (0.07)	−0.01 (0.01)	7.88 (57.45)	240.76 (489.23)
Violent secession	0.07 (0.05)	0 (0.01)	−25.86 (45.95)	−52.38 (380.19)
Peacekeeping mandate	0.01 (0.03)	−0.01** (0)	22.23 (23.01)	18.99 (181.67)
International aid	−0.00* (0)	0 (0)	−0.11 (2.7)	4.59 (20.61)
Natural resource revenue	0 (0)	0 (0)	−0.95 (2.57)	−9.72 (19.52)
Former colony?	0.04 (0.07)	0.02 (0.01)	0.69 (67.22)	−474.48 (545.29)
Constant	0.18 (0.34)	−0.03*** (0.01)	30.28 (60.99)	489.47 (491.53)
Observations	104	104	110	124
Countries	27	27	28	29

Standard errors are in parentheses. *$p<.10$; **$p<.05$; ***$p<.01$.

Table 8.2. Model 2 Regression Results

	Change in Displacement	Change in Infant Mortality	GDP Annual Growth	Battlefield Deaths
Landlocked	−0.71 (1)	0.01	−35.93	11.62
		(0.01)	(40.02)	(259.13)
Violent secession	−0.51	0	−26.28	652.36***
	(0.93)	(0.01)	(35.99)	(232.93)
Peacekeeping mandate	−0.03	0	3.54	137.44
	(0.53)	(0)	(20.95)	(119.18)
Former colony?	0.95	0.02***	−71.73*	−0.79
	(0.99)	(0.01)	(41.79)	(259.74)
Constant	0.46	−0.04***	95.18**	115.53
	(0.91)	(0.01)	(41.28)	(250.79)
Observations	239	295	285	409
Countries	63	61	62	70

Standard errors are in parentheses. $*p<.10; **p<.05; ***p<.01$.

CONCLUSION

This chapter explored what, if anything, we can learn from analyzing dozens of case studies of newly independent states, versus the handful that we analyzed in depth. According to our data, the answer is not so much. The lack of results may seem disappointing at first, but in fact it reinforces just how important historical context, local dynamics, and the impact of unexpected events are to a new state's success. There may be a bit of chance involved as well. The experiences of the five case studies corroborate these findings.

It is not sufficient to say that new countries that are landlocked perform worse than those with sea access. Although it would be logical to assume that sea access provides a wider range of economic opportunities, our data do not reveal it to have any impact on economic growth. However, geostrategic location is a critically significant factor of success because of how it relates to a new state's ability to secure international diplomatic, military, and humanitarian support. If great powers have strong incentives to maintain the stability of the region in which a new state is located, they are likely to devote substantially more support to ensure its stability. On the flip side, great powers rarely devote serious diplomatic attention or resources to new states that are in less important regions.

It is not true that states born out of violence will go on to perform worse. Somewhat counterintuitively, violence seems to produce opportunities as well as risks. Waging a successful armed conflict against a central state often requires a self-determination movement to develop sophisticated administrative capacities that serve it well after it has gained independence. However, the high levels of violence associated with some secessionist struggles mean new states emerge in incredibly challenging circumstances. Our data imply that the negative impacts of violent secession balance out the positives, meaning violent secession ultimately has a limited effect on a new state's overall success.

Even if an international peacekeeping mission with a comprehensive mandate is deployed to a new state, success cannot be assured. The cases of Timor-Leste and Kosovo indicate that if international peacekeeping missions have broad mandates and are sustained over time, they can lead to the creation of viable and democratic states. But our data show that this is not always the case. Therefore, the data support academic studies that have shown that international peacekeeping missions are only successful if they are sensitive to the local context.

Finally, relying on international aid or rent from natural resources is not an inherently bad thing. The absolute amount of aid provided is not the most important factor in terms of its impact. Instead, the decisive factor is how it is spent. Aid must be provided in a coordinated, focused, and sustained manner. Timor-Leste and South Sudan show vastly different experiences with managing resource wealth. Like international aid, revenues from natural resources can prove a boon for new states and help foster economic growth and stability if they are managed effectively. However, if they are not managed in a transparent and accountable manner, they can fuel corruption and unhealthy economic practices.

A few important caveats must be made about the quantitative element of this study. The lack of statistical relationships could be a result of problems with the data, including missing or inaccurate data. It is also impossible to cover all aspects of success in a quantitative manner, but the indicators we chose did cover different facets of a state's authority, capacity, and legitimacy.

The case studies in this volume show that new states can have very different experiences in their infancy. This chapter has ultimately shown that the conclusions from the case studies cannot necessarily be generalized when looking into every state that gained independence since 1960. There is no one-size-fits-all approach for making a new state successful. This puts the onus on leaders of self-determination movements and leaders of world powers to make effective decisions to nurture the conditions that lead to success.

NOTES

1. The year 1960 was chosen for practical rather than theoretical reasons, as many data (such as from the World Bank) are only available for new countries after 1960. At the time of writing, 2016 was the most recent year for which data were available for the world's newest country, South Sudan.

2. For example, Transparency International only has data for the perception of corruption starting in 1995.

3. D. D. Reidpath and P. Alloyet, "Infant Mortality Rate as an Indicator of Population Health," *Journal of Epidemiology and Community Health* 57, no. 5 (2003): 344–346.

4. Many of the states show zero displacement (whether as IDPs or refugees) for the year of record. Because the figures are in the thousands, this does not mean that no people were displaced at all.

5. Jason Sorens, *Secessionism: Identity, Interest, and Strategy* (Montreal: McGill-Queens University Press, 2012).

6. James Fearon and David Laitin, "Ethnicity, Insurgency, and Civil War," *American Political Science Review* 97, no. 1 (2003): 75–90.

7. Cullen Hendrix, "Head for the Hills? Rough Terrain, State Capacity, and Civil War Onset," *Civil Wars* 13, no. 4 (2011): 345–370.

8. Paul Collier and Anke Hoeffler, "Greed and Grievance in Civil War," *Oxford Economic Papers* 56, no. 4 (October 2004): 588.

9. Bridget Coggins, "Friends in High Places: International Politics and the Emergence of States from Secessionism," *International Organization* 65, no. 3 (July 2011): 433–467.

10. Pavel Baev, "Russia's Stance against Secessions: From Chechnya to Kosovo," *International Peacekeeping* 6, no. 3 (1999): 73–94.

11. The study treats a statistically significant relationship as one with a p-value of less than 0.050.

12. Jane Perlez, "After 3-Decade War in Ethiopia, Eritrean Finds Victory Is Somber," *New York Times*, June 10, 1991.

13. Charles Tilly, "War Making and State Making as Organized Crime," in *Bringing the State Back In*, ed. Peter Evans, Dietrich Rueschemeyer, and Theda Skocpol (Cambridge: Cambridge University Press, 1985).

14. Marina Ottaway, "Nation Building," *Foreign Policy* 132 (2002): 16–24.

15. Ryan Griffiths, *Age of Secession: The International and Domestic Determinants of State Birth* (Cambridge: Cambridge University Press, 2016), 48.

16. Barbara Walter, "Information, Uncertainty, and the Decision to Secede," *International Organization* 60, no. 1 (2016): 105–135.

17. Sorens, *Secessionism*, 6.

18. Ryan Griffiths, "Between Dissolution and Blood: How Administrative Lines and Categories Shape Secessionist Outcomes," *International Organization* 69, no. 3 (Summer 2015): 731–751.

19. Michael Doyle and Nicholas Sambanis, *Making War and Building Peace: United Nations Peace Operations* (Princeton, NJ: Princeton University Press, 2006).

20. Jacques Koko and Essoh Essis, *Determinants of Success in UN Peacekeeping Operations* (Lanham, MD: University Press of America, 2012).

21. Lise Morjé-Howard, *UN Peacekeeping in Civil Wars* (Cambridge: Cambridge University Press, 2007).

22. Nicolas Lemay-Hebert, "Rethinking Weberian Approaches to Statebuilding," in *The Routledge Handbook of International Statebuilding*, ed. David Chandler and Timothy Sisk (New York: Routledge, 2013), 3–14.

23. Simon Chesterman, "East Timor in Transition: Self-Determination, State-Building and the United Nations," *International Peacekeeping* 9, no. 1 (Spring 2002): 45–76.

24. Claudia Hofmann and Ulrich Schneckener, "Engaging Non-State Armed Actors in State and Peace-Building: Options and Strategies," *International Review of the Red Cross* 93, no. 883 (September 2011).

25. Mark Mullenbach, "Third-Party Peacekeeping Missions, 1946–2014 (Version 3.1)," *Harvard Dataverse* 1 (2017).

26. Nicolas Lemay-Hébert and Syed Mansoob Murshed, "Rentier Statebuilding in a Post-Conflict Economy: The Case of Kosovo," *Development and Change* 47, no. 3 (2016): 517–541.

27. Achim Wennmann, *Grasping the Strengths of Fragile States: Aid Effectiveness between 'Top-Down' and 'Bottom-Up' Statebuilding*, Working Paper No. 6 (Geneva: Centre on Conflict, Development and Peacebuilding, The Graduate Institute, 2010).

28. Max Boot and Michael Miklaucic, "Reconfiguring USAID for State-Building," Policy Innovation Memorandum No. 57, Council on Foreign Relations, June 22, 2016.

29. Deborah Brautigam, Odd-Helge Fjeldstad, and Mick Moore, *Taxation and State-Building in Developing Countries: Capacity and Consent* (Cambridge: Cambridge University Press, 2008).

9. SELF-DETERMINATION AND U.S. CHOICES
Will Todman

Nine days after the Democratic Republic of Timor-Leste declared independence in late November 1975, Indonesia crushed it. The timing was no coincidence. On December 5, President Gerald Ford and Secretary of State Henry Kissinger visited President Suharto in Jakarta and signaled that the United States would not oppose an Indonesian invasion of the aspiring state.[1] The Americans' logic was that supporting Timorese self-determination would have jeopardized the United States' strategic relationship with Indonesia, a key ally in Southeast Asia and a bulwark against the spread of communism, while bringing no obvious benefits. Permission in hand, Suharto's troops swept into East Timor the following day.

But over the next 15 years, Indonesia's increasingly violent repression of the Timorese and a changing global context ate away at U.S. support. Amid mounting international outrage following the Santa Cruz massacre in 1991, Congress restricted weapons sales to Indonesia. Under the administration of President George H. W. Bush, the State Department and the Pentagon both opposed these punitive measures and strove to maintain strong bilateral ties, given Indonesia's strategic importance. Even so, competing U.S. government priorities often meant bureaucracies pulled policy in contradictory directions. When it came into office in 1993, the Clinton administration conditioned military assistance to Indonesia on human rights performance, and it increased diplomatic pressure to reach an autonomy settlement. The end of the Cold War reduced fears of Timor-Leste emerging as a communist state, and the United States went from being an opponent of Timorese independence to a supporter. Meanwhile, the 1997 Asian financial crisis increased economic pressure on Indonesia, and the financial burden of occupying East Timor became increasingly unjustifiable. The context continued to shift. Finally, with both U.S. and UN support, Timor-Leste gained its independence in 2002.

The United States government can neither engender new states nor prevent them from coming into being, but it does possess a range of policy tools to influence the trajectory of new or aspiring states. While U.S. history creates a certain amount of empathy for self-determination groups, as a general rule the U.S. government views most independence movements skeptically. This is appropriate, in part because few such movements are viable. Economies are small or fragile (or both), the cause enjoys limited internal support, or the forces arrayed against it are too massive.

In addition, the United States is tied diplomatically to some 190 countries around the world, and it usually privileges intergovernmental ties over those with nongovernmental groups. Supporting secession would threaten U.S. relations not only with countries fighting U.S.-backed movements, but also with other countries that feared that the United States might come to support secessionists elsewhere. For the United States, some sort of decentralization or autonomy arrangement is often a less costly option. It is also more agreeable to partner governments and reduces the risk of regional instability. However, exceptions can occur when secessionist movements take root in countries where the United States has more difficult relations, or where repression of minority groups or some other humanitarian factor weighs heavily in the scale.

In order to shape U.S. policy, the United States must first determine if the outcome of an independence movement would have a bearing on U.S. national or strategic interests. For most self-determination movements around the world, the answer is no. If it is yes, U.S. policymakers will then have to confront a series of difficult choices throughout the movement's trajectory. Lessons from the case studies in this volume provide insights into where U.S. influence may be most effective, which tools can be used, and when international partners must be mobilized behind the U.S. strategy.

It is useful to consider three phases through which such movements pass. For the United States, each phase has different tools and presents different opportunities and considerations. In the early phase—when the group first emerges—it rarely makes sense to support independence, and U.S. efforts generally should be dedicated to resolving grievances. In the intermediate phase—when the group is taking serious steps toward independence—the United States has the most options of offering support or discouragement. By the late phase—when independence has been won or nearly so—the United States should focus principally on how to shape the terms under which the fledgling state joins the international system. At each stage, the United States must work to tie regional and international organizations and partners to whatever effort they decide to pursue to share the burdens effectively and add to the weight of its advocacy.

Support for—or opposition to—independence movements is a fraught endeavor for the United States. Like the movement in Timor-Leste, independence efforts tend to outlast both the circumstances and the contexts in which they were born, let alone the U.S. administrations that may take a view on their future. Some movements that took shape in the Truman administration are still struggling for their future today; arguably, several date back to the presidency of Woodrow Wilson. In the meantime, the Cold War began and ended, jet travel became mundane, and what was once considered a supercomputer can be found in almost everyone's pocket.

Throughout, U.S. government consensus has often been elusive. Even the most basic question of assessing whether the situation is something that touches on U.S. national security interests often produces disagreements. Influencing self-determination movements also requires tremendous investments, and irrespective of whether the Executive Branch can reach consensus, Congress is often reluctant to authorize large-scale military or civilian funding for such efforts. And Congress can also seek to move U.S. policy on independence movements in the other direction. Powerful constituencies or effective lobbying campaigns may lead Congress to pressure the administration into acting in a one-sided way, even when it is reluctant to do so. What it all amounts to is unclear. Even if the United States and its partners devote sufficient resources and political capital to a cause, the movements often follow unpredictable trajectories with no guarantee of success.

And yet such movements do provide opportunities. They can advance direct U.S. strategic interests, and they can substantially improve humanitarian conditions among oppressed people. Addressing humanitarian conditions not only serves moral imperatives; it also helps reduce fragility and enhance stability. Many self-determination movements are worthy of sustained attention, even if it is unwise to provide unqualified support.

The following sections synthesize the lessons learned from the previous chapters and outline the principal tools of influence U.S. policymakers possess during each phase. Each of these tools has multiple subparts, and it is not within the scope of this chapter to provide a comprehensive list of the precise tools U.S. policymakers possess. Rather, this chapter serves to frame policymakers' choices when approaching self-determination movements and encourage policymakers to think outside their given areas. At the end of the chapter, we present a checklist of factors policymakers can use as a reference to facilitate a more holistic assessment of a new state's performance.

PHASE ONE: THE MOVEMENT EMERGES

When a self-determination movement emerges in an area of importance to U.S. interests, policymakers—in most cases—should work with international partners to bolster the original state's capacity to meet its international commitments and advance the rule of law. In addressing perceptions of economic or political discrimination, the United States can help remove the root causes that animate secession movements. Simply by engaging on the issue, the United States signals its attention, which represents an important aspect of its diplomatic influence.

History shows us that even when significant U.S. resources are committed, independence movements rarely yield outcomes that are aligned with U.S. interests. Still, the United States may benefit in certain cases from encouraging a secessionist movement as a means of countering an adversary, supporting a partner, or advancing other specific interests.

Influencing the Original State

If a leader is struggling to consolidate his or her power within a state, the mere fact of U.S. engagement can confer significant legitimacy and bolster the leader's standing. In addition to diplomatic engagement, the United States can also work to mobilize international partners to join it in providing the original state with economic incentives. Offers of increased military support could also encourage the original state to live up to its international commitments. Concurrently, U.S. policymakers can raise the cost of the original state's persecution of a minority or a region by threatening to implement punitive political or economic measures.

However, threats should be measured because maintaining bilateral ties with the original state is essential to sustaining influence. The case studies show that at this early stage, self-determination groups are unlikely to represent a serious threat to U.S. strategic interests.

Influencing the Self-Determination Group

Secessionists gain stature when international powers engage them. U.S. policymakers should be particularly aware of what actions enhance secessionists' legitimacy, and they should be alert to what signals they are sending about the possibility of more substantial U.S. assistance in the future. Given the United States' diplomatic power and political influence, even hints of support may encourage a group to radicalize its aims and to accelerate a push toward independence. Raising the specter of independence could have dangerous implications for the United States' relations with its allies. For example, U.S. support for Syrian Kurds fighting the government of Bashar al-Assad in 2017–2018 raised Turkey's fears of Turkish Kurds' secession, prompting the Turkish government to take military action against the Syrian Kurds and drastically increasing the chance of a direct military confrontation between two NATO allies. The Syrian Kurds also withdrew for a time from the U.S.-led battle against the Islamic State group to defend themselves from the Turkish assault, weakening the U.S. military effort.

At the early stage, U.S. officials should gather as much information as possible from open sources, intelligence reporting, and diplomatic engagement to assess a group's aims, capabilities, and level of unity at this stage. They can then judge the speed at which a group may attempt to pursue independence and the likelihood of its success.

In certain situations, it may be in the United States' strategic interests to provide quiet support to a self-determination group to encourage it to mobilize. An adversary's ability to pursue policies that counter U.S. interests is reduced when it is forced to commit political and economic resources to preserve domestic stability. Weakening the original state may also be a means of reducing a rival great power's influence in an area of strategic competition. However, Congress may prove unwilling to support these efforts, and this kind of support also carries great risks. The United States could inadvertently get drawn into a civil war that is out of its control, as was the case with Syria; it could result in an alliance with an unsavory partner, as was the case with apartheid South Africa through the United States' support for UNITA in Angola; and it could risk emboldening violators of human rights and destabilizing the broader region, as was the result of support for the Contras in Central America.

Protecting Regional Interests

It is essential that U.S. policymakers consider the politics of neighboring states when assessing their options. Nearby states may host groups from the same minority and could fear a domino effect as they also agitate for self-determination. If the United States opposes the group's independence, U.S. diplomats must clearly articulate that opposition to neighboring states and to key regional powers. The U.S. government should use its memberships in multilateral organizations and its relationships with regional organizations to mobilize the international community to help maintain regional stability.

In situations in which policymakers determine that it is beneficial for the United States to support a group's secession over its relationship with the original state's government, U.S. diplomats, together with other parts of the U.S. government, should seek to secure the support of key regional allies and friends, especially those powers that share borders with the separatist region. The case studies show that these states will become critical conduits of U.S. and international support to the self-determination group, for example, through military training, funneling arms to separatists, providing their leaders with safe haven, and exerting other forms of diplomatic and economic pressure on the original state. Policymakers should consider whether it is beneficial or necessary to offer increased economic or political incentives to regional states bordering the secessionist region to support U.S. aims.

PHASE TWO: APPROACHING INDEPENDENCE

If grievances are not effectively resolved, a group's efforts may gain momentum and it could take concrete steps toward independence. At this intermediate stage, the United States has a wide range of options to offer support or discouragement, and its overriding priority should be to protect U.S. security interests given the heightened risk of armed conflict. U.S. policymakers should wield tools of influence more forcefully with both the original state and the self-determination group. As the stakes rise, disputes between U.S. principals regarding approaches are more likely, with some favoring the use of more carrots and others more sticks. Gaining the support of Congress for the U.S. government's preferred approach often becomes more delicate at this stage, as civil society groups and other constituencies seeking to influence U.S. policy coalesce and become more public.

Influencing the Original State

U.S. policymakers can attempt to influence the situation by increasing U.S. government support to the original state. Often, the United States, in collaboration with its international partners, should continue attempts to address the root causes of the group's grievances. One option is to offer the original state substantial diplomatic or economic incentives in exchange for granting the minority greater political rights or a more equitable share of the state's economic resources. Meanwhile, increasing military support for the original state or sharing intelligence with friendly services raises the costs to rebels, and this may encourage secessionists to pursue their aims peacefully or even put their push for secession on hold.

If the original state resists calls to improve the minority's situation, the United States can turn to tools of coercion to pressure it to address their grievances. The threat of punitive diplomatic or economic measures may encourage the original state to provide the self-determination group with more rights, an autonomy settlement, or even a legal path to independence. The Obama administration used sanctions (and the promise of sanctions relief) as part of a carrot-and-stick approach to encourage Sudan to end violence in Darfur and the semi-autonomous south, and to allow southerners a referendum on secession. However, the United States should only encourage a legal path to independence when an autonomy arrangement would no longer be sufficient to quell demands for self-determination given the risks and costs associated with independence. As previously mentioned, the case studies show that newly independent states require vast amounts of international support, and even with that support, their trajectory is unpredictable. As such, an arrangement that falls short of independence is nearly always preferable. After legislative mechanisms for secession have been established and the original state has committed to a democratic referendum on independence, international powers lose a key aspect of their influence, as they are forced to support whatever the democratic process delivers. Once the United Kingdom granted Scotland an independence referendum, it was difficult for the Obama administration to make public statements dissuading Scottish independence, even though that outcome would have weakened its key ally.

If the United States is especially favorably disposed to the group seeking self-determination (or especially hostile to the state from which it is seeking independence), the United States has the option to provide direct or indirect military support to the group, overtly or covertly. This can be done independently or in conjunction with allies, with a view to forcing the original state to the negotiating table. Although President Bill Clinton did not favor direct U.S. military action against Sudan, he authorized arms sales to neighboring states that then were funneled covertly across the borders to support southern separatists, increasing pressure on Sudan to negotiate.

When humanitarian considerations weigh most heavily on the scale, direct U.S. military intervention can also be considered. Former secretary of state Madeleine Albright was one of the foremost proponents of armed intervention against Slobodan Milosevic to end the humanitarian crisis in Kosovo. She believed that Milosevic himself was the problem and that engaging in negotiations with Yugoslavia would simply prop him up. The NATO bombing campaign forced Milosevic to withdraw from Kosovo and was ultimately successful in ending severe human rights abuses.

Influencing the Self-Determination Group

U.S. policymakers should quietly begin to build interpersonal relationships with the leaders of the self-determination group and members of its diaspora. Such relationships will prove an important source of influence at a later stage if the self-determination movement continues to mobilize. However, the United States should remain cautious in promising any degree of support to a self-determination group at this stage. The prospect of U.S. support would embolden secessionists, perhaps even to the extent that it makes settlement impossible. A lower-cost option would be for U.S. policymakers to offer to exert diplomatic pressure on the original state to improve the group's rights or to help negotiate an autonomy settlement on certain conditions. Support should encourage the group to maintain a peaceful struggle, to achieve internal consensus on its ambitions, and to commit to pursuing realistic goals. These tools of leverage grant the United States influence over the group's aims and methods. U.S. policymakers should also consider whether providing indirect military or covert support for the self-determination movement would be an effective means to the objective of self-determination success. In the late 1990s, the Central Intelligence Agency (CIA) reportedly trained and supported the Kosovo Liberation Army before the NATO bombing of the Socialist Federal Republic of Yugoslavia (SFRY), providing American military training manuals and field advice to enhance the secessionists' capabilities.[2] Encouraging Kosovo's secession advanced the United States' strategic interests in the broader region as a way to weaken a Russian client preying on U.S. allies.

Protecting Regional Interests

As a group takes steps to approach independence, the U.S. government should devote greater diplomatic pressure to align regional and global powers with the U.S. strategy. In cases of violent struggle, the United States can offer humanitarian support to neighboring states to help them cope with influxes of refugees. Obtaining the support of neighboring states greatly enhances the effectiveness of U.S. policy because a neighboring state could undermine U.S. influence in various ways. For example, it could harbor rebel fighters or allow adversaries to circumvent sanctions. As part of the U.S. strategy, policymakers have the option to consider punitive measures, including economic sanctions, against neighboring states that frustrate U.S. objectives.

PHASE THREE: DECLARING INDEPENDENCE

When a self-determination group declares independence, the United States' principal focus should be on how to work with international partners to shape the terms under which the fledgling state enters the international community. A key element of U.S. leverage is the decision to recognize the new state or not. Without formal U.S. recognition, a new state cannot join the United Nations and is barred from accessing critical support from international financial institutions such as the World Bank and the International Monetary Fund. Somaliland has suffered this fate, despite fulfilling many of the functions of an independent state. If U.S. policymakers decide to recognize the new state, they should be cognizant of the high costs of supporting its development and seek to advance U.S. interests in conjunction with other states by sharing the burden with international and regional allies.

Influencing the Original State

If U.S. policymakers decide that it is in its national security interest to recognize the new state's independence, in most cases they should attempt to maintain bilateral ties with the original state. The case studies show that original states often continue to exert significant influence over the new state. Maintaining all possible sources of leverage and influence over the original state is important. Working with the international community, the United States can provide the original state with incentives to recognize the new group's independence and may consider pursuing coercive action if it resists. In certain historical cases, the threat of military action—either by arming secessionists or conducting air strikes—has proved decisive. For this approach to be successful, the administration will likely need to work with congressional representatives to achieve their backing—if Congress restricts the freedom of military operations to a significant measure, the effectiveness of the military approach will be greatly jeopardized. Without international backing, military action lacks legitimacy and can result in the new state being heavily dependent on the United States, as was the case with Kosovo. Russia continues to block Kosovo's entry into the United Nations, contributing to this dependence. If the United States fails to achieve the backing of the United Nations, U.S. policymakers should at least work to build a substantial international coalition to support its military objectives. However, the military option should be taken with extreme caution. It may be so decisive that it negates the need for negotiations, meaning sensitive issues go unresolved. In Kosovo, military action left no room for serious negotiations about the future of the Serb population, and this has continued to represent a significant challenge for Kosovo's government.

Threats of punitive economic or military measures against the original state, such as sanctions or halting arms sales, may help tip the balance and convince it to recognize the new state's independence. Threats should be combined with incentives, such as promises of humanitarian support, political support, direct investment, and military cooperation, to help incentivize positive behavior and assure the original state of the United States' desire to maintain strong bilateral ties after the group has seceded.

In certain cases, if the group's secession is judged to harm U.S. strategic interests, U.S. policymakers can work with the original state to block secession. As with Indonesia's invasion of East Timor in 1975, providing either tacit or direct support for the original state to quash a secession attempt militarily can prove decisive. Once unleashed, forces that drive a group to seek independence are often difficult to silence. The United States should consider how the group may continue its struggle and weigh the potential impact of a prolonged insurgency on regional stability. If the original state resorts to extreme violence to quash the self-determination group, as Indonesia did in East Timor, it may prove no longer in the United States' interests to continue to provide support.

Influencing the Self-Determination Group

The range of tools of leverage the United States can employ to influence a self-determination group shifts significantly if it is no longer acting to deter independence but rather to shape its entry into the international community. As previously mentioned, the United States can provide strong diplomatic support by choosing to recognize the new state's independence and establishing formal diplomatic relations. The United States should continue to encourage the group's unity, the rule of law, and the creation of mechanisms for peacefully resolving internal disputes, as the case studies show that divisions often arise soon after independence has been won. Such divisions proved especially destructive in South Sudan. Diplomats and other U.S. policymakers should carefully and attentively evaluate leaders' effectiveness, ascertain the level of support they actually enjoy and from where, and be careful not to equate English-language skills or charisma with moderation.

Economic tools are a key way to advance U.S. interests, and the United States has many options regarding the level of support, even if securing consensus within the government to commit the necessary resources is often challenging. At a minimum, the United States should work with the international community to ensure the new state receives humanitarian relief, as well as a means of providing the new state with the necessary conditions of security. In the first instance, this assistance should come through a U.N. or other regional organization. Such support helps prevent the emergence of power vacuums that could threaten regional stability and U.S. security interests. Although policymakers should consider contributing to these activities, building a broad multilateral international coalition is often preferable as it helps share the burden. There may be certain situations in which the stakes for U.S. national security interests are so high that the United States wishes to have a more direct role. In such situations, it should be wary of losing its influence by being part of too broad a coalition with competing interests. Policymakers should also ensure that economic support acts to enhance the new state's capabilities rather than effectively creating a rival bureaucracy that is unaccountable and undermines the state's authority. The case studies show that new states frequently suffer from debilitating corruption, and U.S. policymakers should be careful to ensure that legal checks and balances are implemented to keep it in check. Beyond direct aid, nurturing bilateral trade with the new state and encouraging U.S. investment increases the United States' economic leverage, while also promoting the new state's economic stability.

The United States can also draw upon the Department of Defense to help shape the new state. Specifically, building military-to-military ties with the new state's security apparatuses can reinforce diplomatic efforts to ensure the emergence of effective and accountable government institutions. It can also enhance U.S. officials' ability to detect divisions within those institutions early on and then act to bridge them. Timor-Leste's rapid descent into violence in 2006 reveals how serious such splits can be. The United States also can offer to provide expertise to build the new state's capabilities, encouraging the security services' professionalization and preventing politicization. If the decision is made to build the capacity of the new state's military institutions or support military training and education, the Department of Defense should utilize the U.S. military to do so rather than relying on private contractors, because that will more effectively reinforce the deepening of ties.

Protecting Regional Interests

The United States must also use its tools of influence and mobilize the international community to promote stability in the broader region. Neighboring states should be offered diplomatic or economic incentives for recognizing the new state's independence, where potentially effective. It is in U.S. interests for these states to institutionalize relations, something that failed to happen between Eritrea and Ethiopia and contributed to the return to conflict shortly after independence. The United States should also work with international partners and regional organizations to encourage economic integration in the region as a means of raising the cost of future conflict. The United States can use its diplomatic influence to encourage the international community to join it in offering emergency humanitarian support to neighboring states to lessen the burden of refugees and encourage their return. U.S. policymakers should be attentive to the need for an effective mediator between the new state and its neighbors, helping resolve border disputes and disagreements over natural resources. Such mediation can be performed by the United Nations or a regional organization with U.S. support. Options will need to be evaluated carefully.

Neighboring states have various ways to frustrate U.S. efforts to support a new state. If they refuse to recognize the new state or continue to harbor armed actors, its stability will be jeopardized. In such situations, the United States could turn to the punitive diplomatic or economic measures described above.

SIGNS OF SUCCESS: CHECKLISTS AS POLICY TOOLS

Although the United States can help shape the outcome of self-determination movements in various ways, nothing is assured when it comes to new states. The following thematic checklists draw on the lessons from the case studies and are intended as a reference point to help policymakers identify areas where a new state may be underperforming. They cover eight themes: international environment, regional environment, economic context, institutions, security context, social context, political climate, and leadership.

Judging the performance of a new state is an art and not a science, and the various factors presented here are not evenly weighted. This is not intended as a mathematical exercise. However, these checklists seek to visualize a new state's performance in a more holistic and systematic way to help identify unexploited possibilities and areas of particular concern.

When we used the checklists to investigate how the case study states fared at independence and then again six years after independence, we noticed how many states suffered a crisis in the early years. Bangladesh struggled with a series of bloody coups; Eritrea's border dispute with Ethiopia led to renewed conflict; divisions between Timor-Leste's security forces precipitated a nationwide conflict; and South Sudan descended into full-scale civil war. These crises underscore new states' fragility, even when they receive large levels of international support. As a result, U.S. policymakers should constantly evaluate performance across various sectors. The following checklists are designed to facilitate such evaluations.

Figure 9.1. Bangladesh 1972

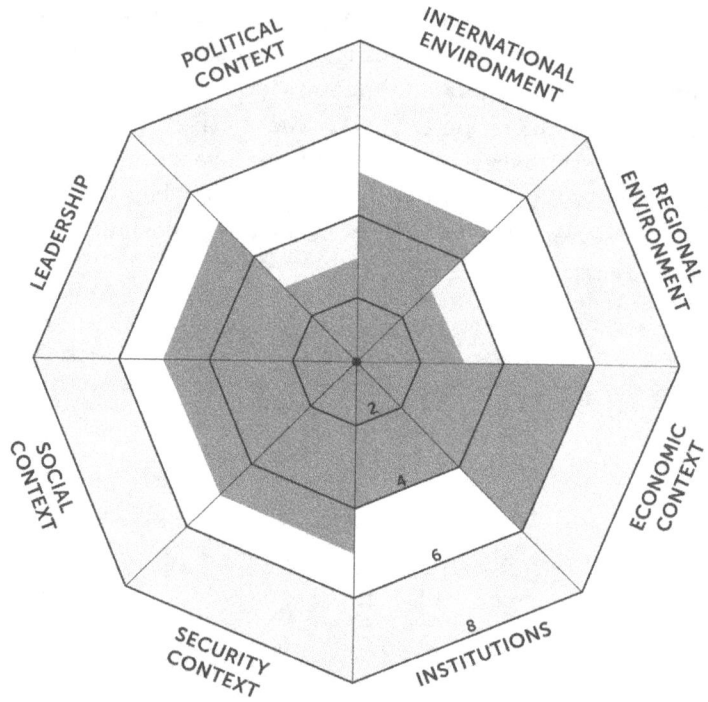

Figure 9.2. Bangladesh 1977

SELF-DETERMINATION POLICY TOOL
BANGLADESH *in* 1977

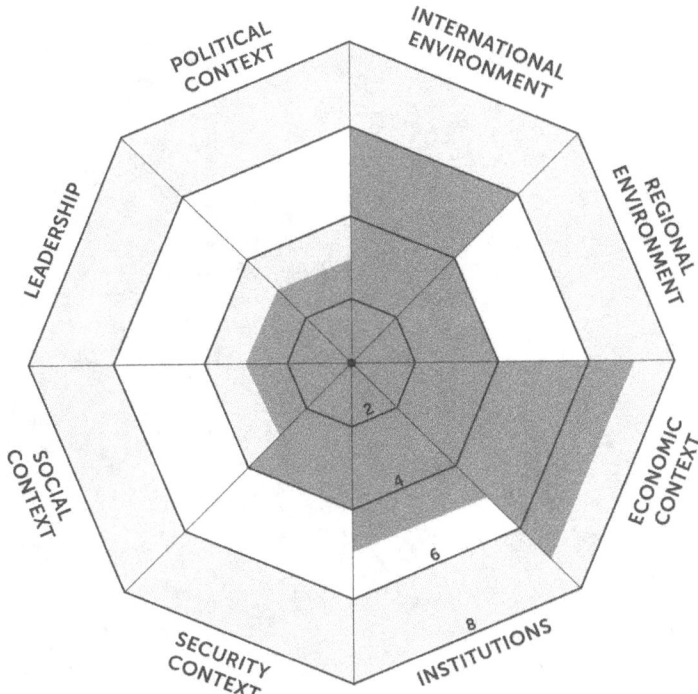

176 Will Todman

Figure 9.3.   Eritrea 1994

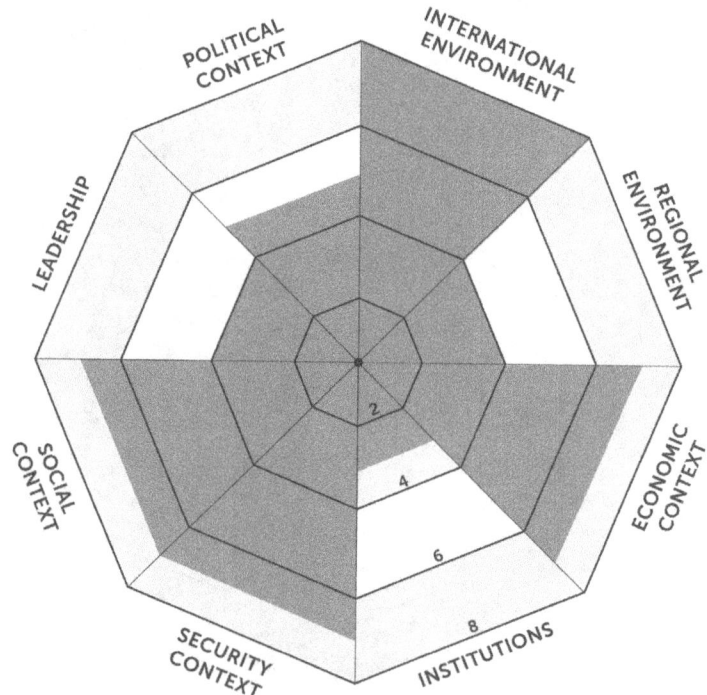

Figure 9.4. Eritrea 1999

SELF-DETERMINATION POLICY TOOL
ERITREA *in* 1999

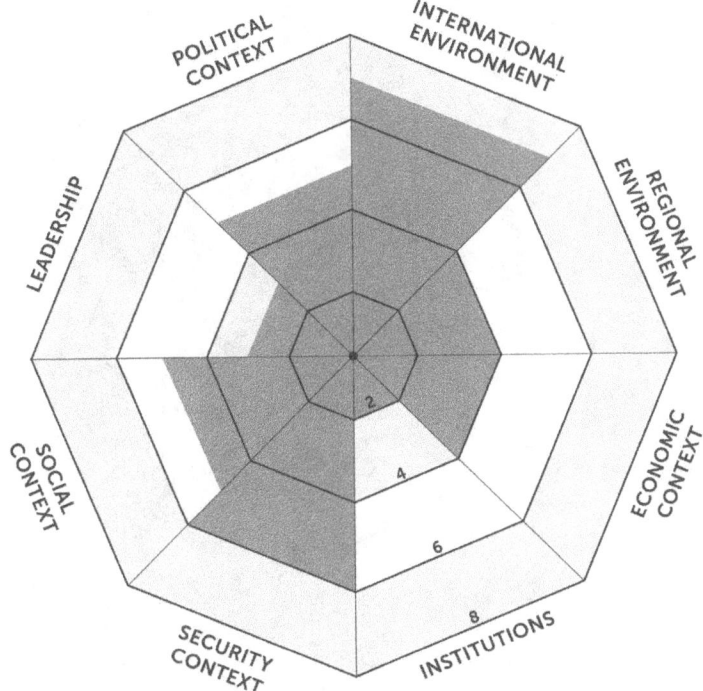

178 Will Todman

Figure 9.5. Timor-Leste 2002

SELF-DETERMINATION POLICY TOOL
TIMOR-LESTE in 2002

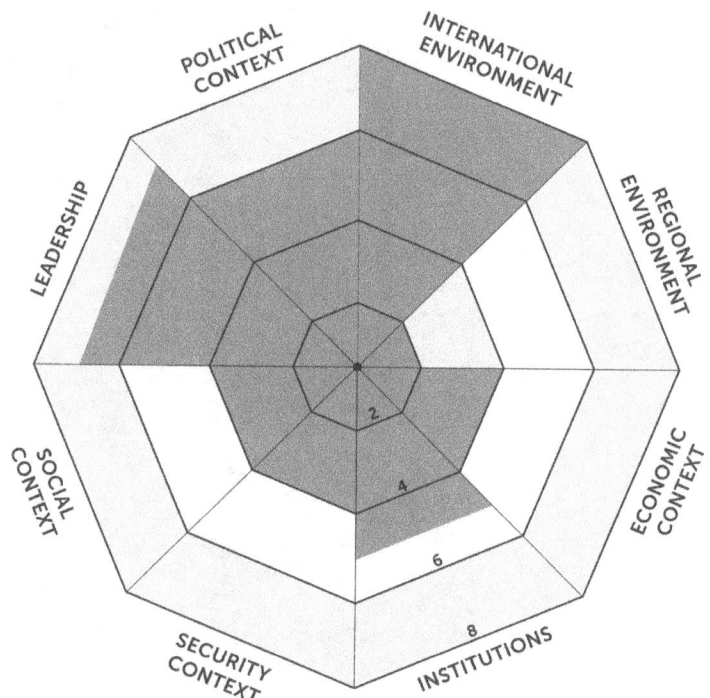

Figure 9.6. Timor-Leste 2007

SELF-DETERMINATION POLICY TOOL
TIMOR-LESTE *in* 2007

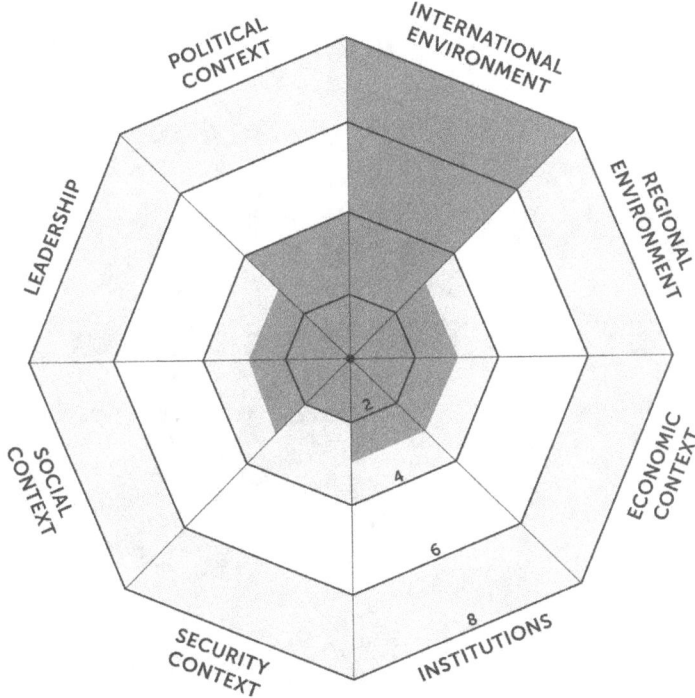

180 Will Todman

Figure 9.7. Kosovo 2009

SELF-DETERMINATION POLICY TOOL
KOSOVO *in* 2009

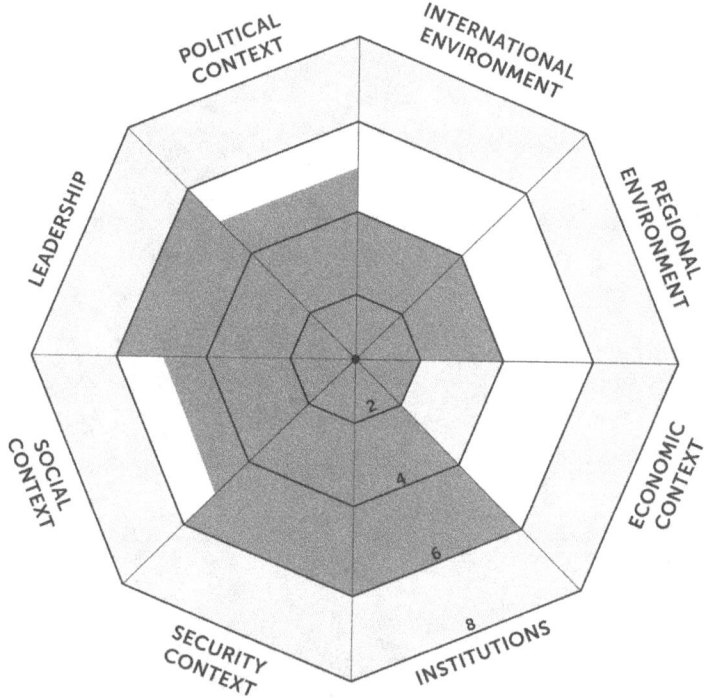

Figure 9.8.   Kosovo 2014

SELF-DETERMINATION POLICY TOOL
KOSOVO *in* 2014

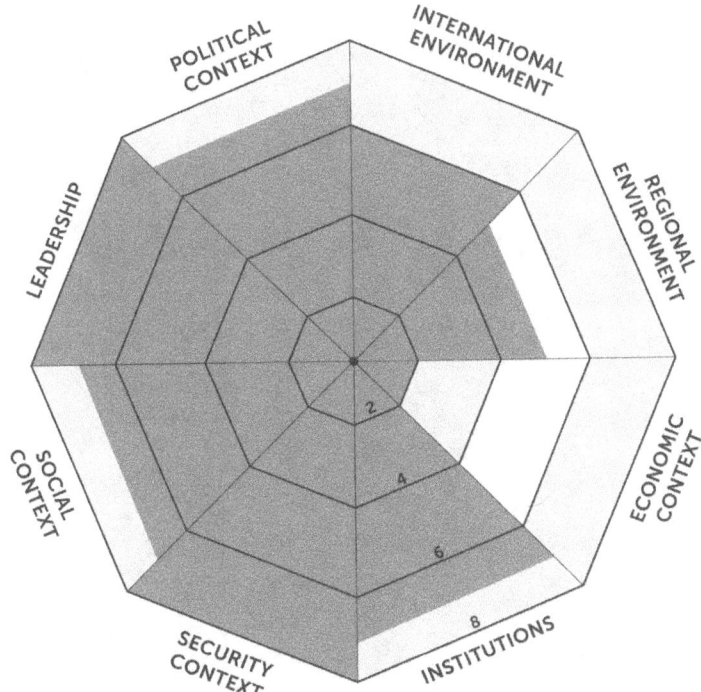

182 Will Todman

Figure 9.9. South Sudan 2011

SELF-DETERMINATION POLICY TOOL
SOUTH SUDAN *in* **2011**

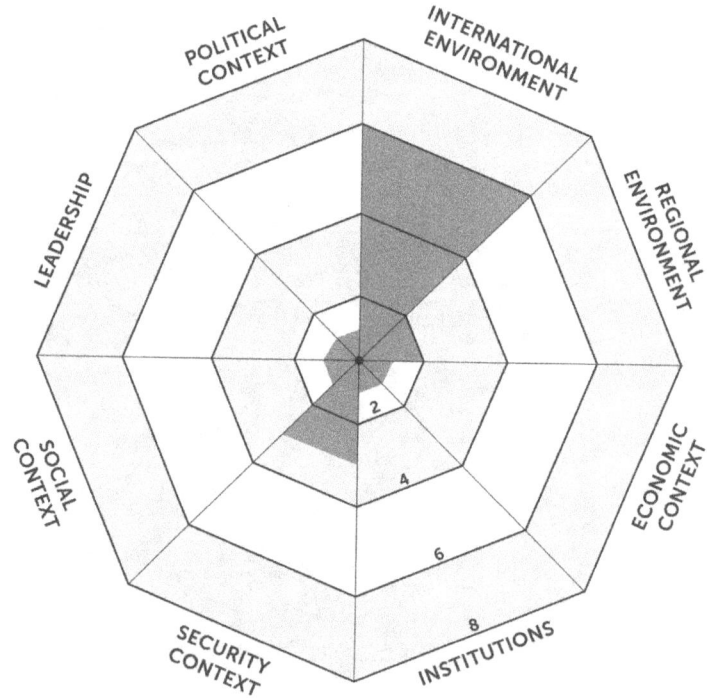

Figure 9.10. South Sudan 2016

SELF-DETERMINATION POLICY TOOL
SOUTH SUDAN *in* 2016

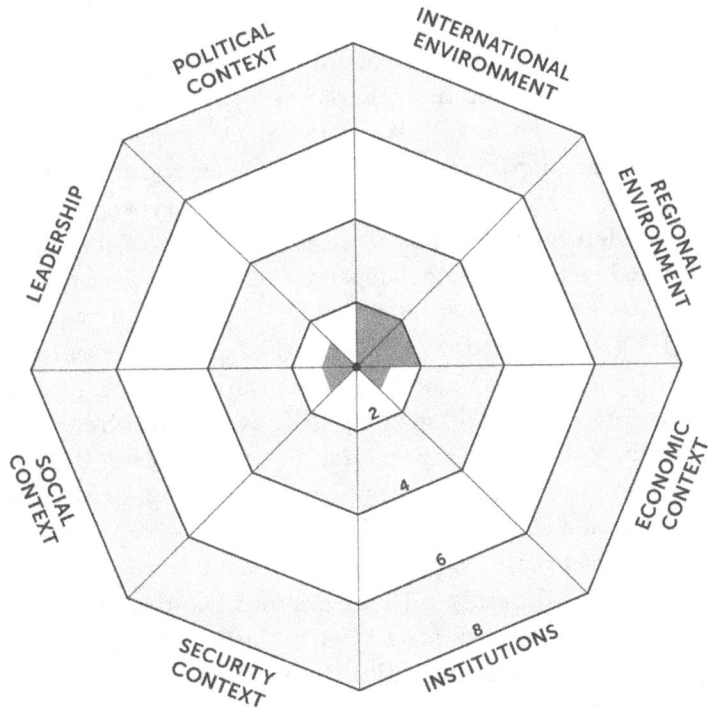

Thematic Checklists

For each theme, tick the number of statements that apply to the new state. If a statement is not applicable, tick so as not to penalize. Tally the scores (with 0 the lowest figure and 8 the highest) and fill them in on the diagram. Connect the dots between each of the thematic lines. The larger the area inside the markers, the more likely the new state will succeed.

INTERNATIONAL ENVIRONMENT

- ☐ *Membership in the United Nations.* As well as the legitimacy associated with UN membership, UN members gain access to economic assistance from the World Bank, the International Monetary Fund, and other forms of assistance through UN agencies such as the World Health Organization. This international support was a great boost to Bangladesh.
- ☐ *Support of great powers for independence.* If a great power opposes independence, as Russia has done for Kosovo, it can problematize or block the path to independence and then act as an irritant to the newly independent state by blocking international resolutions.
- ☐ *No close links between great powers and opposition groups in the new state.* If a great power has close links to an opposition group in the new state, the opposition group will have greater ability to challenge the state's authority and legitimacy. Indonesia's links with the opposition in Timor-Leste continued to represent a challenge to the new government.
- ☐ *International willingness to provide political or military support to the new state.* As the cases of Timor-Leste and Kosovo show, international support for a new state, often in the form of a peacekeeping mission, can prove critical. International support can help end conflicts, maintain peace, and build the capacity of local bureaucrats and nascent institutions.
- ☐ *Coordination between international donors.* If donors have competing priorities that dictate what aid targets, they can pull a new government in contradictory directions and reduce its effectiveness. The lack of coordination between donors in South Sudan was particularly acute.

- *International aid provided with benchmarks.* International aid is more effective when donors have clear benchmarks by which to monitor the effectiveness of aid provided. Better-defined benchmarks could have helped combat corruption in South Sudan.
- *Sustained attention by international community.* Timor-Leste's descent into violence in 2006 shows that if the international community does not sustain its support beyond the short term, conditions in a new state can deteriorate rapidly.
- *A politically and economically supportive diaspora.* Kosovo's active diaspora exemplifies the key form of political and economic support a diaspora can provide by lobbying foreign powers and sending remittances to the new country.

REGIONAL ENVIRONMENT

- *Membership in a regional organization.* A regional organization can provide an important arena for solving disputes that arise between neighboring states, while often bringing trade benefits and the diplomatic support of foreign powers. Bangladesh's membership in the Organization of Islamic Cooperation and the Asia Pacific Trade Agreement afforded some of these benefits.
- *Recognition by neighboring states.* If a neighboring state does not recognize the new state, as Serbia has done with Kosovo, it may challenge the new state politically or militarily, and economic ties will be harder to develop.
- *Institutionalized relationship with neighboring states.* If a relationship with a neighboring state is built on personal rather than institutional ties, it can break down swiftly in the event of a change in leadership or a change in conditions, as was the case with Eritrea and Ethiopia when the border war broke out.
- *No unresolved border disputes with a neighboring state.* Unresolved border disputes can problematize border security and the provision of state services to the disputed area. Border disputes continue to be a challenge for South Sudan.
- *No unresolved dispute over ownership or management of natural resources with a neighboring state.* Disputes over natural resources limit a state's

ability to capitalize on wealth from natural resources and raise the threat of broader political disputes. Timor-Leste has had an ongoing dispute with Australia over oil deposits in the Timor Sea.
- ☐ *No minority groups with irredentist aims with neighboring state.* If a minority group has ethnic ties with a neighboring state, it may attempt to secede and join with the neighboring state through violent means. The Serb population in Kosovo has provided an ongoing challenge for the government.
- ☐ *No large refugee population in a neighboring state.* As has been the case with South Sudan, if a large refugee population remains in a neighboring state, it represents a waste of potential manpower for the new state and could be the cause of negative relations with the host state.
- ☐ *No armed rebels being harbored in a neighboring state.* If a neighboring state harbors armed rebels, they can continue to undermine the new state's authority and prove difficult to oppose, as was the case with Timor-Leste and armed rebels who took refuge in Indonesia.

ECONOMIC CONTEXT

- ☐ *Broad economic parity between different regions.* If a certain region is marginalized, economic grievances could evolve into a security challenge if its population becomes restive. Perceptions of economic discrimination contributed to the outbreak of civil war in South Sudan.
- ☐ *Perception of a positive climate for foreign investment.* A climate that is favorable to foreign investment can help produce new economic opportunities and ties with foreign powers. Eritrea's slide into authoritarianism is a key factor dissuading foreign investment.
- ☐ *High levels of trade with neighboring states.* Developing robust trade relationships increases neighbors' dependency on a new state and so reduces the possibility of conflict breaking out, as Bangladesh did.
- ☐ *Diversified economy.* Relying on natural resources too heavily can foster corruption and exposes new states' economies to the impact of fluctuations in the global economy, as has been evident in South Sudan.

- ☐ *No overreliance on remittances.* As Eritrea's experience shows, relying on remittances to too great an extent can stifle the growth of the local economy by reducing the necessity of creating jobs.
- ☐ *No significant outflow of educated migrants.* New states need highly skilled individuals to help build the local economy, and if there is a brain drain they lose crucial human capital. Both Eritrea and South Sudan have suffered from their most educated citizens fleeing the country.
- ☐ *Low levels of unemployment.* If states have large populations out of work, it reduces government revenues and individuals' spending power, and increases the chances of social unrest.
- ☐ *Stable population growth.* A stable birthrate reduces the likelihood of a youth bulge that could place a high degree of pressure on government services and increase unemployment levels. Bangladesh effectively implemented a family planning program to slow its rapid population growth.

INSTITUTIONS

- ☐ *Government able to provide services to the population.* If a government is unable to provide services to its entire population, it is more likely that it will experience opposition from marginalized communities, as was the case in South Sudan.
- ☐ *Power concentrated in institutions rather than individuals.* As Bangladesh experienced in its early years, when power is concentrated in individuals rather than in institutions, the peaceful transition of power is more complicated.
- ☐ *Executive power is checked.* A lack of checks and balances on the executive makes the emergence of an authoritarian leader more likely. Eritrea's descent into authoritarianism revealed the lack of these checks.
- ☐ *Rule of law.* It is not only important that a constitution be drafted; it must also be formally adopted and institutions must be required to implement it. Eritrea's constitution was never effectively implemented even though it was drafted.
- ☐ *Experienced bureaucrats in place.* Experienced bureaucrats increase a government's capacity by improving the state's efficiency. After

Timor-Leste's severe brain drain, bureaucrats were trained effectively with international support.
- ☐ *Government implements well-sequenced plans across functions.* A government that is able to adopt and implement broad-scale plans across different agencies and institutions is likely to be more effective. Timor-Leste has successfully implement various development plans using carefully managed natural resource revenues.
- ☐ *Local institutions act in conjunction with national institutions.* State institutions are more effective when they integrate local practices, as occurred in Timor-Leste when local customs were institutionalized. When these are not integrated into the state institutions, they can act in competition, reducing efficiency.
- ☐ *No continued presence of international administrators.* If international administrators are deployed in a country for an extended period, local bureaucrats will take longer to take control of the institutions. Local populations can grow resentful of international advisers, as they have done in Kosovo, if they do not have a clear timeline and benchmarks for their withdrawal.

SECURITY CONTEXT

- ☐ *Security forces are disciplined.* If security forces are not well trained and led, as was the case in South Sudan, they are less likely to be able to enforce law and order in the new state, consistent with protection of the rights and security of individuals, and this will undermine a new state's authority.
- ☐ *Sense of solidarity and unity prevails in armed forces.* A strong sense of insider/outsider dichotomy in security services based on the pre-independence struggle, as occurred in Bangladesh, can lead to divisions between the security forces that undermines their efficiency.
- ☐ *Security apparatuses not closely associated with individual politicians.* Close personal links between different elements of the security apparatuses and individual politicians can result in the politicization of the armed forces. Such relationships led Timor-Leste's political disputes to escalate into armed conflict.

- ☐ *Civilians maintain oversight of armed forces.* To reduce the likelihood of a military dictatorship emerging, as it did in Bangladesh, civilian oversight of the military places the ultimate responsibility for a country's strategic decision making in the hands of the civilian political leadership.
- ☐ *Opposition armed groups demobilized.* If the groups that fought against the new state in its struggle for independence are not demobilized, they can continue to represent a challenge to the new state's authority. Pro-Indonesia militia roamed Timor-Leste after it gained independence and killed over a thousand people.
- ☐ *Pro-independence militias demobilized or integrated into the armed services.* Unless pro-independence armed militias are demobilized or integrated into the armed services of the new state, they can continue to represent a challenge to the new state's authority. It took three decades to integrate these forces in Bangladesh.
- ☐ *Security forces tolerate peaceful opposition.* To encourage an environment of healthy political debate, opposition figures must not be removed by armed forces. The regime in Eritrea has ruthlessly quashed opposition.
- ☐ *No state of emergency in place.* An ongoing state of emergency stifles the establishment of an open political environment and raises the possibility of human rights abuses. Sheikh Mujib increased his authority after declaring a state of emergency in Bangladesh in 1974.

SOCIAL CONTEXT

- ☐ *Shared sense of history and heritage.* A shared sense of history and heritage can help unite the population of a new state and prevent serious divisions. In Bangladesh, the new constitution made significant use of symbolism to help strengthen Bangladeshi identity.
- ☐ *Local governing practices integrated into new state's legal system.* The population is more likely to follow the laws and regulations of a new state if local practices of conflict resolution are integrated into the legal system. In Timor-Leste, state authority was bolstered by

adopting a hybrid legal system that integrated aspects of customary law.
- ☐ *Peace dividends distributed.* States that deliver peace dividends early build confidence in the political process, strengthen the state's core capacity, and reduce the risk of descending into violence. In Timor-Leste, the government introduced several social protection mechanisms that helped resolve the IDP issue within a few years.
- ☐ *War criminals equally held to account for their actions.* If war criminals on both sides are equally held to account for their actions, populations that suffered during conflict are less likely to harbor resentment that could result in violence. In Kosovo, the prime minister was tried for war crimes in the former Yugoslavia at The Hague.
- ☐ *Minorities recognize legitimacy of central government in new state.* If minorities reject the central government, as some Serbs do in Kosovo, they can represent a significant challenge to the new state's authority.
- ☐ *Inclusion of minorities and citizens from all regions in politics and the bureaucracy.* If minorities are represented in politics and in the bureaucracy, they are less likely to encourage the government to respond to their communities' needs, and minorities are less likely to feel marginalized. A Kosovo Serb minority party has served in a coalition government.
- ☐ *No significant human rights abuses.* Human rights abuses undermine a government's legitimacy and could lead to international condemnation and sanctions, while also inspiring alienation and unrest. Eritrea has some of the worst human rights abuses in the world.
- ☐ *Society enjoys access to information.* A population benefits from its ability to identify, retrieve, and use information effectively. Eritrea is frequently ranked as one of the most censored countries in the world.

POLITICAL CLIMATE

- ☐ *Insignificant levels of corruption.* As South Sudan showed, high levels of corruption reduce a government's capacity to deliver services, while also damaging its legitimacy.
- ☐ *Politics are not highly polarized.* An environment of highly polarized politics, such as in Bangladesh, increases tensions in society and

Self-Determination and U.S. Choices 191

leads to situations in which large sections of society feel marginalized by the government.
- ☐ *No ethnic outbidding between different political factions.* If different political factions attempt to attract support from certain groups by proposing more radical policies, as occurred in Bangladesh, it can increase social divisions and lead to violent nationalism.
- ☐ *Civil society organizations able to operate.* Civil society organizations can provide important economic and social functions, and fill gaps when the state lacks the capacity to act. Civil society played a particularly important role in Bangladesh.
- ☐ *Free and fair elections.* Free and fair elections enhance a government's legitimacy and help ensure that a population's wishes are represented. Timor-Leste has been celebrated for its democratic elections, which have helped ensure the peaceful transition of power.
- ☐ *Opposition leaders able to act freely.* An environment that tolerates political opposition is more conducive to a government that tailors its policies closer to the needs of the population and is held to account more effectively. In South Sudan, opposition parties have not been allowed to develop beyond personality-driven groupings.
- ☐ *Peaceful protests permitted.* If governments allow peaceful protests and permit their populations to assemble, they are less likely to turn to violence to air their grievances.
- ☐ *No calls for separatism.* New states are more likely to be successful if there are no minority groups themselves seeking independence. The Serb population in Kosovo continues to represent a challenge to the central government.

LEADERSHIP

- ☐ *Leader is charismatic.* A leader who is charismatic is better placed to unite the population behind certain goals and reduce disenfranchisement. Sheikh Mujib gave millions of Bangladeshis hope, leadership, and unity.
- ☐ *Leader articulates a national vision.* A leader who can articulate a clear national vision is better placed to manage the population's expectations and inspire hope for the future. Before his death in 2005, John Garang laid out a clear vision for a New Sudan as an

inclusive, well-governed polity that could accommodate its diverse peoples.
- ☐ *Leadership demonstrates capacity.* Leaders can only be successful if they have the appropriate skills to lead. Such leadership skills include courage, flexibility, and compromise. Salva Kiir arguably lacks these skills, ruling in an increasingly autocratic, narrow, and exclusive manner.
- ☐ *Leader enjoys support of trusted advisers and deputies.* A leader who feels able to delegate to trusted deputies and seek counsel from advisers is more likely to be successful. The political system in Timor-Leste has facilitated such delegation.
- ☐ *Leadership is able to interact effectively with global leaders.* Leaders who can work well with global leaders are more effective at advocating for international support for the new state's priorities. José Ramos-Horta was an effective advocate for the Timorese on the international stage, winning the Nobel Peace Prize for his efforts.
- ☐ *Leadership entertains debate over policy.* If there are mechanisms for exchanging ideas within the leadership, leaders' policies are likely to be placed under greater scrutiny and so be better tailored to their population's needs. As the leadership in South Sudan grew increasingly autocratic, little debate was permitted.
- ☐ *Dissent over policy in leadership is permitted.* An environment that tolerates disagreements within the leadership is likely to produce more effective policies, and less likely to descend into authoritarianism. In Eritrea, the regime became increasingly repressive and isolationist after government officials criticized Isaias in a letter that was leaked.
- ☐ *No cult of personality.* A cult of personality ties the national identity to the leader, inhibiting state institutions from functioning independently or having longevity beyond the leader's tenure. Isaias dominates all aspects of political, economic, and social life in Eritrea, and power is concentrated in individuals, not institutions.

NOTES

1. "Embassy Jakarta Telegram 1579 to Secretary State, 6 December 1975," Gerald R. Ford Library, Kissinger-Scowcroft Temporary Parallel File, Box A3, Country File, Far East-Indonesia, State Department Telegrams 4/1/75–9/22/76.

2. Paul Aranas, *Smokescreen: The US, NATO and the Illegitimate Use of Force* (New York: Algora, 2012), 126.

10. CONCLUSION
Jon B. Alterman

Americans, especially in the twenty-first century, tend to underestimate the perils associated with changes in government. The American Revolution was an unlikely triumph. The independence movement simmered for less than a decade before war broke out, and the war lasted less than a decade, too. The yield was a heterogeneous republican polity that had little precedent, but that became a global model in the following centuries. The U.S. Civil War was a bloody, wrenching conflict, but a one-time event. The outcome produced a union with enough local autonomy to prove resilient, even if it countenanced pockets of intolerance. The nation that arose from the Civil War grew into a global economic and military powerhouse, and no violent transfer of political power has ever followed.

Hundreds of other independence movements around the world have not fared as well. Conflicts have dragged on for decades, sometimes precipitating massacres and forced migrations. If they ever yielded governments, those governments were often unsteady and subject to constant threats from within and without. Economies lurched from crisis to crisis, police and courts emerged as antagonists in society rather than arbiters, and security remained fleeting. These independence movements do not achieve stability; instead, they contribute to instability, and the population suffers. The worst emerged as failed states, with their hard-fought autonomy under threat from a loose amalgam of fiefdoms and foreign proxies who, collectively, impose some kind of order.

It is not a fate many would seek, but it is all too common. The goal of this volume has been to explore different outcomes that independence movements have achieved and to try to discern what tends to lead to better outcomes and what tends to lead to worse ones.

To maximize the potential for a good outcome, populations and leaderships considering independence should explore two things in depth. The first is a fair assessment of what independence is likely to yield. Revolutionaries and secessionists promise they will deliver everything that the population currently enjoys, and more. In practice, merely maintaining current levels of wealth and security is difficult for new governments, even in impoverished and insecure places. With expectations raised by advocates of independence in the pre-independence period, the challenge of meeting public demands can swiftly turn into a political crisis for a new entity and can devolve into scapegoating of political opponents. Things can quickly spiral downward from there.

A clear-eyed assessment of the unalterable aspects of the new state—the size and composition of the population, the geography and geology of the land, water availability, resources, and a host of other factors—is vital. Those characteristics will cast a long shadow over the chances of a new and independent state. While a cadre of activists in any population will be determined to pursue independence, it is important that some portion of the aspiring polity continually evaluate the wisdom of the act, comparing its outcome to various levels of autonomy and levels of independence that do not sever ties of sovereignty.

Even if that results in a conclusion that independence remains desirable, a second task is necessary: understanding the circumstances that make it most likely that independence will produce positive results. Movements rarely can determine the moment that independence is reached, but they can exert strong influence over the context in which it occurs. Allies can be won over and skeptics reassured. Economies can be developed, domestic institutions can be built, and internal rifts can be healed. If independence comes too swiftly, important elements may not be in place, imperiling the project. With planning, success is not assured, but chances for success can be enhanced significantly.

Looking at the cases studied here, and significant examples outside this sample, several aspects of the context seem to have a significant effect on the success of post-independence societies. The first is the *international environment*. While small independence movements cannot shape the international environment, they can judge its general contours. Is there a wave of interest in self-determination, or acceptance of self-determination, or a broader concern with faltering sovereignty? In the

Balkans, for example, the breakup of Yugoslavia created an expectation that new states would arise, and questions were all about how many would arise and when. The normal resistance of states to the rise of new states was in abeyance.

South Ossetia and Abkhazia, aspiring breakaway republics from Georgia, have been unable to join a historical wave. In addition, they have relied heavily on a single international patron—Russia—and incurred the opposition not only of all of the Western countries, but virtually all the other states in the world. In this instance, the obstacle was not global solidarity with the state from which they sought to secede, Georgia, but rather wariness about the chief advocate of their independence, Russia. The absence of broad international support, and the presence of narrow international support, is consequential.

International attitudes toward statehood can change, both in general and in specific cases. For example, the United States and Australia were united for many years in their opposition to independence for East Timor, and that greatly inhibited chances for Timorese independence. The end of the Cold War diminished U.S. opposition, and in time, the United States helped to bring Australia around to supporting independence. This was a change in the very broad international context that Timorese did not influence, but upon which they could capitalize. Bangladesh's independence was spurred by a more intricate dance—Pakistan's assistance to President Nixon's opening to China brought the United States and Pakistan closer, alarming Prime Minister Indira Gandhi, who feared Pakistan might displace India as the most powerful nation on the subcontinent. To counter Pakistan's rise, Gandhi drew closer to the USSR, and she stepped up Indian support for Bangladeshi separatism. In this case, it was not greater U.S. support that spurred the independence movement, but instead a neighbor's alarm at U.S. diplomacy.

It is not just states that matter. Broad international support and multilateral organizations can play a vital role in the early years of statebuilding, having a dramatically positive effect on the process. For example, in Kosovo and Timor-Leste, sustained UN support was critical to the new states' success. Money, training, and security assistance all played a key role, both in early days and in the years that follow. In the current international environment, support of a similar scale, intensity, and duration seems unlikely for fledgling states. Donor coordination, when possible, can be a large multiplier for new states receiving aid. In South Sudan, donors' competing aims and requirements posed a significant challenge for the new government.

Finally, beyond the state, diasporas can play a significant role. In some cases, such as Northern Ireland in the 1970s and 1980s, diaspora support for combatants can prolong conflict and reward more violent elements of an opposition movement. While some see diasporas hastening independence in that circumstance, they also boost the fortunes of armed groups that may handicap a peaceful post-conflict environment. Post-independence, diasporas can be an important source of funding for new states. Jews around the world have poured money into Palestine and then Israel for more than a century, and donations currently run at billions of dollars per year.[1] The Eritrean diaspora is a critical source of national revenue and continues to shape in significant measure the economy and politics of the country. It does not always work out that way. The Palestinian expatriate community has been relatively reluctant to invest in Palestine even after the Oslo Accords seemed to pave the way to statehood.[2]

The second important piece of the context is the *regional environment*. Some new states have supportive states on their borders (even if the state from which they are seeking to break away resists independence). India, for example, strongly supported Bangladeshi independence and was vital to its success. Prime Minister Indira Gandhi gave safe haven to Awami League separatists from Bengal, helped mediate rifts within the Bangladesh independence movement, and established a joint military command with separatists. In Eritrea, the Eritrean People's Liberation Front (EPLF) gained power almost simultaneously with a new government taking power in Addis Ababa, and the new Ethiopian government was actually supportive of Eritrean independence from Ethiopia. In fact, Ethiopia was the first state to recognize Eritrea after its independence referendum.

Having positive relations with a neighbor does more than allow those agitating for independence easy access to a safe zone, although that is important. Warm relations also allow for the development of trade and investment ties that can boost the new economy. The opposite is true as well. While many factors contributed to the misery of South Sudan, the profound weakness of the new country's economy (both in overall output as well as its dependence on oil revenues, which were diverted to enrich a tiny few) was among the most important. So, too, was the immediate dispute with Sudan about oil revenues, which created the new country's first economic crisis.

On the other side, threatened states may seek to play the role of spoilers. In Timor-Leste, for example, militia groups operating from Indonesia were a sustained challenge. Serbia's military tried to prevent an independent Kosovo from emerging, and only the intervention of NATO forces made independence possible. In Eritrea, relations with Ethiopia initially were warm, providing a positive environment for success. Those relations deteriorated six years after independence and dissolved into a conflict that set Eritrea on a path to authoritarianism.

The third element is the *economic context*. Populations of new states often have high expectations for services the new government will provide (perhaps none so much as in South Sudan, where an immiserated population had wholly unrealistic expectations of a strong and immediate economic boost after independence). Managing those expectations, and delivering economic welfare, requires advanced skills from new governments, and those skills are as much political as they are economic.

If well managed, natural resources can provide a crucial source of wealth for a new government. For example, Timorese leaders recognized the need to manage with great caution the oil wealth they inherited. They swiftly enlisted Norwegian experts, who provided valuable guidance. But natural resources can also be a curse, often engendering corruption and creating economic distortions that can inhibit the growth of the labor force.

Corruption is endemic in any society but can be especially corrosive in fragile new countries. War economies produce opportunities for profiteering, so countries that emerge out of warfare have especially difficult times stamping out corruption. The large international presence in both Kosovo and Timor-Leste did not prevent corruption but helped limit its extent. South Sudan swiftly fell victim to corruption, and the entrenchment of that corruption continues to fuel conflict to this day.

Finally, industries can often be developed with independence, and that can have a dramatically positive impact on conditions. For example, Bangladesh moved quickly to improve its investment climate after initial economic disaster, and the country's vibrant garment industry is a product of very deliberate policy choices by a relatively new government.

The fourth element is the *political context*. Often but not always, a political party championed independence and has dominance in the immediate aftermath. This was true, for example, of the Awami League in Bangladesh and the EPLF in Eritrea. In those cases, it can be difficult to adapt to more pluralistic governance. In South Sudan, politics already were deeply polarized by the time of independence. Continued conflict has increased that polarization. Where military forces played a key role, as they did in Bangladesh, it can be difficult to transition to genuine civilian rule. Indeed, in Bangladesh, a brief period of civilian rule led to a series of coups that left the army in charge.

The politics that emerge are, in part, a function of the quality of the *leadership* that new governments have, which is the fifth element. Charismatic leaders can both rally populations to the new state and unify them. Leaders with good diplomatic skills can build crucial support for the new state with neighboring countries, with donor nations, and with international institutions. José Ramos-Horta, for example, was a principal East Timorese diplomat from the age of 25. He later won the Nobel Peace Prize for his efforts, and served as Timor-Leste's foreign minister, prime minister, and president, building both domestic and international support that proved vital to his country's success. The repressive turn of Eritrean president Isaias Afewerki and the spiraling corruption around President Salva Kiir in South Sudan, have dealt a blow to both countries. Bangladesh has a somewhat mixed record. Independence brought in a charismatic leader, Sheikh Mujib, who turned more authoritarian when the economy weakened. His assassination in 1975 led to more than a decade of military rule, which was finally displaced by a popular movement.

The quality and capacity of the new state's *institutions* are the sixth element. Below the leader, new governments do not come to power with equal capacity. Some inherit institutions, a skilled bureaucracy, and a skilled workforce. In Timor-Leste, severe violence triggered a devastating brain drain, yet a number of Timorese bureaucrats played important roles in the new state's administration. In Bangladesh, many senior government officials returned to West Pakistan after independence, leaving relatively junior officials to cope with awesome responsibilities, contributing to economic problems that plagued Bangladesh upon independence, but providing a basis for stabilization in years that followed.

The seventh element is the *security context*. When new states come to power through armed struggle, it may be difficult to demilitarize the society. Armed groups that participated in the fight for independence may seek to increase their share of power in the aftermath. Elements that opposed independence in the first place, often with the support of the rump state, may not go quietly. The Balkans have particularly struggled with this challenge, but they are in no way unique. Military officers sought power in Bangladesh soon after independence and controlled the country for decades afterward. Eritrea was relatively successful in making the transition from a long-running insurgency to an independent civil state, but the eruption of a border war with Ethiopia five years after independence put Eritrean politics into an authoritarian tailspin from which they have still not recovered. Singapore was expelled from Malaysia but benefited from the British military presence for the first six years of its independence. While there was considerable fear of unrest due to economic dislocation, the United Kingdom's interest in supporting order in Singapore was a significant security asset. On the purely domestic side, poor security can exacerbate political polarization, as it has done in South Sudan.

The last piece of the context is a bucket of *social issues*. In many new states, a large part of the population believes that it shares a heritage and a history. Shared histories of repression and common grievances were critical in uniting and mobilizing communities in Bangladesh, Eritrea, Kosovo, South Sudan, and Timor-Leste. And yet a shared history of repression is not sufficient. Social unity in a new state is important and is often dependent on how well the new state deals with minorities and with how well these minorities deal with the new state. The western Balkans in particular are shot through with minority communities, often with ties to surrounding states. Balkan case studies are a particularly rich vein to mine to understand how national identity can be built, and the different political outcomes in Bosnia, Macedonia, and Kosovo are, in part, a reflection of how each government has dealt with its minority communities. They present cautionary tales not to be too generous nor too miserly.

While it is hard to quantify the cultural legacy that new countries bring to their independence struggles, it surely has a role. Some communities cherish their images as warriors, others as traders and entrepreneurs. These ideas surely imprint themselves on the new state. On the more local level, customary practices of dispute resolution at the village level proved a boon to Timor-Leste's reconciliation efforts, providing an important asset on which the new nation could build.

The only place where we studied the success of movements that stopped short of independence is in the western Balkans. There, arguably similar states took different approaches to protecting the interests of minority communities and achieved different outcomes. There certainly are alternatives to complete independence, and some seem to work well.

By and large, however, this study has not focused on the management of self-determination movements that stopped short of independence. Québec, for example, has flirted with independence for decades and seems to have arrived at a modus vivendi with English-speaking Canada, at least for now. Iraqi Kurdistan and Catalonia might have been judged a year ago to be managing their negotiations well, until things seemed to unravel in the fall of 2017. Scotland's future in the United Kingdom seems newly uncertain, especially with the British decision to leave the European Union. Myriad other efforts continue around the globe.

We did not include these efforts because autonomy seems never fully satisfying. Demands wax and wane.

Our goal is not to make an absolute judgment of whether groups should seek autonomy or independence, nor is it our goal to describe the kind of autonomous relationships that are durable. Some seem to work well, at least for a time. At the same time, it seems that self-determination movements are seeking much more than that, and we sought to inform the choices that such movements make.

Albert O. Hirschman famously observed the utility of the "hiding hand" in development projects. Referring to three schemes that had an especially bumpy start, he argued,

> If the project planners had known in advance all the difficulties and troubles that were lying in store for the project, they probably never would have touched it ... [and] in some, though not all of these cases advance knowledge of these difficulties would therefore have been unfortunate, for the difficulties and the ensuing search for solutions set in motion a train of events which not only rescued the project, but often made it particularly valuable.[3]

Self-determination movements are far more complex than mere economic development projects. They have multiple vectors of success, from political to economic to social to security, and they almost by definition take place in a fraught environment.

There is a utility in the "hiding hand," or, seen alternatively, the willingness to pursue independence even when success is not guaranteed. That is different than pursuing independence regardless of conditions, whether in the aspiring independent entity itself or globally. As the studies gathered here suggest, the level of success we should expect from independence movements is not random. There are things that movements can do to improve their chances. Chances are only that, though. Nothing guarantees success, and events inevitably take their own course.

In a follow-up to Hirschman's study almost 50 years later, two prominent professors analyzed more than 2,000 projects. They found that a hiding hand was often at work, but that planners overestimated the benefits of projects more than they underestimated the costs.[4] Particularly striking is their assertion that cost overruns are common, but "benefits overruns" are rare. There are many incentives to overpromise results. There are fewer reliable pathways to deliver them.

Several remarkably successful independence movements have inspired the world, and a few quite unsuccessful ones have distressed it. The success of any movement is never foreordained. Each movement is, as in the memorable title of one book on the American independence movement, "a leap in the dark."[5] But two things seem clear. The first is that the single most important determinative factor in the success of any independence movement is often beyond the control of such a movement. It has to do with the historical context, with great power actors, or with unpredictable events that emerge on the scene. Movements can capitalize on these moments, but they cannot manufacture them. The second is that a whole host of important factors are well within the control of such a movement, but movements do not always seek to act on many of them. Activists become so convinced in the justness of their cause that they do not do everything they might to increase its likelihood of success.

It is all a gamble, but shrewd gamblers do what they can to improve their odds.

NOTES

1. Revital Blumenfeld, "U.S. Jews' Donations to Israel Double in Past 20 Years, Study Shows," *Haaretz*, March 25, 2012.
2. Kate Gillespie, Edward Sayre, and Liesl Riddle, "Palestinian Interest in Homeland Investment," *Middle East Journal* 55, no. 2 (Spring 2001): 237–255.
3. Albert O. Hirschman, *The Principle of the Hiding Hand* (Washington, DC: Brookings Institution, 1967), 12–13.
4. Bent Flyvbjerg and Cass R. Sunstein, "The Principle of the Malevolent Hiding Hand; or, the Planning Fallacy Writ Large," *Social Research* 83, no. 4 (Winter 2016): 979–1004.
5. John Ferling, *A Leap in the Dark: The Struggle to Create the American Republic* (New York: Oxford University Press, 2003).

INDEX

Note: Information in figures is indicated by page numbers in italics.

AAK. *See* Alliance for the Future of Kosovo
ABRI. *See* Indonesian National Armed Forces
Academy of Rural Development, in Comilla, 29, 35n41
Addis Ababa, 36, 43–44, 46, 49, 196
Addis Ababa, Agreement of 1972, 100, 104
African Union (AU), 37, 48, 100, 106, 115
Agreement on the Resolution of the Conflict in the Republic of South Sudan (ARCSS), 101, 112, 114
Ahtisaari, Martti, 82, 92, 130
Ahtisaari Plan, 92, 123, *125–26*, 130, 137n42
Albanian National Liberation Army (NLA), 121–22
Albanians: in Kosovo, 81, 82–86, 88–89, 90–94, 96–97, 122–23, 132; Macedonians and, 121–22
Albanian Self-Determination Movement, 96
Albright, Madeleine, 167
Algerian National Liberation Front (FLN), 40–41
Algiers Agreement, 37, 47
Alkatiri, Mari, 65, 67–68, 71–72
Alliance for the Future of Kosovo (AAK), 93
Anglo-Egyptian condominium, 100, 103
ARCSS. *See* Agreement on the Resolution of the Conflict in the Republic of South Sudan
Armed Forces of the Republic of Kosovo (FARK), 87
army. *See specific armies*
ASDT. *See* Timorese Social Democratic Association
ASEAN, 70–71

Asian financial crisis, 160–61
Asmara, 36, 41, 43, 44, 46, 48, 49
assassinations, 12, 26, 27, 198
AU. *See* African Union
Australia, 54, 58, 59, 60, 70–71, 78n54, 195
Awami League, 10–11, 18–21, 23, 25, 31
Awami Muslim League, 16
Ayub Khan, Mohammad, 10, 17–18, 33n8, 33nn10–11

Balkans, 3, 81, 87, 95, 199. *See also* West Balkans
Bangladesh, *11*, *13*, 198–99; army, 23, 27–29, 34n36, 34n37; Ayub and, 17–18; constitution written for, 24, 26; corruption in, 31; economy, 27, 29–32; establishment of, 23–25, 34n23; governance, 25–26, 27, 31–32; property nationalization by, 25, 30; recognition of, 25; self-determination movements in, 5; self-determination timeline of, 10–12; two-winged Pakistan, 14–16; United Pakistan end, 19–20; U.S. policy relating to, 12; Zia (Ziaur Rahman) as president of, 26–27, 28, 30.
Bangladesh Nationalist Party (BNP), 31
Bangla language, 14–15, 16, 24
Basque country, secession movements in, 3
Battle of Adwa, 39
Battle of Kosovo Polje, 81, 83–84, 85
Belgrade, 88, 92–94, 96, 119, 123, 130–32, 137n48
Bengalis, 11, 14–15, 17, 18; in Bangladesh army, 27–28; as civil servants, 23–24; interned, 24; killing of, 20
Bhutto, Zulfikar Ali, 11, 19, 25

203

BMA. *See* British Military Administration
BNP. *See* Bangladesh Nationalist Party
Bosnia and Herzegovina, 83, 86, 87, 88, 89, 91, 199; minority empowerment of, 127–28, 136n35; self-determination movements, 117, 118, 127; West Balkan settlements of, 119–21, 124, 125–26, 131, 135n11
British Military Administration (BMA), 39
Brussels Agreement of April 2013, 123

Catalonia, secession movements in, 3, 200
Catholicism, 39, 59, 67, 74
CAVR. *See* Commission for Reception, Truth, and Reconciliation
Center for Systemic Peace, 139, 141
Central Bank (of Timor-Leste), 64, 78n41
Central Intelligence Agency (CIA), 168
Central Powers, 2, 3
Chechens, secession movements of, 3
China, 12, 20–21, 22, 70, 79n57, 195
CIA. *See* Central Intelligence Agency
civilian police (CIVPOL), 62, 63
Clinton, Bill, 59, 60, 88, 113, 160, 167
CNRT. *See* Timorese National Resistance Council
Cold War, 6, 20–21, 55, 58, 60, 73, 87; end of, 160, 195
colonialism, 3
Commission for Reception, Truth, and Reconciliation (CAVR), 64
Commission for Truth and Friendship (CTF), 70
Commission on Human Rights, 60
communism, 15, 60, 160
Community of Portuguese Language Countries (CPLP), 71
Community of Serbian Municipalities in Kosovo, 123, 136n25
Comprehensive Peace Agreement (CPA), 100, 103, 106–8, 115
Congress, U.S., 88, 105, 164, 166, 169
consociationalism, 118, 120, 124, 135n7
Constituent Assembly, Bangladesh, 10, 14–15, 16, 24
Constituent Assembly, Timor-Leste, 65
constitution: for Bangladesh, 24, 26; interim, for South Sudan, 101
Correlates of War project, 139
corruption, 7, 143, 154, 197; in Bangladesh, 31; in East Timor, 57; in Kosovo, 95; in South Sudan, 111, 138; in Timor-Leste, 69

Council of Europe's Framework Convention for the Protection of National Minorities, 129
CPA. *See* Comprehensive Peace Agreement
CPLP. *See* Community of Portuguese Language Countries
"Creeping Coup," in Ethiopia, 40
Croatia, 81, 83, 85, 89, 120
Croats, 119
crony capitalists, 18, 33n9
CTF. *See* Commission for Truth and Friendship

Darfur, 107, 166
dataset, analysis of: dependence on natural resources, 153–55; geostrategic location, 143–46; international aid, 151–53; method of gaining independence, 146–48; peacekeeping missions, 148–51
dataset, quantitative methodology for: annual change in GDP per capita, 140; annual change in infant mortality rate, 141; change in displacement, 141, 158n4; criteria for, 139, 158n1; factors for, 140; large-scale violence, 141–42; limitations of, 142; variables for, 139–40, 158n2
Dayton Accords. *See* Dayton Peace Agreement (DPA)
Dayton Peace Agreement (DPA), 82, 86, 120, 121, 124, 125–26, 127
decentralization, 122, 129, 161
Declaration of Independence: of Bangladesh, 23; of Bosnia and Herzegovina, 119; of East Timor, 57, 73, 160; of Kosovo, 85, 92, 119, 132; of Macedonia, 121
decolonization, 56
Democratic League of Kosovo (LDK), 86, 87, 90, 93–94
Democratic Party of Kosovo (PDK), 93
Democratic Republic of Timor-Leste, 54, 57, 65, 160
Department of Defense, U.S., 171, 172
Department of State, U.S., 34n26, 88, 160, 192n1
Derg regime, in Eritrea, 36, 40, 43, 44
Dhaka, 10–11, 14, 17, 19, 22, 25, 32
Dili, 54, 57, 59, 62, 72
Dinka, in South Sudan, 106, 109, 112

displacement, change in, 141, 158n4
DPA. *See* Dayton Peace Agreement

East Bengal. *See* East Pakistan
East Pakistan, 6, 10, 11, 20, 23–24, 33n13; economic concerns of, 15–16, 33n3; marginalization of, 3
East Pakistan Legislative Assembly, 16
East Pakistan Rifles, 28
East Timor, 55; Catholicism in, 39, 59, 67, 74; corruption in, 57; FRETILIN relating to, 53, 56–58, 63, 65, 68–69, 72–73, 75n10, 147; human rights violations in, 73; Indonesian occupation of, 57–61, 68, 70, 73, 76n11, 79nn55–56, 170; invasion of, 57–58; Portugal relating to, 53, 56–58, 61, 75nn2–3; self-determination movements in, 5–6, 74, 117; UNAMET relating to, 61, 62; United States and, 58–59, 60. *See also* Timor-Leste
East Timor Police Service (PNTL), 54, 63, 72
economic context checklist, 186–87
economy. *See specific countries*
EEBC. *See* Eritrea-Ethiopia Border Commission
ELF. *See* Eritrean Liberation Front
Emergency Relief Desk, 42
Enterprise, USS. 22
EPLF. *See* Eritrean People's Liberation Front
EPRDF. *See* Ethiopian People's Revolutionary Democratic Front
Equatoria Corps, 103–4
Eritrea, 51n23; BMA relating to, 39; Derg regime in, 36, 40, 43, 44; ELF with, 36, 40–41, 49; EPLF relating to, 37, 41–44, 196, 198; EPRDF relating to, 36, 43–44, 51n16; Ethiopian border war with, 37–38, 46–50, 51n25, 51n27; Ethiopia relating to, 36, 44–46; ethnic groups in, 38–39; independence struggles of, 36–38; international recognition of, 44, 49; 1993 independence of, 37; as oppressive regime, 48, 51n28; PFDJ relating to, 45–46, 49; refugees during, 42; religious groups, 39; self-determination movements in, 5, 37, 117; self-determination timeline of, 36–37; Tigre population, 39; Tigrinya population, 38–39; TPLF with, 36, 43; UN relating to, 44

Eritrea-Ethiopia Border Commission (EEBC), 37, 47, 50
Eritrean diaspora, 42, 45, 49
Eritrean-Ethiopian Federation, 39–40
Eritrean Liberation Front (ELF), 36, 40–41, 49
Eritrean People's Liberation Front (EPLF), 37, 41–44, 196, 198
Ershad, H. M. (general), 12, 27, 28–29
Ethiopia, 6, 36, 37, 39, 44–46
Ethiopian border war, Eritrea with, 37, 38, 46–50, 51n25, 51n27
Ethiopian People's Revolutionary Democratic Front (EPRDF), 36, 43–44, 51n16
Ethiopian Student Movement, 40, 41
ethnic rioting, in Kosovo, 82, 92
European Union, 5, 8, 58, 95, 97, 130–31

FARK. *See* Armed Forces of the Republic of Kosovo
FDI. *See* foreign direct investment
F-FDTL. *See* Timorese Defense Force
First Civil War, Sudan, 100, 104
FLN. *See* Algerian National Liberation Front
Forcibly Displaced Populations dataset, 141
foreign direct investment (FDI), 57, 66–67, 95–96
Freedom Fighters (Mukti Bahini), 28–29, 34n36
FRETILIN. *See* Revolutionary Front for an Independent East Timor

Gandhi, Indira, 21, 195, 196
Garang, John, 100, 104, 105, 107
GDP. *See* gross domestic product
geostrategic location: domestic vulnerabilities of, 144–45; impact of, 143; natural resources of, 143–44; strategic importance of, 144, 145
Globalization, 8
Great Britain, 3
gross domestic product (GDP), 15–16, 66, 95, 140, 154
guerrilla organizations, Bangladesh, 28
Gusmão, Xanana, 57, 63, 65, 67–68, 71–72

Haile Selassie (emperor), 40, 44
Haq, Fazlul, 16, 17, 33n5
Hasina, Sheikh, 12, 23, 26, 27, 29
Hindu, 15, 16, 21

Hirschman, Albert O., 200
Homeland Calling, 87

ICO. *See* International Civilian Office
IGAD. *See* Intergovernmental Authority on Development
IMF. *See* International Monetary Fund
independence movements. *See specific movements*
India, 6, 11, 20; British in, 13; diplomacy with, 22; intervention in East Pakistan of, 22; Ministry of External Affairs in, 21; Muslim population in, 14; Pakistan and, 12, 21–22, 24–25; partition of, 19; refugees in, 21; Treaty of Friendship and Cooperation with the Soviet Union of, 21
Indian and Pakistani diplomacy, 21–22
Indian Punjab, 22
Indonesia, 54; East Timor occupied by, 57–61, 68, 70, 73, 76n11, 79nn55–56, 170; economic pressure on, 60; strategic importance of, 160; U.S. aid to, 60
Indonesian National Armed Forces (ABRI), 57, 59, 61, 62
infant mortality rate, 141
institutions: checklist for, 173, 187–88, 198
Interethnic Council, Macedonia, 122
INTERFET. *See* International Forces for East Timor
Intergovernmental Authority on Development (IGAD), 100, 106, 115
international aid, 22, 25, 29, 64, 74, 91, 151–53, 157, 188–89, 195–96
International Civilian Office (ICO), 92
international environment checklist, 172, 184–85, 194–95
International Forces for East Timor (INTERFET), 54, 62
International Monetary Fund (IMF), 11, 25, 66, 169
International Organization, 148
International Organization for Migration (IOM), 62–63, 91
intervention: of India, 22; of NATO in Kosovo, 87–89, 96–97
invasion, of East Timor, 57–58
IOM. *See* International Organization for Migration
Iraqi Kurdistan, 1, 200
Isaias Afwerki, 36, 38, 44, 46, 48, 146

Jakarta, 54, 70, 73, 160
Japan, 53, 56
Jatiyo Rakkhi Bahini, 26, 28
Jinnah, Muhammad Ali, 10, 14
Joint Interim Administrative Structure, Kosovo, 90

Khartoum, 103, 104, 106–8, 110, 111, 113
Kiir, Salva, 100, 101, 108, 109, 110–12, 114, 115
Kissinger, Henry, 6, 20–21, 22, 160
KLA. *See* Kosovo Liberation Army
Kosovo, 83, 169–70, 199; Albanians in, 81, 82–86, 88–89, 90–94, 96–97, 122–23, 132; building new state of, 90–94; Congress relating to, 88; corruption in, 95; economic growth of, 95–96; ethnic background of, 82–83; ethnic rioting in, 82, 92; GDP of, 95; government of, 93–94; grievances in, 85; international intervention in, 87–89, 96–97; majority empowerment in, 129–31; mineral deposits of, 96; movement origins of, 82–85; NATO and, 82, 88–89, 90, 97; in 2009, 180; in 2014, 181; nonrecognition of, 95; ongoing challenges for, 94–96; self-determination timeline of, 81–82; Serbs in, 81, 82–89, 90–92, 94, 122–23; sovereignty of, 94–95, 96; UN and, 88, 123, 195; violence in, 90–91; West Balkan settlements of, 122–23, 124, 125–26, 131–32
Kosovo Albanian liberation struggle, 85–86
"Kosovo and Metohija," 84
Kosovo Liberation Army (KLA), 82, 87, 90–91, 94, 97, 123, 168
Kosovo Police Service, 91
Kosovo Protection Corps (KPC), 91
Kosovo Security Forces, 94
Kosovo Transitional Council, 90
KPC. *See* Kosovo Protection Corps
Krishak Sramik Party (KSP), 16
Kurds, 117, 164

LDK. *See* Democratic League of Kosovo
leadership checklist, 173, 191–92, 198
League of Communists of Yugoslavia, 119
Libya, 1

Macedonia, 88, 89, 90, 118, 132, 199; Albanians and, 121–22; decentralization in, 122; empowerment of, 128–29, 130–31,

136n40; NATO and, 121–22; self-determination movements in, 117; West Balkan settlement of, 121–22, 124, 125–26, 135n13, 135n15
Machar, Riek, 101, 105, 109, 111, 112, 114, 115
majority empowerment, 129–31
Marxism-Leninism, 40
Melanesian Spearhead group, 71
Menelik (emperor), 39
Mengistu, Haile Mariam, 43, 44
Milosevic, Slobodan, 81, 85–90, 94, 97, 167
Ministry of External Affairs, in India, 21
minority empowerment, 127–29, 131–33, 136n35, 137n51
Mother Teresa, 82
Mother Teresa Society, 86
Muhith, A. M. A., 23, 34n27
Mujib, Sheikh (Sheikh Mujibur Rahman), 10, 11, 16, 19, 33n12; assassination of, 12, 26, 198; in jail, 18, 20, 23; return of, 24; state-in-waiting of, 23, 34n24
Mukti Bahini. See Freedom Fighters
Muslim League, 14, 16, 26, 39

National Assembly, Pakistan, 19–20, 24
nationalization, of Bangladesh property, 25, 30
National Recovery Plan, Timor-Leste, 72
national security, of United States, 169
National Security Service, South Sudan (NSS), 112
NATO, 118; Kosovo and, 82, 88–89, 90, 97; Macedonia and, 121–22
NATO-Yugoslav war, 88, 90, 120
natural resources, dependence on, 153, 155, 156
negotiated settlements, 117–18, 133–34. See also West Balkan settlements
Nigerian, Igbo, secession movements of, 3
Nimeiri, Gaafar, 100, 104, 105
Nixon, Richard, 19, 20–21, 22
NLA. See Albanian National Liberation Army
nonrecognition, of Kosovo, 95
North American colonies, 3
NSS. See National Security Service, South Sudan

OAU. See Organization of African Unity
Ohrid Framework Agreement (OFA), 122, 124, 125–26, 128–29, 130, 133

OIC. See Organization of the Islamic Conference
oil: in Sudan, 3, 101, 104, 110–11; in Timor-Leste, 66, 75
Organization for Cooperation and Security in Europe (OSCE), 91, 97
Organization of African Unity (OAU), 42, 44–45
Organization of the Islamic Conference (OIC), 24–25
OSCE. See Organization for Cooperation and Security in Europe
Oslo Accords, 196
Osmany, M.A.G. (general), 23, 28

Pacific Islands Forum, 71
Pakistan, 6, 10, 31, 32n2; Ayub Khan as president of, 17–18; Bangla, 14–15, 16, 24; Bangladesh relating to, 14–16; economic grievances with, 15–16, 33n3; GDP relating to, 15–16; India and, 12, 21–22, 24–25; language issue of, 14–15; military with, 15; Muslim population in, 14; United Pakistan, 19–20; Urdu, 14–15; United States and, 20–21, 195. See also East Pakistan; West Pakistan
Pakistan Army, 20, 21–22, 27–28
Pakistan Partition, 14, 32n1
Pakistan People's Party, 19
Pancasila philosophy, 59
Paris Peace Conference, 2
partition: of India, 19; Pakistan Partition, 14, 32n1
PDK. See Democratic Party of Kosovo
peacekeeping missions: mandate for, 149; success of, 149–50; UN involved with, 148–49
Peace Research Institute, 142
People's Front for Democracy and Justice (PFDJ), 45–46, 49
People's Republic of China, 22
Petroleum Fund, Timor-Leste, 66
PFDJ. See People's Front for Democracy and Justice
PISG. See Provisional Institutions of Self-Government
PNTL. See East Timor Police Service
policy tool, 8, 172–73; checklist for: Bangladesh, in 1972, *174*; Bangladesh, in 1977, *175*; economic context, 172–73, 186–87, 197; Eritrea, in 1994, *176*; Eritrea,

policy tool (continued)
   in 1999, *177*; institutions, 173, 187–88, 198;
   international environment, 172, 184–85,
   194–95; Kosovo, in 2009, *180*; Kosovo, in
   2014, *181*; leadership, 173, 191–92, 198;
   political climate, 173, 190–91, 198;
   regional environment, 172, 185–86,
   196–97; security context, 173, 188–89,
   199; social context, 173, 189–90, 199;
   South Sudan, in 2011, *182*; South Sudan,
   in 2016, *183*; thematic, 184–92; Timor-
   Leste, in 2002, *178*; Timor-Leste, in
   2007, *179*
policy tools, of United States, 161, 163,
   166–68, 170, 172
political climate checklist, 173, 190–91, 198
Portugal, 53, 56–58, 61, 75nn2–3
Provisional Institutions of Self-
   Government (PISG), 82, 90, 91

Québec, 3

Rahman, Ziaur. *See* Zia (Ziaur Rahman)
Ramos-Horta, José, 54, 60, 68, 72, 73, 198
ready-made garments industry, of
   Bangladesh, 30
Red Sea, 39, 45–46
refugees, 14; during Eritrea armed
   struggle, 42; in India, 21; Timorese, 60,
   62, 76n16
regional environment checklist, 172,
   185–86, 196–97
Repatriates, 28, 34n37
Republic of Kosova, 85
Republika Srpska (RS), 127–28, 131
Revolutionary Front for an Independent
   East Timor (FRETILIN), 53, 56–58, 65,
   68–69, 72–73, 75n10, 147
Round Table Conference, 10, 18
RS. *See* Republika Srpska
Rugova, Ibrahim, 81–82, 85, 90, 94
Russia, 88
Russian Federation, 2

SAA. *See* Stabilization and Association
   Agreement
sanctions, 104, 116n3, 166, 167, 170
Santa Cruz massacre, 54, 59–60, 160
Sayem, A. S. M. (chief justice), 12, 26
Scotland, 3, 167
Second Civil War, Sudan, 100, 104, 105, 113

secularism, with Bangladesh governance,
   31–32
security context checklist, 173, 188–89, 199
Serbia, 81, 82–89, 90–92, 94, 119; minority
   empowerment of, 128, 131–33, 137n51
Serbs, 119, 120, 132; in Kosovo, 81, 82–89,
   90–92, 94, 122–23; migration of,
   129–30
settlements. *See* negotiated settlements;
   West Balkan settlements
SFRY. *See* Socialist Federal Republic of
   Yugoslavia
Simla Agreement, 24–25
Six Point Program, 10, 18, 19
social context checklist, 173, 189–90,
   199
Socialist Federal Republic of Yugoslavia
   (SFRY), 84, 119, 121, 168
South Sudan, 1, *102*, 117, 195–97, 198, 199;
   corruption in, 111, 138; CPA for, 100,
   103, 106–8, 115; democratic
   development in, 112; Dinka in, 106, 109,
   112; failures of, 109–14; with history of
   conflict and brutality, 109–10;
   independence for, 100–101, 104, 106–8;
   interim constitution of, 101;
   marginalization of, 3; national identity
   of, 103–6; oil in, 3, 101, 110–11; political
   pluralism in, 112; self-determination
   timeline for, 100–101; short
   honeymoon of, 108–9; U.S. support in,
   113–14, 116nn16–17
Soviet Union, 3, 12, 22, 88, 117
SPLA, 105, 107, 110, 111, 112
SPLM. *See* Sudan People's Liberation
   Movement
SPLM/A. *See* Sudan People's Liberation
   Movement/Army
Sri Lankan Tamils, secession movements
   of, 3
Stabilization and Association Agreement
   (SAA), 128, 130
Sudan, 101, 103; First Civil War in, 100,
   104; neighbors of, 105; oil deposits in,
   104; Second Civil War in, 100, 104, 105,
   113; U.S. sanctions against, 104, 116n3,
   167. *See also* South Sudan
Sudan People's Liberation Movement
   (SPLM), 102, 105–8, 110–12, 113, 115
Sudan People's Liberation Movement/
   Army (SPLM/A), 100, 104, 105

Suhrawardy, Huseyn Shaheed, 16, 17, 33n4

TGoNU. *See* Transitional Government of National Unity
thematic checklists, 184–92
Tibetans, secession movements of, 3
Tigrayan People's Liberation Front (TPLF), 36, 43
Tigre population, of Eritrea, 39
Tigrinya population, of Eritrea, 38–39
Timorese Defense Force (F-FDTL), 54, 63, 71–72
Timorese Democratic Union (UDT), 56–57, 68
Timorese National Resistance Council (CNRT), 54, 60, 65, 67–68, 74, 76n18, 78n46
Timorese refugees, 60, 62, 76n16
Timorese Social Democratic Association (ASDT) party, 56, 75n4
Timor Gap Treaty, 58
Timor-Leste, 55, 76nn24–26, 195, 197, 199; China and, 70, 79n57; corruption in, 69; Gusmão in, 57, 63, 65, 67–68, 71–72; military coup relating to, 56; Muslim community in, 69; resolution of 2006 crisis, 71–73, 79nn61–63, 80nn66–67; self-determination timeline of, 53–54; U.S. policy in, 160–61, 162. *See also* East Timor
Timor Sea, 59
TPLF. *See* Tigrayan People's Liberation Front
Transitional Government of National Unity (TGoNU), 101, 112, 114
Transparency International Corruption Perceptions Index, 31
Treaty of Friendship and Cooperation with the Soviet Union, 21
Turco-Egyptian empire, 103
2006 crisis (in Timor-Leste), resolution of, 71–73, 79nn61–63, 80nn66–67

UCDP. *See* Uppsala Conflict Data Program
UDT. *See* Timorese Democratic Union
UNAMET. *See* United Nations Mission in East Timor
UNESCO, 91
UNHCR, 62–63, 91
United Front, East Pakistan, 16, 17

United Kingdom, 106, 117, 167, 199, 200
United Nations, 2, 25, 37, 44, 106; Commission on Human Rights of, 60; Kosovo and, 88, 123, 195; peacekeeping missions and, 148–49; Special Committee on Decolonization of, 58
United Nations Mission in East Timor (UNAMET), 61, 62
United Nations Peace Implementation Council, 121
United Nations Security Council, 22, 53, 95, 112, 114; Resolution 37/30, 58, *58*; Resolution 1244, 82, 90, 92, 123, 129; Resolution 1246, 54, 61; Resolution 1264, 62
United States (U.S.): Bangladesh with policy of, 12; Bengalis in, 23, 34n26; East Timor and, 58–59, 60; Pakistan and, 20–21, 195; South Sudan lack of support from, 113–14, 116nn16–17; Sudan sanctioned by, 104, 116n3, 167.
UN Mission in Kosovo (UNMIK), 82, 90, 91, 124, 129–30, 132, 151
UN Transitional Administration of East Timor (UNTAET), 54, 62–63, 64, 67
Uppsala Conflict Data Program (UCDP), 142
Urdu, 14–15
U.S. *See* United States
USAID, 152

Vatican, 59
Versailles Treaty, 3

wars: famine and, 5; with India, 15, 18. *See also specific wars*
West Balkan settlements, 118, *120*, 125–26, 200; Bosnia, 119–21, 124, *125–26*, 131, 135n11; Kosovo, 122–23, 124, *125–26*, 131–32. *See also* Macedonia
West Pakistan, 6, 11, 15, 16, 198; Ayub Khan and, 17–18
West Timor, 61, 76n21
WHO. *See* World Health Organization
World Bank, 11, 25, 29, 66, 145, 169; database from, 139, 140, 141
World Health Organization (WHO), 91
World War I, 2, 3
World War II, 3, 13, 53, 56, 75n2

Yahya Khan, Agha Mohammad (general), 10, 11, 19–20, 21

Yugoslavia, 3, 81, 84–86, 92, 97, 167, 195; self-determination movements in, 117, 118
Yugoslav League of Communists, 84–85
Yugoslav Republic of Bosnia and Herzegovina, 119

Zia (Ziaur Rahman): assassination of, 12, 27; as Bangladesh president, 12, 26–27, 28, 30; BNP created by, 31; issues with, 26–27
Zia, Begum Khalida, 12, 27, 29

ABOUT THE AUTHORS

Jon B. Alterman is a senior vice president, holds the Zbigniew Brzezinski Chair in Global Security and Geostrategy, and is director of the Middle East Program at the Center for Strategic and International Studies (CSIS). Prior to joining CSIS in 2002, he served as a member of the Policy Planning Staff at the U.S. Department of State and as a special assistant to the assistant secretary of state for Near Eastern affairs. Before entering government, he was a scholar at the U.S. Institute of Peace and at the Washington Institute for Near East Policy, and worked as a legislative aide to Senator Daniel P. Moynihan (D-NY), responsible for foreign policy and defense. He is the author or coauthor of numerous publications on the Middle East, including four books, and the editor of five more. He received his PhD in history from Harvard University.

Richard Downie was deputy director of the CSIS Africa Program from 2009 to 2018. He has conducted research for CSIS in more than a dozen African countries on topics as diverse as security sector reform, political risk, religious trends, and economic development. He joined CSIS following a decade-long career in journalism. He has conducted research and completed writing projects on Africa for the Council on Foreign Relations and the U.S. Institute of Peace, and is a contributor to the Africa section of Freedom House's annual report, *Freedom in the World*. He holds a master's degree in international public policy from the Johns Hopkins School of Advanced International Studies (SAIS) and a BA in modern history from Oxford University.

Beáta Huszka is assistant professor at the Department of European Studies of ELTE University, Budapest. From 2013 to 2017, she led the work package on regional partnerships and bilateral cooperation of

Fostering Human Rights among European Policies (FRAME), funded under the EU Seventh Framework Programme. She is the author of the book *Secessionist Movements and Ethnic Conflict: The Development and Impact of Nationalist Rhetoric* (Routledge, 2014). Her more recent articles focus on the role of human rights in EU policies in the Balkans, media freedom, the framing aspect of nationalist movements, and EU enlargement policy. She completed her PhD in international relations at the Central European University in 2010.

Erin Jenne is a professor of international relations and European studies at Central European University in Budapest. Her research focuses on ethnic conflict and secessionism. She has received numerous grants and fellowships, including a MacArthur Fellowship at Stanford University and a Belfer Center for Science and International Affairs fellowship at Harvard University. Her first book, *Ethnic Bargaining: The Paradox of Minority Empowerment*, is the winner of Mershon Center's Edgar S. Furniss Book Award in 2007. Her second book, *Nested Security: Lessons in Conflict Management from the League of Nations and the European Union*, published in 2015, explores how emerging domestic struggles can be contained through soft power mediation. She received her PhD in political science from Stanford University.

Terrence Lyons is an associate professor of conflict resolution at the School for Conflict Analysis and Resolution at George Mason University. His research focuses on comparative peace processes and post-conflict politics, with a regional emphasis on Africa. He has written or cowritten five books and coedited a further four. He has consulted with the U.S. Department of State, the U.S. Agency for International Development, the United Nations, and key think tanks. He was the senior adviser to the Carter Center in Liberia and Ethiopia. In March 2017, he testified before the House Subcommittee on Africa and Global Health on the crisis in Ethiopia. He received his PhD in international relations from Johns Hopkins University.

Miks Muižarājs is a sustainable development practitioner who focuses on community-driven development projects in Southeast Asia and West Africa. He has spent several years working in Timor-Leste and served as lead researcher of a World Bank technical assistance project to the Timorese government. He has conducted extensive fieldwork in the country and is the author of several publications that focus on the East Timorese security situation, local governance, and public service delivery. He has consulted with other World Bank projects in Togo, the European Commission, and the NATO Strategic Communications Centre of Excellence. He holds a master of public administration degree from Columbia University and was a Fulbright scholar at Ohio University's master of international development studies program.

Howard Schaffer served in the U.S. Foreign Service for 36 years, holding posts at embassies in India and Pakistan before serving twice as deputy assistant secretary of state for South Asia. He was appointed U.S. ambassador to Bangladesh in 1984 and helped organize the distribution of U.S. aid, encouraged the Bangladeshi government to shift from martial law toward democracy, and participated in lengthy textile trade negotiations. After retiring from the foreign service in 1991, he taught at Georgetown University, where he was for 15 years director of studies at the Institute for the Study of Diplomacy. He has written numerous books on South Asia and biographies of diplomats Chester Bowles and Ellsworth Bunker. He received a BA in American history and literature from Harvard University.

Teresita Schaffer is an expert on South Asia and serves as a senior adviser to McLarty Associates, a Washington-based international strategic advisory firm. During her 30-year career in the U.S. Foreign Service, she served in Pakistan, India, and Bangladesh, and from 1992 to 1995 as U.S. ambassador in Sri Lanka. She was previously a nonresident senior fellow at the Brookings Institution. Prior to that, she created the South Asia program at CSIS and directed it from 1998 to 2010. Her most recent book, *India at the Global High Table: The Quest for Regional Primacy and Strategic Autonomy*, which she coauthored with her husband, was published in 2016. She received a BA from Bryn Mawr College and did graduate work in economics at Georgetown University.

Daniel Serwer directs the conflict management program at the Johns Hopkins School of Advanced International Studies (SAIS). Professor

Serwer is also a senior fellow at its Center for Transatlantic Relations and is affiliated as a scholar with the Middle East Institute. He was previously vice president of the Centers of Innovation at the U.S. Institute of Peace and its vice president for peace and stability operations. As a minister-counselor at the Department of State, he directed the office of European intelligence and research and also served as U.S. special envoy and coordinator for the Bosnian Federation, mediating between Croats and Bosniaks and negotiating the first agreement reached at the Dayton peace talks. He received his PhD in history from Princeton University.

Will Todman is an associate fellow in the CSIS Middle East Program and a fellow at the Syria Studies Centre at St. Andrews University. His research, analysis, and translations have been published by Lawfare, Mercy Corps, the Middle East Institute, and the Middle East Research and Information Project, and he has commented in print and on television. He previously lived in Beirut, where he worked for the British embassy and the office of the United Nations special envoy to Syria. He holds a master's degree in Arab studies from Georgetown University's School of Foreign Service and a BA in Arabic and modern Hebrew from Oxford University.

ADVISORY BOARD MEMBERS

Professor Henri Barkey, Bernard L. and Bertha F. Cohen Professor of International Relations at Lehigh University

General Wesley Clark (USA Ret.), CEO of Wesley K. Clark & Associates and NATO's former supreme allied commander

Ambassador Marc Grossman, vice chairman of the Cohen Group and former U.S. undersecretary of state for political affairs

Dr. Claudia Hofmann, professorial lecturer at the School of International Service at American University

Ambassador Beth Jones, adviser with ExxonMobil and former U.S. assistant secretary of state for European and Eurasian affairs

Clare Lockhart, director and cofounder of the Institute for State Effectiveness

Ambassador Princeton Lyman, senior adviser to the president of the U.S. Institute of Peace and former U.S. special envoy for Sudan and South Sudan

Dr. Jodi Nelson, senior vice president for policy and practice at the International Rescue Committee

Ambassador Thomas Pickering, vice chair of Hills & Company and former U.S. undersecretary of state for political affairs

Ambassador David Pressman, partner at Boies, Schiller, & Flexner and former deputy U.S. ambassador to the United Nations

Professor Nicholas Sambanis, Presidential Distinguished Professor of Political Science at the University of Pennsylvania

Ambassador Alan Solomont, Pierre and Pamela Omidyar Dean of the Tisch College of Civic Life at Tufts University and former U.S. ambassador to Spain

Anne Witkowsky, former U.S. deputy assistant secretary of defense for stability and humanitarian affairs

ABOUT CSIS

For over 50 years, the Center for Strategic and International Studies (CSIS) has worked to develop solutions to the world's greatest policy challenges. Today, CSIS scholars are providing strategic insights and bipartisan policy solutions to help decisionmakers chart a course toward a better world.

CSIS is a nonprofit organization headquartered in Washington, DC. The Center's 220 full-time staff and large network of affiliated scholars conduct research and analysis and develop policy initiatives that look into the future and anticipate change.

Founded at the height of the Cold War by David M. Abshire and Admiral Arleigh Burke, CSIS was dedicated to finding ways to sustain American prominence and prosperity as a force for good in the world. Since 1962, CSIS has become one of the world's preeminent international institutions focused on defense and security, regional stability, and transnational challenges ranging from energy and climate to global health and economic integration.

Thomas J. Pritzker was named chairman of the CSIS Board of Trustees in November 2015. Former U.S. deputy secretary of defense John J. Hamre has served as the Center's president and chief executive officer since 2000.

CSIS does not take specific policy positions; accordingly, all views expressed herein should be understood to be solely those of the author(s).

www.ingramcontent.com/pod-product-compliance
Lightning Source LLC
Chambersburg PA
CBHW052040300426
44117CB00012B/1899